W9-ACP-770

Pleasure in the Eighteenth Century

Pleasure in the Eighteenth Century

Edited by

ROY PORTER *and* MARIE MULVEY ROBERTS

NEW YORK UNIVERSITY PRESS
Washington Square, New York

First published in the U.S.A. in 1996 by
NEW YORK UNIVERSITY PRESS
Washington Square
New York, N.Y. 10003

Library of Congress Cataloging-in-Publication Data
Pleasure in the eighteenth-century / edited by Roy Porter and Marie
Mulvey Roberts.
p. cm.
Includes bibliographical references and index.
ISBN 0–8147–6644–7
1. Pleasure in literature. 2. Literature, Modern—18th century–
–History and criticism. I. Porter, Roy, 1946– . II. Roberts,
Marie Mulvey.
PN56.P534P54 1996
809'.93353—dc20 96–12952
CIP

Printed in Hong Kong

To Helen and Vivian
for being such endless sources of pleasure

Contents

Preface

Pleasure is the only thing worth having a theory about.

Oscar Wilde

When Oscar Wilde, the doyen of the pleasurable, wrote 'I adore simple pleasures. They are the last refuge of the complex',[1] he was acknowledging one of the many paradoxes that pervade the history of pleasure. Simple pleasure can not only be complex but may also be the last refuge of the nostalgia-monger, who is unable to resist the comfortable notion that the pleasures of the eighteenth century had managed to escape the complexities of modernity. As we are all only too aware nowadays, the pleasurable can often be a site of unease, against which we must ask such questions as: is it environmentally safe, morally acceptable, ideologically sound or politically correct? But were there not similar constraints surrounding pleasure during the eighteenth century, particularly when the enjoyment lay in transgression? Has not pleasure always been encumbered by the weight of its own inner complexities, ideology, discourse and paradoxes? The notion of simple pleasure has been too often a simplification of the past and a disavowal of the complexities of which it is constituted. On the other hand, problematising pleasure, whether simple or otherwise, may be part of a response to the perversities it can incite. It could also be, as Michel Foucault suggests, an indulgence in the discursive pleasure which is inherent within the 'pleasures of analysis':

> It is often said that we have been incapable of imagining any new pleasures. We have at least invented a different kind of pleasure: pleasure in the truth of pleasure, the pleasure of knowing that truth, of discovering and exposing it, the fascination of seeing it and telling it, of captivating and capturing others by it, of confiding it in secret, of luring it out in the open – the specific pleasure of the true discourse on pleasure.[2]

The editors of this volume hope that the reader will enjoy a Foucauldian 'true discourse of pleasure' which is long overdue. Considering how important eighteenth-century pleasure was to its participants, it is surprising that so little has been written directly on this subject. For the first time, this collection of essays brings together material history, theoretical perspectives and literary studies to explore the complexities surrounding the theory and practice of pleasure during this period. Here a number of leading scholars have broken through the taboo of writing about pleasure. To a great extent, its history has been marginalised by the more acceptable subjects of happiness or desire. Because of its associations with immediate gratification, the pleasurable has been devalued partly because it has been seen as being more accessible to the populace than to the elite. The class-bias in regard to prioritising desire over pleasure as a philosophical category is indicated by Roland Barthes who notes that 'the "populace" does not know Desire – only pleasures'.[3] When anyone dares to address the pleasure of the text, Barthes claims that there are two policemen ready to pounce on the transgressor; 'the political policeman and the psychoanalytical policeman: futility and/or guilt, pleasure is either idle or vain, a class notion or an illusion'.[4] He goes on to complain about the way in which epistemologies of pleasure have been neglected:

> Pleasure is continually disappointed, reduced, deflated, in favor of strong, noble values: Truth, Death, Progress, Struggle, Joy, etc. Its victorious rival is Desire: we are always being told about Desire, never about Pleasure: Desire has an epistemic dignity, Pleasure does not.[5]

Trivialised and over-simplified remains the popular view of the pleasure-seekers of the eighteenth century – one that reinforces the stereotype of an Arcadian of simple pleasure. The prevailing image is of a large pleasure garden wherein lusty Boswellian males stalk white-thread-stockinged 'nymphs', where club-men consume claret with gusto and jolly hearty eaters gorge themselves, patriotically, on beefsteak. The eighteenth century was the era of the belly-laugh. Even though one of its most amusing writers, Jonathan Swift, is applauded for having laughed only once, the fact that someone was counting is, in itself, significant. It is appropriate that it was during a performance of Henry Fielding's *Tom Thumb* (1730) when Swift erupted into laughter, since the taking of pleasure in company was regarded as the proper theatre of human enjoyment. As William Hogarth's engraving of a laughing audience on the front cover of this book signifies, the social face of pleasure was etched into a notion of enjoyment that was shared. While solitary mirth and delight were regarded as miasmic, the happiness arising from collective humour was seen to be healthy. For example, the pleasures of conversation, that had been refined to such arts as those of raillery and repartee, were represented best as a dialogue as opposed to a monologue. As an expression of communality, pleasure was predicated upon conviviality, and institutions such as the playhouse, the club and the coffee-house were formed in order to consolidate the joys of social intercourse. But to what extent was pleasure stage-managed in order to make it socially, morally and politically acceptable? Was it, in part, a performance, or was it a moral desideratum in being allied to notions of the social good, civic virtue and rationality?

The pleasure of doing good is the subject of Carolyn Williams's essay. The rise of organised charities provided a catalyst for turning the abstracted cult of sensibility into the hands-on culture of the worthy cause. She concentrates on the aptly named Royal Humane Society, which specialised in life-saving and was therefore able to provide intense pleasure both for its Lazarus-like beneficiaries and for its benevolent members. As a further inducement to the pleasure of resuscitating a victim rescued from drowning, there were cash rewards for the lower classes and medals for their social superiors. The link between virtue and pleasure is one nexus in the web of philosophical underpinnings that are unpicked by Roy Porter in his essay on 'Pleasure and the Enlightenment'. Here, he also looks at the new hedonism that had emerged from the *philosophes*, which was posited upon the new materialistic doctrines arising from the Scientific Revolution. Pleasures were sanctioned by being redefined in the light of innovative ideologies. The revival of Classicism, which encompassed the pleasures of the Ancients, also granted a licence to the Epicurean, provided that it was tempered by the Augustan emphasis upon moderation.

Yet the excesses described in Simon Varey's guide to Georgian feasting suggest that the upper classes threw aside all restraint when gorging themselves upon Bacchanalian delights. Varey traces the great chain of food down from the aristocrats' banquet with its pyramids of sweetmeats, to the middle classes' penchant for a comfortable soup, through to the lower classes' more modest fare of potatoes and fatty pork. Gastronomic warfare was waged between the English and the French, which turned the dinner table into a battleground over nationalist pickings on both sides. Unlike France, which retained a greater variety of regional cooking, there developed in England a national cuisine. This tended to standardise tastes between the town and country, even though there was a sharp divide in regard to the quality of food available. While the rural communities enjoyed fresh nutritional products, the townsfolk often had no option but to buy over-ripe fruit and vegetables and stale meat from the urban market.

Consumerism is the theme of Roy Porter's other essay, which is on material pleasures. He points out that increasing affluence facilitated the growth of a consumerist society which helped characterise England as a nation of shoppers to the detriment of folk merrymaking. Forms of enjoyment that had once been the exclusive property of the elite were now becoming more accessible to the majority. His focus is upon how and why the middling classes aspired to buy into aristocratic pleasures and the emergence of a quintessentially bourgeois realm of enjoyment. The location of Georgian jollifications in the pleasure garden represents a matrix wherein the classes, nature, art, artefact, fashion, courtship and consumerism converged on common ground.

It was at Vauxhall Pleasure Garden where the elements of water and fire were celebrated through the first performance of Handel's *Water Music* and *Fireworks Music*. Derek Alsop discusses the influence of Handel on Italian opera, which was a spectacular, lavish and foreign import into London society. The absurd plots, sensuality, strutting tenors with their falsettos and, worse still, the castrati performers were all feared by patriots as un-English and by moralists as eroding the standards of popular taste. In an age when travesty was the 'norm', the permutations for sexual ambiguity were inexhaustible, as when castrati would masquerade as women playing the roles of men disguised on stage as women.

Marie Mulvey Roberts looks at the cross-dressing 'Mollies' as another source of voyeuristic pleasure in her survey of clubs of Augustan and Georgian England. These various and varied clubs catered for the pleasures of their members as in providing them with roast beef, a place to consume claret and conversation with abandon, or to incite rakes and rogues in Mohock mayhem. Such was the vogue for clubs, that pleasure was to be found even in their fabrication, as in the Ugly Club, the No Noses Club and the Beaus' Club, also known as the Lady's Lapdog Club. She argues that single-sex clubs provided men and women with the opportunity to appropriate the characteristics of the opposite sex as well as focusing on the absent other. As contemporary taxonomies reveal, there was a club, real or imaginary, for almost every kind of pleasure, from the Lying Club for the mendacious to the Surly Club for the misanthropist.

It may be too simple to regard the pleasures taken during the eighteenth century as a reaction against earlier ideologies, religious hegemony and social mores. The pleasures of the Augustans have been viewed as a rejection of the killjoys of the previous century. Since they had to contend with plague, fire, and civil war, it is hardly surprising to find that for them life was often nasty, brutish and, in view of such misery, mercifully short. Likewise, the prurience and puritanism of the Victorians have been represented as a backlash against the rollicking Georgians. It is easy to discredit these views by pointing out that the puritan and the libertine co-existed during the eighteenth century and that the Victorians were not averse to having a good time. But although no period can claim to have had a monopoly on enjoyment, neither has there been, during the course of history, a particular group of recipients who have had an automatic entitlement or inalienable right to it. For example, the rational Enlightenment was seen to endorse the pursuit of both pleasure and happiness as the prerogative of the reasonable man. Women, even when they were not blatantly regarded as *machines de plaisir*, were generally perceived as more of a source than a subject of pleasure.

The notion that pleasures became more refined the higher one advanced up the social hierarchy was an illusion that the 'well-bred' liked to cultivate. The polluting pleasures of the bawd house and bordello were not enjoyed exclusively by any one class. Individuals who were able to indulge in pleasurable activities could find that their delight was compromised by the moral or immoral burdens with which their pleasure could be loaded. The rationalising of forms of enjoyment into hierarchies and taxonomies can lead to a danger of the kind of exploitation of the powerless that characterised the division of labour which has been formulated by Adam Smith. Such divisions of pleasure can be seen to have distilled and intensified certain kinds of pleasurable activity, which helped incubate the seeds of Victorian fetishism.

The Enlightenment's high-priest of the perversity of pleasure was the Marquis de Sade, whose credo – that there should be a right to pleasure beyond guilt – disrupts the laws of reciprocity between even the most dangerous of acquaintances. Such an ideology was grafted on to some of the plots of popular fiction. Vivien Jones explores the perversities of the transgressive pleasures arising from conduct literature by juxtaposing it with the seduction plots of contemporaneous novels. She shows how conduct books can be titillating in the way that they stimulate the disruptive desires they seek to curtail. Although these prescriptive manuals could scarcely be regarded as progressive for women, as providers of subversive pleasures they expose an ideological instability within literature.

An antidote to the literary instability represented by the Gothic novel can be seen to have been provided by the flood of treatises on the sublime, that sought to explain the paradoxical pleasure of terror. Emma Clery draws on Edmund Burke's notion of the terrible sublime to argue that, once terror ceased to function as a guardian of civic virtue, it became domesticated through the Gothic novel into a commodity for the consumption of private pleasure. Although some writers in the terror mode took the civic responsibilities Burke indicated seriously, the majority were interested only in saleable sensationalism, and the notion of civic terror collapsed under the weight of its contradictions. Since Burke formulated many of the ideas that were developed by the Romantic poets, it is appropriate that the following essay, which concludes the book, is a textual analysis of the pleasures to be found in the poetry of Burns and

Wordsworth, culminating in 'The Pleasure which there is in life itself'. Susan Manning shows how simple pleasure is captured within Wordsworth's Romantic poetry, as that which does not aspire to the abstract or transcendent, but is grounded in the immediacy of the here and now.

As readers are doubtless eager to begin their vicarious enjoyment of the pleasures of the eighteenth century, they should be delayed no longer by this preface. Considering that the pursuit of happiness has already been given centre stage by scholars such as Peter Quennell,[6] the time has arrived for the curtains to open and pleasure to be reclaimed from the wings. This urgency is particularly pressing when we consider how many of the pleasure-seekers of the eighteenth century would have agreed with Wilde in his 'Phrases and Philosophies for the Use of the Young', that 'Pleasure is the only thing one should live for. Nothing ages like happiness.'[7]

MARIE MULVEY ROBERTS

Bristol

1. Enlightenment and Pleasure

ROY PORTER

It is a presupposition of this book that pleasure came into its own in the eighteenth century. But it would be quite misleading to give the impression that, before the Enlightenment, the pleasures of the flesh and even the mind were universally frowned upon, or that there were no philosophies of pleasure. In Antiquity, Epicurus and his followers devoted themselves to the cultivation of hedonism, with an accent if not exactly on gratification of desire, at least upon the avoidance of physical pain (thus the popular image of an epicure as a gourmet *bon viveur* is somewhat misleading).[1] The drunken and orgiastic saturnalia of the Romans were well known to the Renaissance.[2] In literary traditions, pastoral poetry pictured an idyllic, bucolic golden age in which fertile Nature freely yielded up her fruits, the climate was mild, and relations between master and man, and mankind and the animals were blissfully harmonious.[3] And even Christian culture had its occasions for festivity and carnival, associated in particular with the religious calendar – Christmas wassailing, Shrove Tuesday or All Souls.

Familiar themes – the cornucopia, the flowing bowl, the revels of Bacchus and Venus – attest the fact that, at least in mythology, art and folklore it was easy to conceive of times and places of holiday release, in which humans should be free to abandon themselves to enjoyment. Witness the pastoral verse of such Jacobean or Caroline poets as Ben Jonson, Richard Lovelace and Richard Carew, or Breughel's paintings with their uninhibited peasant merrymaking.[4] It would, in other words, be utterly erroneous to picture the medieval or early modern centuries as unremittingly negative in their attitudes towards sensual pleasures.

Yet it is also important to stress that before the eighteenth century compelling objections were officially raised to the idea that the pleasures of the senses were legitimate, fulfilling and to be encouraged. In Antiquity it was held, notably by Plato and Aristotle, that gratification of appetite was a lower form of activity than rational pursuit of goodness. Plato, in particular, depicted conflict between vulgar emotions and noble reason. Like mutinous troops over whom a commander had to enforce stern discipline, Plato saw the pleasure-seeking senses as an anarchic and self-destructive rabble; the dictates of reason, curbing sensual appetites, formed the only basis for virtue, truth and the good life.[5]

Stoic philosophers, for their part, asserted that sensuous pleasure was insubstantial, impermanent and, at bottom, illusory. Hedonism was in many respects a form of false consciousness. Stoicism urged the wise to rise above passing pleasures and seek a higher truth that was immaterial, unchanging and ideal.[6] In rejecting mere hedonism for a loftier form of good, the tenets of Stoicism in many respects anticipated the Christian creed that the so-called pleasures of the flesh were shallow, base and sinful; and the consequent conviction that true blessedness would come only from renouncing baser corporeal urges, seeking virtue in obedience to God, and finally attaining true fulfilment in Heaven.

Christian theology did not deny the possibility of happiness; but that was to be attained only through the reunion of the immaterial spirit with its heavenly Maker.[7] The itch for physical pleasure on earth was the consequence of original sin at the Fall, and the formulation of the Seven Deadly Sins in the Middle Ages emphasised that terrestrial pleasures were evil, self-defeating and self-destructive. Christians were taught from the pulpit and through omnipresent images of the *danse macabre* and the *memento mori*, that this life was in a vale of tears, in which there was much to be endured and little to be enjoyed. Mortification of the flesh was thus in order. Only by renouncing the body could the spirit be released.[8]

Mainstream Christianity cast lapsarian man as a sinner through and through. Labour was a curse, a constant reminder of the sin for which Adam and Eve had been expelled from Paradise. Theologians denounced egoism as evil: it was God and one's neighbour who were to be loved. Pride and vanity had to be cast out of the heart by denial; mortification should stun the self. Though oddly silent on violence and cruelty, the Seven

Deadly Sins singled out for censure envy and avarice (signalling the Christian Church's iconoclastic anxieties about the seductive pleasures of objects), lust, and even, somewhat bathetically, gluttony. The anathematisation of gluttony points to the importance of eating and drinking as releases – perhaps for many people the *only* and, even then, extremely rare releases – in a feudal, agrarian world which afforded, for the great majority of peasants, a life of grinding poverty.

Christian theology commended abstinence and self-denial, symbolised each year by Lent and its obligation to fast; by the example of Christ ('take that thou hast and give to the poor'), by apostolic poverty and the monastic vows (poverty, chastity, obedience). If the Reformed confessions did not hold with monasticism, Protestantism owed its very existence to protests against the worldly greed of a Medieval Catholicism whose very headquarters spelt greed (ROMA = *Radix Omnium Malorum Avaricia*: Avarice, the Root of All Evil). There must be no place for money-changers in the Temple. As the parable of the needle's eye made plain, the empire of things was a hindrance to Heaven. Puritans waged war against pagan pleasures.

In other respects, too, pleasure-seeking was deplored in traditional Christian culture. The aesthetic and libertine tendencies stimulated by the Renaissance and erupting in England in the aesthetic court of Charles I and the bawdy court of Charles II, were fiercely denounced by moralists and preachers as ungodly examples of aristocratic debauchery.[9]

The background was thus complex: there were traditions of enjoyment, yet hedonism was wholly deprecated within Christianity. What marks the innovativeness of the eighteenth century is its new accent upon the legitimacy of pleasure – not as occasional release, aristocratic paganism or heavenly bliss, but as the routine entitlement of people at large to seek fulfilment in this world rather than only in heavenly salvation, to achieve the gratification of the senses not just the purification of the soul.

This transformation came about partly *within* the culture of Christianity, for during the eighteenth century Christian theology modified its priorities and developed the notion that a rational and benevolent God had created a universe in which earthly ends were desirable as well as Heavenly bliss.[10] But a new hedonism also emerged beyond Christian teachings, thanks largely to the philosophies of the Enlightenment, to a reinstatement of Classical ideas, and to the impact of the new science, creating the science of man, the science of the mind.[11]

New scientific outlooks pictured man essentially as a self-contained machine or physical organism, governed by a tendency to pursue pleasure and avoid pain. Initially, such daring egoistic models were highly contested. Two intellectual figures above all were widely attacked for their advocacy of selfish views of human nature and society. One was Thomas Hobbes. In *Leviathan* (1651) and elsewhere, Hobbes advanced an essentially mechanistic vision. Like Nature in general, man was a machine, moved by fear and programmed to avoid pain. Hobbes's vision of man the hedonist was couched in negative terms: dread of death was the main motivation for the creation of society, morality, law and all other human institutions. His was a bleak hedonism, concerned less with fulfilment than with the avoidance of pain: life in the state of nature had severe limitations – 'No arts; no letters; no society, and which is worst of all, continual fear and danger of violent death; and the life of man, solitary, poor, nasty, brutish, and short.' Many saw in Hobbes's philosophy a shameless denial of the more noble spiritual aspects of man, especially the soul – an assumption that there was nothing to man but bodily reflexes.[12] He was accused of atheism and materialism.

Attracting almost as much hatred as Hobbes was Bernard Mandeville, a Dutch-born physician who came to live in London in the late seventeenth century, writing a succession of satirical works dealing with politics, morality, sexuality and social conduct.[13] A supreme cynic, Mandeville's aim was to anatomise man, unmasking pretensions and assertions of higher motivations and virtues. Behind such hypocritical facades, Mandeville maintained, lay a rather Hobbesian selfishness, a desire for power or the quest for reputation and honour. All supposedly disinterested morality was veiled self-seeking, all trumpeted altruism disguised hedonism. Behind every human action and institution lay unremitting selfishness, an insatiable itch for gratification.

Like Freud later, Mandeville was acutely aware of the systematic denial of desire governing public morality and religion. Sharing the lubricity of the Restoration, he was fascinated by sexual thou-shalt-nots and the economy of erotic restraint. He viewed males and females alike as creatures perennially on heat; both sexes craved satisfaction of sexual hunger. Yet social *mores*, as Mandeville explained in his *The Virgin Unmask'd*, dictated elaborate techniques for impeding or deferring erotic gratification. In particular, 'modest' women had to remain chaste, or at least cultivate a reputation for so being.

Mandeville frequently returned to matters sexual, but the focus of his non-medical writings was another kind of desire and denial: the itch for gain and glory. Time and again, he addressed what he identified as the central paradox of his age. The nation was obviously availing itself of every opportunity to get rich and accrue esteem and status. Money, possessions, display and conspicuous consumption all conferred power and prestige. Yet this ingrained acquisitiveness was pursued against a blanket disapproval of gold, gain and greed; enjoyment was denounced as luxury. How so and why? What was to be made of this? Was something to be done about it? These were the issues addressed in Mandeville's most notorious work, *The Grumbling Hive: or, Knaves Turn'd Honest* (1705), a moral tale in doggerel hexameters, later decked out with lengthy prose commentaries as *The Fable of the Bees: or Private Vices, Public Benefits* (1714), a work that expanded with every edition.[14]

Mandeville imagined a successful 'hive'. All the bees were ambitious egoists, busy, buzzing to get on by all possible means: labour, trade and other ways to turn an honest penny, but also more shady enterprises, such as the chicanery of the law, and unabashed swindles, frauds, roguery and theft on top:

> All trades and Places knew some Cheat,
> No Calling was without Deceit.[15]

On the grand scale, the conduct of the nation replicated individual behaviour: it was, in other words, a proud, aggressive, warlike hive. Busy and bustling, both individuals and community flourished:

> Thus every Part was full of Vice,
> Yet the whole Mass a Paradise;

Flatter'd in Peace, and fear'd in Wars,
They were th'Esteem of Foreigners,
And lavish of their Wealth and Lives,
The Ballance of all other Hives.
Such were the Blessings of that State;
Their Crimes conspired to make 'em Great.[16]

So what was the secret, the grand arcanum, of the thriving hive? Mandeville's challenging answer was: Vice – that is, translated from the terminology of Christian moral condemnation into plain-speaking, self-interest:

Thus Vice nursed Ingenuity,
Which join'd with Time, and Industry
Had carry'd Life's Conveniences
Its real Pleasures, Comforts, Ease,
To such a Height, the very Poor
Lived better than the Rich Before;
And Nothing could be added more.[17]

Or rather, that is, until moral rigorism had its say. All was corruption, insisted self-righteous grumblers; the system fed on and fostered vanity and greed, it created artificial desires that ran before strict needs. It was wanton and wasteful. It excited the appetites of the flesh instead of chastising them. It begat luxury and debauchery. All this, insisted the virtuous and godly, must be extirpated.

Such rigorism had its way in the 'grumbling hive'. In the name of purity, a regime of self-denial was inaugurated. Frugality became king, double-dealing was stopped. The consequence? Abject decline. Rectitude and thrift had no need for a market economy, and therefore opportunities dried up for the myriad services and commercial and manufacturing activities that went with it. If righteousness was to rule, Mandeville concluded, you had to abandon pleasure and be prepared to feed off acorns.

So there was a choice. It was possible to have wealth, employment, a booming society and pleasure, by the pursuit of what morality-mongers dubbed 'vice'. Or one could be (in the classic phrase) poor and honest. What riled Mandeville was the myopic folly or hypocrisy of those who preached against profligacy but took no heed of the implications of their rhetoric.

The morality of rigorous self-denial obviously led to untoward consequences. Why so? It was, Mandeville agreed, because it involved false consciousness about the nature and purposes of morality itself. Hence he added to the 1723 edition of the *Fable* a 'Search into the Nature of Society', to explain the true origins and functions of ethics. Properly understood, in his view, true morality was not a matter of the *denial* of human propensities, but of their more effective *achievement.*

Somewhat like Freud two hundred years later, Mandeville suggested that, at its most elemental, human nature was utterly, nakedly and selfishly drive-directed. In the state of nature, Mandevillian man was essentially Hobbesian man, with an agenda of basic wants (food, survival, sex, etc.), and a propensity to set about realising them in the most direct ways. Such barefaced egoism inevitably created conflict. Hence society had to be initiated, with conventional codes for normalising unsociable appetites and facilitating egoism. The urge to possess was to be regulated by the laws of property; lust was to be tamed by matrimony. The envy that initially led to snatching other people's things was civilised into labour, trade, and the love of lucre. Thus society, properly understood, was an engine for converting naked anti-social egoism into more peaceful and profitable ways for people to get what they wanted, at the cost of a bit of effort, some deferral of gratification and much ostentatious conformity (why not? – after all, even respectability had its pleasures).

Morality was the passport people had to display to prove that they were abiding by the social code. Honour and shame provided the motivations. Those playing by the rules of the game would be crowned in honour; rule-breakers would be covered in obliquy. Since people were moved by vanity, the distribution of acclaim and disgrace provided compelling inducements to ensure that play went by the rules.

Ultimately, the name of the game was 'that strong Habit of Hypocrisy, by the Help of which, we have learned from our Cradle to hide even from ourselves the vast Extent of Self-Love, and all its different Branches'. In short, what official values dubbed immorality was, suitably veiled, a vital social filip. 'Vices are inseparable from great and potent Societies', Mandeville asserted, 'and it is impossible their Wealth and Grandeur should subsist without.' So what was the moral? –

> Then leave complaints; Fools only strive
> To make a great an honest hive . . .
> Fraud, luxury and pride must live
> While we the benefits receive.[18]

Mandeville, in other words, denied contemporaries the easy moralistic options he believed they loved to take. But he was reviled for having had the temerity to come out as the champion of vice:

> T'enjoy the world's conveniences,
> Be famed in war, yet live in ease,
> Without great vices, is a vain
> Eutopia seated in the brain.[19]

Mandeville aimed to provoke, and he did: the critic John Dennis retorted that 'vice and luxury have found a Champion and a Defender, which they never did before'. He forcibly reminded his readers that their moral training taught that human nature was corrupt, that greed and envy were vicious, and love of money the root of all evil.

Mandeville, therefore, was in one respect suggesting that the old Christian preachers were right – man was indeed a fallen and sinful creature – and he took paradoxical pleasure in suggesting that dominant values and institutions were founded upon grotesque hypocrisy. But the thrust of such works as *The Virgin Unmask'd* or *The Fable of the Bees* was not that Man was sinful and *therefore* sin ought to be renounced. Mandeville's message was quite the reverse. Man was selfish, but that was *desirable*: all *should* be pursuing greed, lust, vanity and ambition, though in a socially sanctioned manner. For the consequence of universal selfishness, properly pursued, was social harmony and progress. Private vices, according to Mandeville, would result in public benefits, selfishness would stimulate progress. In other words, two or three generations before Adam Smith and the emergence of the classical political economy, Mandeville was suggesting that individual greed properly socialised worked towards the good of the whole.

Hobbes and Mandeville were ferociously abused because they challenged traditional humanistic, idealist and Christian moralities. But the message was gradually accepted, that self-fulfilment rather than denial should be embraced because it was innate to the constitution of human nature and beneficial to society. Such assumptions became taken up by later moralists and social and political thinkers, who clothed these unpalatable conclusions in agreeable rationalisations propounding the desirability of the pursuit of pleasure and the quest for happiness. These came in several guises, in different fields of discourse.

One lay within theology itself. By 1700, a branch of cosmic philosophising known as natural theology was achieving high prominence, arguing that God was a benign and wise Creator.[20] The Divine Architect, rational theologians argued, had designed a perfect universe in which all elements harmoniously cooperated for mutual benefit and improvement. The Deity had planned an environment benign, blessed and fertile, within which humans could flourish: such was the message of natural theologians like John Ray, William Derham and a succession of pulpit scientists, who followed in the footsteps of Sir Isaac Newton and emphasised that Nature was a law-governed machine working efficiently for mankind's benefit.[21] God, in short, had fashioned the world for human use and enjoyment. Man could garner the fruits of the soil, tame the animals and quarry the Earth's crust for its natural resources.[22]

Such an optimistic vision of Creation as designed for human pleasure of course spelt abundant problems, and it was satirised by Voltaire's *Candide* and Samuel Johnson's *Rasselas,* both published in 1759 after the catastrophic Lisbon earthquake.[23] But the natural theology tradition remained extremely influential throughout the eighteenth century, culminating in the theological utilitarianism of the Revd William Paley, abandoning the view of God as an Old Testament avenger, smiting and scourging His people, in favour of a vision of a Divine Benefactor: the happiness of the terrestrial world was the best augury of future bliss in Heaven.[24]

Of no less importance were new traditions of moral philosophy and aesthetics developing in eighteenth-century England under the stimulus first of the Third Earl of Shaftesbury and then of the Scottish professor of philosophy, Francis Hutcheson, as part of wider attempts to formulate an understanding of human existence within a framework of Nature, reason and the human psyche.[25] Without pursuing anything like a systematic science of the mind, Shaftesbury, who had learned much from Locke, attempted to formulate a natural understanding of the powers of the mind in respect of its activities in moral choices, the pursuit of virtue and the cultivation of beauty. Shaftesbury was a Platonist, with not the slightest inclination for Hobbesian hedonism. Nevertheless, his promotion of the notion of the pleasures of virtue could point the way for those who would later champion the virtues of pleasure. Aesthetics was thus pointing in the direction of psychology. And while Hutcheson deeply disapproved of Mandeville, his formulations – in particular an early expression of the 'greatest happiness' principle – turned morality in the same direction and gave attention to its psychological dimensions.[26]

And, in parallel moves, many of the moral philosophers of the first half of the eighteenth century gave morality a new and, as they saw it, a sounder basis in psychology. Morality had traditionally been understood as a system of universals: objective right and wrong, goodness and justice. Within the English Enlightenment, however, it was increasingly regarded as a matter of conformity to human nature. Ethics was not so much obeying commandments as acting rationally upon desires. And the new philosophers emphasised that – contrary to rigorist Christian teachings – human nature was not corrupt consequent upon original sin; human instincts, passions and appetites rather were naturally benign. There was pleasure to be derived from altruism, sympathy, benevolence and sociability.[27] Virtue was, in short, integral to a psychology of pleasure – indeed its own reward.

Such shifts in perception were bound to emerge as society itself changed. The Christian had traditionally been regarded as a fixed being – the innocent creature planted by God in Eden, the sinner expelled from Paradise. But when the Enlightenment thinker looked around, he saw that civilisation was making rapid and wholesale changes to the physical environment – building cities, draining marshes, constructing harbours,

digging canals, sinking mines, modernising agriculture; he saw the powers over Nature that science and technology were conferring. Such changes were changing people themselves – their physiques and appearance, their ways of thinking, their prospects, their social existence. Viewed in this light, *homo rationalis* was not, after all, some immutable essence, but the malleable product of various forces, influences, stimuli and responses. Man was *homo faber*, but he was also *homo hominis faber*, maker of his own destiny, though with some help from the environment in which he lived.

There is no space here for detailed exploration of the Enlightenment ideas of the 'party of humanity': Montesquieu, Voltaire, Diderot and d'Alembert's *Encyclopédie*, the English moralists and the Scottish professors of progress. But many of the theories promoted and popularised by the *philosophes* in France and by fellow travellers in Britain, Italy, Germany and North America were to have crucial consequences for the philosophy of the pursuit of pleasure and the goal of happiness, and so deserve mention. Central to all Enlightenment thinking was a heightened this-worldliness. With this went a new stress on knowing Nature and Nature's laws; in other words, a more scientific vision. No longer was the Universe a pious mystery, pervaded by occult powers and spiritual destinies, it was a machine that could be taken to bits, put together again, mended, altered and improved.

And so could man – it seemed to Enlightenment thinkers that man was also an engine made up of parts, open to scientific study through the methods of anatomy and physiology, sociology, psychology and any number of other '-ologies'. Whether or not, certain radical *philosophes* claimed, one could speak of *l'homme machine*, many aspects of human behaviour were capable of being analysed in a manner analogous to falling bodies within Newtonian mechanics or the motions of atoms.[28]

Enlightenment thinkers believed that examining human nature made intellectual sense. And this was partly because they set increasing store by individual values – freedom, independence, toleration, choice. Mankind, so many Enlightenment thinkers asserted, was not immutably cemented into some pre-existing social order – the 'Divine Right of Kings' or the 'Great Chain of Being'. Rather, people were born naturally free and could not legitimately be politically enslaved. 'The great and chief end, therefore, of men's uniting into commonwealths and putting themselves under government' – thus spake John Locke – 'is the preservation of their property', and for him 'property' meant both material belongings and personal autonomy.[29]

Eighteenth-century thinkers developed from such assumptions a fierce championing of individualism, a vindication of independence, the right of self-determination, self-improvement – and *happiness.* 'The desire of bettering our condition', remarked the social commentator, Frederick Eden, 'is the predominant principle that animates the world', which 'expanded into action, gives birth to every social virtue'. Daniel Defoe's *Robinson Crusoe* (1719) fictionalised the dilemma of the man set in the state of nature – the shipwrecked mariner on the island – having to (re)invent civilisation single-handedly (except for Man Friday) and map out his own destiny. In fact, it became common to depict society as a congregation (like Mandeville's hive) of individuals each bursting with needs, desires and drives, which sometimes worked together, sometimes collided, but which energised the entire system. 'The wants of the mind are infinite', argued Nicholas Barbon, property developer and self-styled intellectual:

> Man naturally aspires & his mind is elevated, his senses grow more refined & more capable of delight. His desires are enlarged, & his wants increase with his wishes, which is for everything which is rare, qualify his senses, adorn his body & promote ease, pleasure & pomp of life.[30]

A century later in the *Wealth of Nations* (1776), Adam Smith endorsed, in comparable terms, this egoistic, self-centred vision of man, being convinced of 'the uniform, constant and uninterrupted effort of every man to better his condition'. Individual desires for betterment led to general improvement:

> From whence, then, arises that emulation which runs through all the different ranks of men, and what are the advantages which we propose by that great purpose of human life which we call bettering our position? To be observed, to be attended

> to, to be taken notice of with sympathy, complacency, and approbation, are all the advantages which we can propose to derive from it. It is vanity, not the ease, or the pleasure, which interests us. But vanity is always founded upon the belief of our being the object of attention and approbation.[31]

It became common to rephrase the question as to the essence of good and evil, right and wrong, virtue and vice, in terms of an agenda of searching questions to be put to human nature: How do we know? What is right and wrong? Are we mere machines, programmed by mechanics, genetics or chemistry? Or do we have free will? Or, perhaps, do we merely *think* we have free will? Where have we come from? And where are we going? – questions tackled over and again, sometimes teasingly, sometimes tragically.

Eighteenth-century thinkers have often been credited with being the first modern, scientific analysts of society, the first sociologists and anthropologists, the first historians of morals and language, social psychologists, penologists, and so forth. This followed from their view of man as radically pliable, capable of almost unlimited change. Here Locke and his followers proved immensely influential. The history of the human race, suggested many thinkers, following Locke's fundamental *An Essay Concerning Humane Understanding* (1690) and his *Some Thoughts Concerning Education* (1693), could be seen as paralleling the education of an infant. Lockeans believed that fundamentalists were wrong to judge that man was born sinful, and that Plato had been equally mistaken in claiming that people came into the world prepacked with innate ideas (for instance, those of right and wrong).[32]

The human mind rather began as a *tabula rasa*, a clean slate or a blank sheet of paper. It then continually absorbed data through the senses (sight, hearing, etc.), storing this information and shaping it into 'ideas', which crystallised into empirical knowledge of the outside world and also into moral values:

> The senses at first let in particular *Ideas*, and furnish the yet empty Cabinet: And the Mind by degrees growing familiar with some of them, they are lodged in the Memory, and Names got to them. Afterwards the Mind proceeding farther, abstracts

> them, and by Degrees learns the use of general Names. In this manner the Mind comes to be furnish'd with *Ideas* and Language, the Materials about which to exercise its discursive Faculty.[33]

Man's nature, capacities, and knowledge were thus entirely the products of learning from experience, through a process Locke called the 'association of ideas' (the building of complex trains of thought out of simple units). Man was thus the child of his environment; but in turn, driven by the quest for satisfaction, he acquired the capacity to transform those same surroundings.[34]

Engaged thus in energetic interplay with his fellows and environment, man was ever evolving to meet the challenges of surroundings he was continually changing. Hence it is little surprise that admirers of Locke, such as the doctor and scientist Erasmus Darwin – Charles Darwin's grandfather – outlined biological theories of progress and evolution, which presupposed just such a capacity of creatures to adapt, improve and finally transmit their acquired characteristics to their offspring.[35] In the writings of David Hartley, a pious medical practitioner who developed a physiological psychology, such outlooks assumed a materialist, determinist basis;[36] while the eccentric Unitarian, Joseph Priestley, embedded the pursuit of happiness within a Providential theory of progress.[37]

These epistemologies (theories of knowledge and learning) were typically linked by Enlightenment thinkers with psychological models contending that human beings – let Stoical philosophers and Christian theologians say what they will – were essentially driven by their passions, and (more scandalously) that it was right that they should be. Reversing traditional priorities, the Scot David Hume argued that reason should properly be the slave of the passions. It was natural, he maintained, for individuals to pursue pleasure: such egoism would contribute to general social cohesion and advantage. Properly educated and channelled, it would be easy to ensure, in the words of Alexander Pope, that 'self love and social [would be] the same' – a less provocative variant of Mandeville's 'private vices, public benefits' paradox.[38]

This 'sensationalist' psychology – man viewed as an ensemble of stimuli and responses, mediated through the senses –

sanctioned a new hedonism. 'Pleasure is now, and ought to be, your business', Lord Chesterfield instructed his teenage son. The well-tempered pursuit of happiness in the here-and-now – indeed, the *right* to happiness – became a leading theme of moral essayists.[39] For many (though not for Dissenters and Evangelicals) the teachings of *Pilgrim's Progress* became a thing of the past. The mid-century writer, Soame Jenyns, argued that 'happiness is the only thing of real value in existence: neither riches, nor power, nor wisdom, nor learning, not strength, nor beauty, nor virtue, nor religion, nor even life itself, being of any importance but as they contribute to its production'.[40]

Such views were to find their most systematic expression in Utilitarianism, whose high priest was Jeremy Bentham. Replacing the Classical Humanist vision of man as a rational soul warring against brutish appetites, Utilitarians newly envisaged man as a creature prudently programmed by nature to seek pleasure and avoid pain. The true end of enlightened social policy should therefore be to encourage and educate enlightened self-interest, so as to realise what Bentham styled the 'greatest happiness of the greatest number'.[41] Utilitarianism and its 'felicific calculus' had practical applications. Legal reformers argued that a truly scientific jurisprudence needed to be erected upon a psychology of rational selfishness: taking man as a rational hedonist, the pains of judicial punishment must be precisely calculated to outweigh the pleasures of crime. Benthamite Utilitarianism in particular emphasised that the individual should standardly be regarded as the best judge of his own interests, and that human wants could always be expressed in, or reduced to, quantitative terms (ultimately cash values).[42]

Above all, the Utilitarian goal (the greatest happiness principle) chimed with the new political economy, especially the theory perfected by Adam Smith in his *Wealth of Nations* (1776), that the selfish behaviour of individual producers and consumers, if pursued in accordance with the competitive laws of the free market, would result in the common good – thanks to the 'invisible hand'. The *laissez faire* economics advocated by Smith, developed by followers in many nations over the next few generations and implemented (albeit patchily) by governments as part of free-trade policies, finally sidelined the traditional Christian war against greed.[43]

Smith's recommendations were, moreover, democratic in tendency. The economy should not be subject to governmental *diktat* or commanded by mercantilist policy-makers. Protectionist regulation, he argued, was always short-sighted and generally corrupt. Nor should economic power be monopolised by particular, privileged interest groups – corporations, guilds, etc. – because these would always set private above public interest. Market forces must, rather, be supreme, and in the end that could mean nothing but the sovereignty of consumer demand. In Smith's vision, an economic system worked best when producers were kept on their toes, being forced to innovate and introduce economies, so as to compete for consumers. Economic prosperity should thus bring the optimal satisfaction of all.

Smith's demand-driven vision was also consumerist and hedonic in a further important respect.[44] One of the key debates in economic theory revolved around wage levels. Was it desirable that earnings rise or be kept to a minimum? Smith favoured what he called the 'liberal reward of labour'. Good wages would give workers incentives, and help to make the labour force more reliable and respectable. They would also put spending power into pockets, which in turn would create demand, employment and economic activity (inflation is a more modern anxiety). Hence, Smith's economics gave special attention in two important respects to the critical role of consumption – gratification through goods – in boosting a healthy economy. Most economic historians would argue that this reflected the economic realities of the time.

Smith's belief that the liberal reward for labour, by increasing purchasing power, would spur growth was widely echoed. 'It is not . . . an excess of property to the few', contended his fellow Scot, Patrick Colquhoun,

> but the extension of it among the mass of the community, which appears most likely to prove beneficial with respect to national wealth and national happiness. Perhaps no other country in the world possesses greater advantages in this respect than Great Britain, and hence that spirit of enterprise and that profitable employment of diffused capitals which has created so many resources for productive labour beyond any other country in Europe.

Smith's formula – let market forces, the aggregate wishes of the consumers, decide – in some ways epitomises the predilection of many eighteenth-century socio-political thinkers to put their trust in the people and the wider scheme of wants and needs. Could a large measure of individual liberty prove compatible with socio-political stability? Or would constitutional government collapse into either anarchy or despotism? Could the surge of individual prosperity in an age of empire and industrial revolution prove compatible with social cohesion? Or would 'luxury' – that great bugbear – subvert liberty, set class against class, and subvert the constitution – all dangers forefronted in traditional pessimistic 'commonwealth' ideology, anxious about political corruption.[45] Fears about luxury never disappeared but, once again, an optimistic alternative was formulated, which contended that the affluence of individuals would enhance the wealth of nations, and that such prosperity automatically wove webs of interpersonal connections that strengthened, rather than divided, society.

Critics nevertheless feared that 'possessive individualism' (pursuit of private gain) would prove too disruptive, leading to the alienation of man from man. On the contrary, counter-argued an influential current of British thinking, including such late Enlightenment Scottish professors as John Millar and Dugald Stewart. Economic progress would produce a consumer society which would refine manners, promote peace, soften sensibilities and bind men to their fellows by the invisible chains of commerce. Properly understood, the culture of capitalism would prove not the solvent of society but its very cement.[46]

The eighteenth century thus brought the formulation of new models of man and philosophical rationales for the right to individual happiness in the consumer society. There was an emphasis on dynamic change, on human plasticity, on the interaction between individual, collectivity and environment; the notion was advanced that people were continually making and remaking themselves, that they could be educated or conditioned. Such ideas were often grounded in the scientific claim that man was essentially determined by his bodily needs and stimulated by organic sensations. There was, above all, a new legitimising of rational hedonism, a faith that the pursuit of pleasure would advance the general good. Such belief in a new human personality, the man of feeling, pointed towards Romanticism. Not least, confidence grew that the laws and system of Nature would produce order and progress.[47]

By 1800, it was widely contended by propagandists for modernity that human nature was programmed for pleasure, and that individual pursuit of happiness promoted the social good. 'New hedonist' was not the aristocratic rake 'writ large', but the man or woman of sensibility who could pursue satisfaction through sociable behaviour, and whose altruism and benevolence gave pleasure. Here, finally, lies the importance of the writings of Joseph Addison and Richard Steele, and the tradition of moral writings following *The Spectator* (1711–14) and the *Tatler* (1709–11).[48]

The Spectator paraded two old-fashioned images of human conduct as objects of ridicule: on the one hand, Puritan holier-than-thouism and, on the other, aristocratic libertinism. The zealots were sanctimonious killjoys who didn't understand Divine Benevolence, while rakes wore themselves out with drunken debauchery and thereby wrecked the very pleasures they hoped to attain. Addison and Steele by contrast advocated a middle way, in which moderate pursuit of sober and rational pleasures would produce lasting enjoyment. They stressed the importance of urbanity, politeness, rationality, moderation and the heeding of conventions, and gave fashionable sanction to new sorts of pursuits – light reading, tea-table conversation, the pleasures of the town – expected to be personally gratifying while socially harmonious. Their writings were imitated and repeated by scores of other essayists and moralists.

The eighteenth century gave its blessing to the pursuit of pleasure, but it was able to do this precisely because it redefined the nature of the pleasures it was desirable to pursue. Not least, the English ideology, as articulated through Lockean psychology, utilitarianism and political economy, promoted civilised hedonism within the values of rational self-interest in a capitalist system.[49]

2. Material Pleasures in the Consumer Society

ROY PORTER

Every age, every society, it goes without saying, has its own particular forms of pleasure, and only a brave historian would venture that some had more pleasure than others, or even were more pleasure-loving. Jeremy Bentham's 'felicific calculus' notwithstanding, pleasure is hard to measure.[1] But what is indisputable is that the pursuit of pleasure has taken different forms from century to century. This chapter will examine the shifting material bases and expressions of the quest for pleasure in the eighteenth century. It will argue that these alterations were to a large degree responsive to growing affluence within a more commercial, money-driven capitalist economy, which left more people with spare money in their pockets to be spent or squandered on a growing range of amusements and commodities.[2]

Alongside the 'affluence factor', it will also examine how changes in material culture transformed pleasure-taking. By material culture is here meant the physical apparatus of society, the built environment of cities, the availability of pleasure sites, resorts indoor and outdoor, and the 'pleasure machines' through which consumers might find pastime and amusement.[3] It is argued that the interplay of affluence – and hence demand – with developments in material culture gave rise in the Georgian era to new engines of enjoyment. It was, after all, a society in which by the 1780s one could, by paying a sum of money, actually soar into the air, thanks to the invention of the hot-air balloon, or, in Euston Square in 1808, be propelled on rails round and round in a 'steam circus' enclosure in the 'catch-me-who-can', the first steam locomotive to draw passengers, designed by the Cornish engineer, Richard Trevithick.[4]

The third dimension to be explored in this chapter is the social question: *who* could take *which* pleasures? It will be contended that, partly as a result of spreading affluence, enjoyments hitherto restricted to elites became open, certainly to the many and perhaps to the masses.

In earlier times, exclusiveness helped to make up the very relish of pleasure. The ruling class was the leisured class. Only landed aristocrats had the time and money to devote themselves to conspicuous pleasure: in a large measure it was they who traditionally defined what pleasure and leisure were. But, because of their associations with grandees, such goals could be regarded in a negative light – as earmarks of unjust privilege and symptoms of debauchery, the primeval deadly sin of sloth.[5] Indeed, in the thunderings of preachers and moralists, the upper classes were deemed to be 'corrupted' by leisure, while the lower orders were proverbially 'debauched' by idleness.

High Society viewed its relaxations through a value-system imparted by its Classical education. From this viewpoint, free time was the prized privilege of noble birth, the mark of personal glory. Lack of leisure was the penalty of poverty – or it betrayed the contemptible, mercenary spirit of the miserly Scrooge-like tradesman, proverbially obsessed with filthy lucre. The yoke of perpetual toil bespoke dependency; leisure, by contrast, permitted the cultivation of the mind and body, and promoted the nobler, great-souled freedom praised by Aristotle.[6]

Spokesmen for Georgian landed society by no means despised *negotium* (business) as such. They constituted, after all, an immensely ambitious, wealth-accumulating elite, consolidating their political clout at Westminster and in the shires, cultivating economic interests as energetic agrarian capitalists, and exercising their sway as magistrates and military leaders. But they particuarly prized *otium* (ease). They entertained no Puritan contempt for pleasure; they subscribed to Horatian models of the happy pastoral life; not least, as converts to Enlightenment values, they recognised that their enduring authority must depend not upon mere force of arms, but upon cultural hegemony, a conspicuous show of the good life, the excitation of envy and emulation. In that respect, they constituted a 'leisure class' in Thorsten Veblen's definition, an elite devoted to the conspicuous squandering of scarce resources; the pursuit of profligacy proved their good fortune in having so much to spare.[7] For England's ruling class, business and pleasure thus traditionally went hand in glove. If not an end in itself, leisure was essential for the parade of patrician eminence and dignity. The eagerness of the professional, commercial and industrial middle classes to buy themselves into land and leisure, Society and its Season (summer in the shires, winter in London's West End), even at the risk of financial ruin, attests the formidable appeal of this ideal. What this chapter will concentrate upon is the desire of the middling classes to imitate and buy into aristocratic pleasures – if also occasionally to scorn them; and it will also examine the emergence of new realms of pleasure and enjoyment that were quintessentially bourgeois. Pleasure and leisure became commercialised: that was, in large measure, a new development.[8]

Like all other European nations, pre-industrial Britain of course supported highly traditional forms of leisure activity. These had long been organised around Christian festivals (admittedly attenuated by consequence of the Protestant Reformation); around the rhythms of agrarian life; and around the political calendar.[9] 'Old Leisure' wore a bucolic air. The Georgian propertied classes amused themselves on their estates, symbolically through the exercise of the rights of hunting and shooting, almost religiously upheld by ever more ferocious game laws. Immensely extravagant great houses – Holkham, Houghton, Blenheim and so forth – with their paintings and furnishings, libraries and music rooms, elaborate dining habits, vast kitchens and cellars, all maintained by armies of flunkeys, cemented the traditional association of country estate with aristocratic enjoyment, while providing leisure retreats for the grandees' relations and hangers-on. With the notable exception of the grand tour, that youthful *rite de passage*, patrician pleasures were customarily orchestrated around the familial acres.[10]

Under the Hanoverians, however, high society also found it necessary to have an urban leisure headquarters, ideally a residence in the fashionable West End of London, or, for lesser gentry, a base in a stylish provincial city like York. If the sixteenth- or seventeenth-century English town had principally served as a site for trade and guild-based manufactures, in the Georgian age it became a locus of pleasurable consumption, where the affluent could flaunt themselves at the theatre, pump room, coffee-house, assembly and ball, and patronise the elegant shops on the parade. The leisure town was born.[11]

Though 'leisure' had hardly been thought a commodity appropriate to the poor, the lower orders in traditional society gained sporadic release from lives of drudgery through village sports, merrymaking, fairs, and the drinking festivals associated with occupations (for instance, apprenticeship rituals) or the rural calendar (Shrove Tuesday, Twelfth Night, Harvest Home, etc.). These, however, were to face increasing opposition. With the triumph of capitalism, preachers, employers and magistrates expressed hostility to the 'idleness' of the poor and the 'disorder' of their saturnalian bouts of dissipation, accompanied by drunkenness and crime and followed by telltale bastard births. Seeking the 'reformation of popular culture', campaigns were mounted to control or suppress such traditional plebeian sports as bear-baiting and bull-running. Certain recreations like horse-racing and prize-fighting remained popular amongst all social ranks, but by 1800 leisure activities in the countryside were growing more exclusively class-defined and -specific, that is to say, led by landowners. It was essentially in towns that pleasures became thrown open to the many.[12]

The questions of leisure and pleasure – their desirability and accessibility – were hotly debated. In early Georgian times, William Hogarth graphically pointed out the contrast between the industrious and idle apprentice: the former became Lord Mayor of London, the latter ended up hanged at Tyburn. Messages of this kind were endlessly hammered home: the poor had to be disciplined, inured to labour and, above all, to the regimes of work- and time-disciplines demanded by the new industrial system. Josiah Wedgwood, pioneer ceramics manufacturer and intellectual besides, clearly saw what industrial capitalism required of its workforce in stating his aim of turning workers into 'such machines as cannot err'. Popular sports and dissipations stood in the way of this goal, and, like other masters, Wedgwood publicly condemned intoxication, poor timekeeping, fecklessness and the 'leisure preference', the labourer's supposed habit of spending rather than saving, of wasting not working. Respectable public opinion denounced plebeian drunkenness, casual sex and spendthrift attitudes; Daniel Defoe, John Wesley and later moralists argued that the morals and orderliness of the masses could be secured only by instructing them in habits of industriousness, by enforcing long, regular and constant labour, and by penalising lounging and scrounging.[13]

To some extent, social change and commercial opportunism left these moralistic debates about the desirability of pleasure behind. While preachers thundered and magistrates sentenced, new modes of pleasure came into being, driven by opportunity and the profit-motive. The public voted with its feet, going in their droves to the theatre, to cricket matches, prize fights, spectacles, spas and the seaside.[14] What we can call an entertainment industry arose, devoted to satisfying the popular thirst for pleasures. For the first time there emerged sizeable bodies of professional actors, theatre managers, painters, sportsmen, art dealers, journalists, hack writers, and other people whose business was to provide entertainment for the public at large.[15] In England, it was in the eighteenth century that economic and cultural progress supported large numbers of those whose job it was to supply others with pleasure.

All this, of course, had its critics – preachers who thought pleasure was rank hedonism and sin, and therefore jeopardised salvation, moralists who condemned merriment as a bread-and-circuses diversion from the serious business of life and believed luxury would sap social discipline and morale. But the shrillness of such criticisms betrays the fact that the populace was increasingly involved in the pursuit of organised commercial pleasures. It was also a nation in which a lobby of enlightened economists and progressive social commentators began to view culture, sport and leisure as productive and valuable sectors of the economy, as forces for civilisation and social cohesion, and as indices of improvement.[16]

The leisure and pleasure industries could grow, thanks, of course, to economic vigour, above all what has been dubbed the eighteenth-century 'consumer revolution'. Many factors coalesced to make England more commercially successful than hitherto, not least the expansion of Empire and rising world trade, involving massive importation of goods, many coming from exotic parts.[17] Spices, cloths and furniture from the Middle East and the Orient began, for the first time, to grace the households of ordinary people. Homes were increasingly stocked with comforts and 'decencies' which that were shop-bought rather than home-made. From curtains to carpets, tableware to tea-sets, plate to prints, people were acquiring new enjoyments in tangible form – we would say as consumer durables.[18]

This revolution in domestic comforts created daily delights for ordinary folks. Homes grew more comfortable. New kinds of amusements came within reach; for example, the growing numbers of books on people's shelves included not just conventional improving works like the Bible but *belles lettres*, light reading, essays and novels (those 'evergreen trees of diabolical knowledge', in Sir Anthony Absolute's phrase). The spread of newspapers and magazines was highly significant. Up to 1700, all newspapers had been printed in London, but a provincial press soon augmented the metropolitan. The *Norwich Post* began in 1701, and, before the century was out, almost every big town had its own paper. By 1760, 200 000 copies were being sold per week of the thirty-five provincial papers in circulation, and sales doubled by 1800. A successful provincial paper, such as the *Salisbury Journal*, would have a weekly sale running to a few thousand (a flourishing *Paris* newspaper during the Revolution could not expect to sell more). Its readership was probably five to ten times that number, and many more picked up the contents by word of mouth. Provincial newspapers publicised local events, carried scores of commercial advertisements, and conveyed military, political and financial intelligence from London, to say nothing of the latest fashions. Contemporaries recognised that newspapers were great opinion-shapers. 'The mass of every people must be barbarous where there is no printing and consequently knowledge is not generally diffused', observed Dr Johnson. 'Knowledge is diffused among our people by the newspapers.'

If newspapers were, in effect, a novel invention, so too were novels. Alongside old favourites – the Bible, Foxe's *Book of Martyrs*, Horace and Cicero – many other sorts of reading matter became extremely popular: magazines, romances, play-texts, sermons, political pamphlets, almanacs and a host of ephemera, all enhancing a taste for news and novelty, expanding horizons and making people more aware of how the other half lived, thereby creating rising expectations.[19]

Interiors thus became more comfortable as a result of affluence and the capacity of commerce and industry to supply consumer goods to meet demand. Complementing this improvement in home comforts, urban space itself also grew more agreeable. The Georgian city was increasingly a social and cultural centre, designed for the spending of surplus money on enjoyments and entertainments.[20] Of key importance was a great transformation in shops, especially in big cities, London above all. Shops grew in number – by 1750 the 'nation of shopkeepers' had perhaps 150 000 retail outlets – becoming more attractive, bright, airy, and accommodating in layout, designed to allure passers-by and divert customers. Their stock improved. In 1774 one draper was advertising for sale Dutch ratteens, German serges, Wilton stuffs, Silisian cambricks, Manchester velvets, Brussels camblets and twenty other sorts of fabric in a sort of United Nations of haberdashery.

The traditional shop had been a workshop, a place of manufacture where customers placed orders that craftsmen would complete. Increasingly, however, it became a retail outlet displaying ready-made goods. The accent fell upon catching the customer's eye through design and lighting, aided by big bow-windows showing off goods to window-shoppers.[21] The delights of English shops were remarked by foreign travellers. 'It is almost impossible to express how well everything is organised in London', commented the German novelist, Sophie von La Roche,

> Every article is made more attractive to the eye than in Paris or in any other town. . . . We especially noticed a cunning device for showing women's materials. Whether they are silks, chintzes or muslins, they hang down in folds behind the fine high windows so that the effect of this or that material, as it would be in the ordinary folds of a woman's dress can be studied. Amongst the muslins all colours are on view, and so one can judge how the frock would like in company with its fellows. Now large shoe and slipper shops for anything from adults down to dolls can be seen – now fashion articles or silver or brass shops – boots, guns, glasses – the confectioner's goodies, the pewterer's wares – fans, etc. Behind great glass windows absolutely everything one can think of is neatly, attractively displayed, and in such abundance of choice as almost to make one greedy.[22]

Like many foreign visitors, Sophie loved browsing the London shops. 'What an immense stock, containing heaps and heaps of articles!', she exclaimed, visiting Boydell's, the capital's biggest print dealer:

> Here again I was struck by the excellent arrangements and system which the love of gain and the national good taste have combined in producing, particularly in the elegant dressing of large shop-windows, not merely in order to ornament the streets and lure purchasers, but to make known the thousands of inventions and ideas, and spread good taste about, for the excellent pavements made for pedestrians enable crowds of people to stop and inspect the new exhibits. Many a genius is assuredly awakened in this way; many a labour improved by competition, while many people enjoy the pleasure of seeing something fresh – besides gaining an idea of the scope of human ability and industry.[23]

All such developments turned shopping (and window-shopping) into pastimes in their own right.[24] It was Napoleon who remarked that England was a nation of shopkeepers, but it was also a nation of shoppers for whom buying became one of the social pleasures. The 'shop till you drop' mentality had perhaps not yet arrived, but the letters of Jane Austen demonstrate that one of the chief joys she gained from coming up to the capital from her seclusion in darkest Hampshire was to visit London's milliners, hosiers and drapers. She bought her fashionable muslins at Grafton House, New Bond Street, where she would also order gowns for her mother and sister. Another store that gained her custom was Bedford House, also known as as Layton & Shear's, conveniently near her brother Henry's Covent Garden residence.[25]

Alongside the capital, cities such as York, Exeter and Norwich developed institutions devoted to pleasure-taking: assembly rooms, theatres and halls for meetings and performances, with space set aside for clubs, lectures, spectacles, displays and other events. The modern comfortable coaching-inn developed, and every town sported well-appointed taverns, ale-houses and other places for conviviality. Walks were laid out, parks and fashionable bridges designed – in short, amenities were provided encouraging visitors to come to town and linger beyond the calls of business, soaking up the atmosphere of urbane and civilised living.[26]

Certain towns were principally devoted to pleasure. Spas combined the recovery of health with the pursuit of pleasure – a perilous brew! Critics drew attention to the paradox that in Bath, Buxton, Scarborough and, slightly later, Cheltenham, those who ought to have been resting and recovering were dizzied by the non-stop whirligig of pleasure. Resort towns specialised in pump rooms and assembly rooms where tea could be taken, balls held, and gambling indulged – to say nothing of amorous assignations. It was Charles Wesley, one of the founders of Methodism, who described Bath as 'Hell on earth'.[27]

By 1800, the vogue for inland spas was giving way to a fashion for the seaside. Brighton led, partly because the Prince Regent chose to make it his pleasure headquarters, building the exotic Pavilion and creating a fast-living centre for Regency bucks. 'Brighthelmston' was conveniently placed at no great distance from London. His father, George III, preferred Weymouth, and various other seaside resorts sprang up as well, Margate for instance. Jane Austen's final, unfinished novel, *Sanditon*, describes the rise of a fictional seaside resort on the South coast and the attempts of its leisure entrepreneurs to boost amenities such as assembly rooms, hotels, lodgings, shops, and a picturesque harbour, luring tourists.[28]

Nothing could better epitomise the Georgian love of pleasure than the pleasure garden. There were about two hundred or so pleasure resorts dotted amongst London's suburban villages, with their fishponds, fireworks, musicians and masquerades. Amongst the spas and watering places favoured for a Sunday jaunt were Sadlers Wells in Islington, Kilburn Wells (where at the Bell Tavern the 'politest companies could come to drink the water from a nearby spring'), Bermondsey Spa (now marked by Spa Road), and Hockley-in-the-Hole (Clerkenwell), where there were ornamental gardens, fishing, cream teas, grottoes, skittle alleys, fountains and formal walks, purgative waters and sometimes bear-baiting. At 'English Castle', another Clerkenwell pleasure garden, the proprietor advertised a 'Grand Grotto Garden and Gold and Silver Fish Repository', with an 'enchanted fountain' and a beautiful rainbow (admission only 6*d*).[29]

Reputedly once the summer retreat of Nell Gwynne, Bagnigge Wells (near today's King's Cross station) was popular. Its grounds contained honeysuckle-covered tea arbours, a bun house, skittle alley, bowling green, grotto, flower garden, fish ponds and fountains; concerts were held in the pump-room. 'Jenny's Whim' at Pimlico was celebrated for the 'amusing deceptions' in the garden: hidden springs caused harlequins and monsters to jump up before the unsuspecting, while floating models on a lake gave the impression of mermaids and flying-fish. Lambeth Wells had a vogue of more than fifty years, combining the pleasures of purging waters and all-night music – in 1755 its licence was discontinued because of its numerous brawls. Various other gardens were eventually suppressed because of their notoriety – the 'Temple of Flora's' proprietor was given a prison sentence in 1796 for keeping a disorderly house.

Leisure entrepreneurs also created more elaborate pleasure gardens. Long famous were Cuper's (or Cupid's) gardens in Lambeth, notorious for their erotic ambience. Spring Gardens, later known as Vauxhall, opened in 1660 up-river on the south bank: access by boat created a romantic illusion. Laid out with walks, statues and tableaux, Vauxhall became London's most sumptuous resort. Orchestras played, the fireworks were dazzling, there was dancing, or one could sup in gaily decorated alcoves in the gardens – and all for just a shilling. One high spot came in 1749, when a hundred musicians played to an audience of 12 000 – it caused traffic jams as far away as London Bridge; another great event happened in 1802, when a Frenchman made a parachute landing from a balloon.

Adjoining Chelsea Hospital, Ranelagh gardens opened in 1742, vying with Vauxhall. 'Ranelagh looks like the enchanted palace of a genie', commented Tobias Smollett in his novel, *Humphry Clinker*:

> adorned with the most exquisite performance of painting, carving, and gilding, enlightened with a thousand golden lamps, that emulate the noon-day sun; crowded with the great, the rich, the gay, the happy, and the fair; glittering with cloth of gold and silver, lace, embroidery, and precious stones.

Its chief attraction was a rotunda, 150 feet in diameter, an orchestra in the centre and tiers of boxes all round. 'Every night I constantly go to Ranelagh, which has totally beat Vauxhall', declared Horace Walpole, an *habitué* of both. Fairly cheap and open, if not to all, then at least to all with a few shillings to spare, pleasure resorts and gardens perfectly embodied the Georgian pleasure revolution.

Various forms of entertainment were rendered more commercial to make them more attractive to the public at large. Take the theatre. Condemned as threats to morals and good order, playhouses had been closed down by the Puritans at the time of the Civil War. Re-established in 1660 at the restoration of Charles II, the English theatre initially depended upon royal patronage. Restoration drama therefore tended to be court-oriented and highly elitist. The comedies of Congreve, Farquhar, Vanbrugh and Etherege were written for a cliquey audience and were full of in-jokes. In the eighteenth century by contrast, theatre tended to cater for wider tastes.

Drury Lane theatre saw a succession of great playwrights, managers and actors, including David Garrick and Richard Sheridan. It was redesigned in 1773 by Robert Adam and eighteen years later demolished to make way for Henry Holland's new auditorium which cost £150 000 and seated a staggering 3611 (even in Norwich, the theatre held over a thousand). Aiming to appeal to huge audiences, Drury Lane's management presented a mix of entertainments, including light opera, farce, burlesque and 'burlettas', alongside watered-down versions of Shakespeare and melodramas that offered big roles for star actors; its playwrights had to write for mixed middle-brow audiences, their hits being simple and sentimental, with elements of pantomime, farce and music-hall.

Theatre audiences were a veritable social microcosm. 'We have three . . . different and distinct Classes', noted a London guide in 1747:

> the first is called the *Boxes*, where there is one peculiar to the King and Royal Family, and the rest for the Persons of Quality, and for the Ladies and Gentlemen of the highest Rank, unless some Fools that have more Wit than Money, or perhaps more Impudence than both, crowd in among them. The second is call'd the *Pit*, where sit the *Judges*, *Wits* and *Censurers*, . . . in common with these sit the *Squires*, *Sharpers*, *Beaus*, *Bullies* and *Whores*, and here and there an extravagant *Male* and *Female Cit*. The third is distinguished by the Title

of the *Middle Gallery*, where the Citizen's Wives and Daughters, together with the *Abigails*, Serving-men, Journey-men and Apprentices commonly take their Places.[30]

What followed from the vastness of the auditorium was a trend towards more accessible, naturalistic acting styles and the triumph of the theatrical star, since leading actors – who often doubled as impresarios, producers and directors – were able to dominate the stage. David Garrick, Peg Woffington, Sarah Siddons and Edmund Keane achieved a public fame comparable to that of Hollywood stars such as Marilyn Monroe in the twentieth century. Here was theatre not for the elite but as general mass entertainment.[31]

Sport was another kind of pleasure-taking transformed in the eighteenth century. Traditionally it had been part of ritual village activity, integral to the seasonal customs marking the agricultural year. Football for instance had been played on one particular day in the calendar (notably Shrove Tuesday), involving all the men in the village.[32] In the Georgian century, complementing such village games, sport was developed on commercial and professional lines, encouraging the emergence of the paying spectator. In London, for example, there were regular commercial cockpits, and prize-fighting became big box-office too.[33] The old manly traditions of cudgelling and fisticuffs evolved into organised boxing, mainly still barefist but leading to the rise of professional prize fighters like Daniel Mendoza, Tom Cribb and 'Gentleman' John Jackson who topped the bill in widely advertised contests, drawing thousands of spectators, and becoming national celebrities. Cricket and other games also became spectator sports; as with horse-racing, much of their popularity lay in the element of gambling.[34]

Sport was thus becoming organised, commercial, professional and national. So too did other cultural activities hitherto largely home-made or exclusive to the court and nobility. As Derek Alsop suggests in his essay on opera in this volume, Georgian England supported a vast increase of concerts and other public musical occasions. Music formed an important aspect of the attractions offered by the pleasure gardens: Handel's Water Music and Fireworks Music were performed for the first time at Vauxhall. So attractive were the potential rewards thereby offered to composers and conductors and instrumentalists, that top continental musicians chose to come and make concert tours in London and some – Handel above all – settled because the commercial opportunities for a career in music were so much more inviting than those offered as *Kappelmeister* at a continental court.[35]

Other innovations were the shows and spectacles mounted in cities, above all in London. The swathe leading from Fleet Street and the Strand, up through Charing Cross and into Leicester Square, Soho and Piccadilly boasted all manner of halls, booths and displays. There were Robert Powell's puppet shows in the Little Piazza, Covent Garden; Mrs Salmon's waxworks in Fleet Street; the 'wonderful tall Essex woman' at the Rummer tavern in Three King's Court, Fleet Street, who was 'seven feet high'; as well as 'Young Colossuses', 'Tall Saxon Women', and the 'Ethiopian Savage': 'this astonishing Animal', it was reported by the *Daily Advertiser* on 4 June 1778,

> is of a different species from any ever seen in Europe, and seems to be a link between the Rational and Brute Creation, as he is a striking resemblance of the Human Species, and is allowed to be the greatest Curiosity ever exhibited in England.... Also the Orang Outang, or real Wild Man of the Woods... a Calf with eight legs, two tails, two heads, and only one body on display opposite the New Inn, Surrey side of Westminster Bridge at 1*s.* each person.

In Panton Street, Piccadilly, the quack doctor, James Graham, was giving his celebrated displays of healthy nude mud-bathing, aided by a bevy of belles. In 1779, Robert Barker built his 'Panorama' in Leicester Place, and in nearby Lisle Street, James Loutherbourg opened his 'Eidophusikon' (magic lantern) – to say nothing of the 'raree' shows at the menageries at the Tower and Exeter Change in the Strand and at Bartholomew Fair, Smithfield every September.[36]

Appealing to the more serious-minded was the growth of museums. The British Museum itself was founded in 1753, as a result of the bequest to the nation of his vast collections by the physician and scientist, Sir Hans Sloane. Originally set up in Montagu House, Bloomsbury, it grew considerably, requiring the erection of the present building at the dawn of the nineteenth century. Alongside this public museum, many private museums were open for an entrance fee as, for example, Sir Ashton Lever's museum in Leicester Square, a vast collection of curios, anatomical specimens, antiquities, archaeological finds, paintings, coins and knick-knacks.[37]

In most developments of this kind it was the market – or in other words commercial opportunism – that led the way in providing new forms of entertainment for the paying crowd.[38] In Victorian times, the Great Exhibition (1851) was a state-promoted enterprise, as were the museums set up with the proceeds – the Victoria and Albert Museum, the Natural History Museum, the Science Museum were all state-funded. By contrast, comparable initiatives in Georgian England came from leisure entrepreneurs, bent upon bringing their wares to the people, seeking to make money out of every new sensation, freak and commercial opportunity.[39] The state rarely intervened.

This commercialisation of leisure did not, of course, instantly put a stop to traditional folk pleasures. People carried on playing village sports and making merry at home and in the tavern. Indeed, the process of commercialisation in some ways encouraged amateur and community-based activities. For example, with the publication of sheet-music, developed by the extremely enterprising publisher, John Walsh, it was easy for home music-makers to be playing Handel on their viols, harpsichords or flutes shortly after such music had been composed. High culture was thereby channelled down to the people.[40]

Yet this commercialisation of pleasure probably tended, in the long run, to undermine traditions of folk merrymaking, mumming and the like. And such trends were enhanced by campaigns against what were stigmatised as vulgar or violent forms of pleasure – bear-baiting, bull-running, pugilism, cudgelling and other characteristically physical lower-class amusements. These were increasingly the target of attack from self-styled 'friends of civilisation' and from evangelical Christians hostile to brutality.[41] Moves were afoot to encourage more *civilised* forms of pleasure. Looking back in 1801 on the development of Bath, the Reverend Richard Warner bemoaned that 'the sports which sufficiently satisfied our ancestors of the sixteenth and seventeenth centuries' had been

> the pranks of mountebanks, the feats of jugglers, tumblers, and dancers, the jests of itinerant *mimes* or mummers, and the dangerous amusement of the quintane, diversified occasionally by the pageant and the masque, or the *elegant* pastime of bull-baiting, cock-fighting, cock-scaling, pig-racing, bowling, football, grinning through a horse-collar, and swallowing scalding hot frumenty. . . . But as national manners gradually refined, the ideas of elegance were proportionally enlarged, and publick amusements insensibly approximated to the taste and splendour which they at present exhibit; balls, plays, and cards, usurping the place of those rude athletick sports, or gross sensual amusements, to which the hours of vacancy had before been devoted.[42]

In Warner's time moral crusaders formed societies designed for purifying pleasures. The Proclamation Society, in particular, attempted to render Sundays sober: entertainments should be closed on the Sabbath to induce church-going.

Yet it would be a mistake to give undue emphasis to the killjoys. Hedonism remained unabashed. It was a time, for example, as is shown elsewhere in this volume by Simon Varey, when enormous delight was taken in food – partly as a result of low prices, partly thanks to the increasing importation of new and exotic foodstuffs such as pineapples. The pleasures of the table loomed large – diaries like that of Parson Woodforde suggest something like an obsession with eating. Almost every single day of his journals includes a reference to meals, above all dinner. Even in the very last entry before his death, he managed to record that, although extremely weak and almost unable to get downstairs, there was, nevertheless, 'roast beef, etc.' for dinner.[43]

The pleasures of the table were washed down by those of the bottle. The century was notorious for heavy alcohol consumption, indeed for public and often unashamed drunkenness. Politicians such as Pitt the Younger and Richard Sheridan were notoriously heavy drinkers. It was manly to be inebriated, and drinking one's friends under the table was a proper and honourable ambition, as is evident from the memoirs of William Hickey. Samuel Johnson called drinking life's second greatest pleasure.[44]

In respect of eating and drinking, there is little sign of strong public criticism before the close of the century. Indeed, the reverse seems to be the case. During the French Wars, aristocratic mores were to the fore. Under the Regency (1811–20) especially, when the Prince Regent (the 'Prince of Pleasure') led fashion, there was more conspicuous consumption and greater public drunkenness than ever. The Prince's insatiable appetite for food and liquor, his sexual foibles, adoration of fine clothes and exorbitant tastes in building – he built Regent Street and Regent's Park and rebuilt Buckingham Palace – all created a climate of pleasure-seeking.[45]

It may be argued, of course, that the truest barometer of the pleasures of a civilisation lies in its sexual activity. Sex – for Samuel Johnson the number-one pleasure – however, leaves few records, and is unusually subject to sensationalist distortion. Nevertheless, recent scholarship has shown that sex was publicly flaunted in eighteenth-century England in a manner that bears comparison with the second half of the twentieth century. The most visible index was, of course, prostitution. There were anything up to 30 000 public streetwalkers in London. The diaries of James Boswell suggest it was impossible to walk down Fleet Street or the Strand or to saunter in St James's Park without encountering the clamorous attentions of scores of harlots, which he found extremely difficult to resist.[46]

An early best-seller was James Cleland's book, popularly known nowadays as *Fanny Hill* but significantly entitled *Memoirs of a Woman of Pleasure* (1749). The very notion of a 'woman of pleasure' betrays macho prejudices – woman as sex object – but it perfectly conveys the belief that erotic gratification was a legitimate mode of enjoyment. Cleland turned the 'harlot's progress', which for Hogarth had been a tragedy, into a triumph. His whore, Fanny Hill, enjoys her profession, and derives pleasure from promiscuous fornication, while also falling in love with her very first client, whom she finally marries. Fanny thus united pleasure, profit, love and romance all in one completely implausible fiction.[47]

Prostitution aside, there is plenty of evidence to suggest that Georgian men and women devoted themselves with gusto to the pleasures of bed, not yet inhibited by Victorian scruple and the demands of strict respectability. Rather than condemning sexuality as sinful, as in Augustinian theology, or regarding it as primarily functional – merely the means of procreation – much eighteenth-century sexual advice literature maintained that sexuality constituted a pleasure in its own right, a civilising force and a legitimate fountain of enjoyment. Dr Erasmus Darwin, a leading physician, called sex 'the purest felicity in the otherwise vapid cup of life'. And he would know, because he produced twelve children, ten legitimate and two illegitimate. One of his legitimate children became the father of Charles Darwin, the founder of evolutionary theory.[48]

It is difficult in retrospect to gauge the hedonic temperature of an era and feel the pulse of its merrymaking. One window, however, is through the visual evidence it leaves. Hogarth's prints provide plentiful evidence that the English did not merely indulge in pleasure-taking, but wanted to be *recorded* enjoying themselves. Hogarth shows us, for example, images of Southwark Fair with all sorts having a good time, eating, getting drunk, amusing themselves around stalls and theatrical performances: likewise his print, Beer Street. But he also depicts respectable bourgeois families, not, as they might have been shown in the seventeenth century – or even in the nineteenth – at prayer or engaged in solemn improving activities; but enjoying themselves, drinking tea, playing with their children or pets, taking a stroll, visiting pleasure gardens – often with happy expressions on their faces. Rowlandson, equally, loved recording popular fun.[49] It is no accident that the Victorians, who prided themselves on the importance of being earnest and whose Queen was not amused, looked back with stern disapproval at their pleasure-loving grandparents.[50]

3. The Pleasures of the Table

SIMON VAREY

To celebrate the coronation of George II, which took place on 11 October 1727, three loyal tables in Westminster Hall groaned beneath the accumulated weight of seventy-five different dishes, thirty of which were replaced with yet more food as the repast continued, so that 105 different taste sensations were available in one place. With platters crowding the tables, some piled on top of others to give the image of food rising along the middle of each table, everything was calculated to please the palates, the eyes and the appetites of hundreds of guests. Each table contained a characteristic combination of savouries and sweets. 'Leeches' (chequered jellies) nestled against collared veal, geese à la daube, crabs, cheesecakes, bombards and friçandos, venison pasties, polonia sausage, and numerous plates marked 'Sweetmeats' and 'Fruit', with four 'grand pyramids' of sweetmeats every few feet along the length of each table, and one especially grand grand pyramid 'of Wet & Dry Sweetmeats' in the very centre. No fewer than fifty separate plates of garnish were provided on each table to set off the opulence of the main attraction. The banquet lasted for three days, as it would have had to, if every guest were to taste, just taste, a sample of each dish. The architect of this banquet was Charles Carter, proud of his credentials as former cook to a string of noblemen.[1] Carter was no ordinary cook, but then this was no ordinary occasion.

Apart from the sheer scale of a banquet, this of course was not how many people, even the privileged, customarily ate. An ordinary family living in a cottage on perhaps £30–£40 a year

would probably have been making do with a plate of potatoes, a few green peas, or most likely the ubiquitous bread and cheese, and possibly a small piece of fatty pork or bacon. People who lived a little more comfortably than that might have entertained

their guests with as many as two courses, each consisting of two dishes: the heavier course first, perhaps boiled beef and a pudding, followed by roasted fowl and a tart.[2] At the banquet, young wine, tasting probably rather like Beaujolais nouveau, was poured in copious quantities. In the cottage, the drink of preference was beer or, if the family could afford it in 1727, tea.[3] It is hard to say who took the more pleasure from their dinner, harder still to say why.

Eating is visibly a social activity. Eighteenth-century eating either falls into the category of subsistence, or it is hailed as an opportunity for the pleasures of convivial company. Boswell was not alone in using the tavern or the ordinary as a place of assignation, nor is this the only connection between the pleasure of food and the pleasure of sex. (I promise at this point not to revisit the 1963 film of *Tom Jones.*) There is an obvious correlation between food and sex, for both of which we do, after all, have appetites. English slang furnishes obvious examples: lamb pie (for which there are straightforward recipes everywhere) meant roughly the same in the eighteenth century as a bit of crumpet in the twentieth. If the English had a passion for oysters, lobsters, mushrooms, ginger, the French knew about avocados, de Sade (ever hopeful) knew the reputation of chocolate, and everyone seems to have rated asparagus alongside the peach tree as a food blessed by Venus herself. As Milton hardly needed to remind us, fruit (loaded word) is the ultimate aphrodisiac: it was Milton who decided to place all the blame on the apple, perhaps because it was the most English of fruits (sixty varieties were commercially available). And that New World import, the tomato, was always known as the love apple. Perhaps the most enduring pleasure of the table was the paradox that it does not endure. Eating stimulates the appetite for more eating.

As all cooks worth their salaries know, we eat with our eyes. The madness of King George's coronation banquet can hardly be typical of a national preference for the arrangement of plates on a table, which is all we can learn about presentation of the food from Carter's diagrams. But we have some sense of how cooks arranged food on the plate, if only because there is advice on the subject of garnishing to be found scattered throughout the cookery books. Generally speaking, large meals were not served on the plate, but on platters from which diners helped themselves, in an unexpected anticipation of the cafeteria. Table decorations would have been uncommon for an everyday dinner, but they did find their way into everyday cookery books, such as Elizabeth Raffald's *The Experienc'd English Housekeeper, for the use and ease of Ladies, Housekeepers, Cooks, &c.* Raffald's decorations include a fishpond made from jelly, a hen's nest and, most striking of all, Solomon's Temple in flummery, which is essentially a cream-based mousse. This last decoration was, like so many things, plagiarised by John Farley, proprietor of the famed London Tavern.[4]

Let us consider some of the attitudes to food and dining that caused eighteenth-century English people to enjoy what they ate. First, a caveat: there is little evidence that can usefully document the eating habits of the poorer half of the population; we do know a good deal about what kinds of food were consumed and roughly in what quantities, but we have a much less certain picture of what so many people liked to eat. The poor ate simple food, in marked contrast to the elaborate combinations of ingredients that created Farley's notion of progress.[5] It is striking just how often writers accustomed to rich food, and lots of it, would express enormous pleasure and great surprise when they were served an extremely simple dish, often in humble surroundings. A typical example occurs in Henry Fielding's semifictional late work, *A Journal of a Voyage to Lisbon.* Waiting on the Isle of Wight, Fielding remarks on the splendid fish he and his wife are induced to buy:

> I bought [a John Dory] of at least four pounds weight, for as many shillings. It resembles a turbot in shape, but exceeds it in firmess and flavour. The price . . . was, in truth, so very reasonable when estimated by its goodness, that it left me under no other surprise than how the gentlemen of this country, not greatly eminent for the delicacy of their taste, had discovered the preference of the dorée to all other fish.[6]

Fielding expresses his surprise that such a plentiful source of nourishment as fish should be so difficult to obtain in London, where 'not one poor palate in a hundred . . . knows the taste of fish'.[7] He was echoing Defoe, who had eaten salmon in Devon for twopence, when fish no bigger and certainly not so fresh was going in London for six shillings and sixpence (thirty-nine times the Devon price).[8] Fielding attributed the scarcity of good fish in the capital simply to money and the fashionable tastes that money generates or attracts. Recognising that there is not much a cook needs to do to a fish, Fielding continues:

> It is true indeed that this taste is generally of such excellent flavour that it exceeds the power of French cookery to treat the palates of the rich with anything more exquisitely delicate.[9]

For Fielding, 'Vanity or scarcity will always be the favourite of luxury', so that for those suffering from a terminal case of vanity, the pleasure of eating almost anything is directly proportional to the cost or rarity of the ingredients.[10] For the preternaturally vain, a simple John Dory would clearly never do, in any company, but for Fielding and many like him, one additional reason for pleasure in eating was surprise, a change, simple variety: the pleasure of the unfamiliar.

Perhaps the key to this repeated culture clash is that the writers tend to be urban, the purveyors of such simple food, rural. Hardly any of the food supply since the early modern period has been grown or cultivated in cities, so that the urban population becomes increasingly alienated from the environment in which food is grown, and fresh food becomes almost an oxymoron in the city. Most English towns and cities in the eighteenth century were surrounded by a ring of market gardens that provided fruit and vegetables, yet visitors to London were continually disappointed by the poor quality and flavour, especially of the vegetables.[11] The rule in the country kitchen was that the cook would use whichever vegetables and fruits were in season, whichever herbs were grown outside the back door. For all we know, the poor might have preferred to eat food they could not afford, but the better off had to be satisfied with what they could get, too. To supply the demand in the cities, fruits and vegetables could be picked before they were ripe, and then shipped, which would not result in ripe produce of good quality in the cities until hardy hybrid varieties had been developed, late in the nineteenth century. The only alternative was that the produce would be picked when ripe and then transported, quite slowly along dreadful roads, to the urban markets. Fruits and vegetables thus supplied to the cities were likely to be overripe, and therefore best suited for cooking methods that would exploit their softer texture. Purees of vegetables were common, either as garnish or as the basis of a sauce, and the English had long had a particular liking for pies and tarts, which usually required fruits to be cooked.

The urban meat supply did not have to suffer from the same problem, because animals could be transported alive, fattened with turnips or cabbages and slaughtered closer to the point of sale. That this procedure did not result in fresh meat as often as it might is witnessed by the advice, successively plagiarised from one cookery book to another, to be cautious when buying meat at the market. Properly aged beef is purple, with cream-coloured fat. The taste, certainly in England and France, was for very red beef, probably meaning young ox meat. Cookery books occasionally dispense the mysterious advice that saltpetre should be rubbed into raw beef prior to roasting or boiling. Aside from imparting a faint flavour of gunpowder (rather like a smoked tea), saltpetre would affect the colour of the meat once it was cooked, helping to prevent the destruction of the florid colour', but toughening it dreadfully.[12] Raw veal, on the other hand, was to be as white as possible, from 'bleeding, and giving them Chalk, as in *Essex*', according to Sir Hans Sloane.[13]

The pleasure of eating could certainly be the pleasure of somehow experiencing the country. Smollett's Matthew Bramble tends to idealise his life on a Welsh country estate, but really the point of his description of his food supply is that it is all fresh, natural, unsophisticated and unadulterated. His cider and bread are home made; his claret 'of the best growth, imported for my own use, by a correspondent on whose integrity I can depend'; his sheep and calves (actually he refers to the *animals* as mutton and veal) raised on 'fragrant herbage' and 'the mother's milk' respectively.[14] In reality, few could rely on food raised as he describes it, but Bramble nicely points up the contrast with city dwellers whose mutton 'is neither lamb nor mutton, but something betwixt the two, gorged in the rank fens of Lincoln and Essex, pale, coarse, and frouzy'.[15] While Londoners swallow contaminated water, Bramble drinks 'the virgin lymph, pure and crystalline as it gushes from the rock'.[16]

The urban experience of food lies behind Smollett's commentaries as well as those expressions of the unexpected pleasure of eating simple dishes. Bramble's preference can probably be explained as the pleasure of eating fresher food that is untouched by any of the problems inherent in providing the urban food supply. The most problematic foodstuff of all was milk, which was so perfectly disgusting in London that it is a wonder anyone drank it at all, and that anyone who did drink it did not drop dead.[17] There are no urban panegyrics to milk, no expressions of pleasure in its consumption. Swift's early poem, *Baucis and Philemon,* testifies to the freshness of milk in the country. In Austen's day, though not, I think, in her experience, milk could be had at the doorstep in fashionable parts of London, taken direct from the udder, literally bringing the country to the city and incidentally making genuinely fresh syllabub possible. This brief fashion can scarcely be attributed to a renaissance of demand for the most symbolically nutritive and nurturing of foods. The motive was the lower one of ostentation, a pleasure in itself to some. Seldom the style of the rural (or urban) poor, ostentation had long ago taken the unfamiliar a step further by providing the attraction of the truly exotic.

Perhaps no one ever really imitated the grandest of feasts, Trimalchio's, but there was much pleasure to be derived from providing guests with the shock of the unfamiliar, the exotic, or the plain expensive. Trimalchio's Feast surely satisfied some pleasure requirement vicariously, as Petronius describes the guests washing their hands in fine Opimian wine before consuming such 'trumpery' as a wild boar stuffed with live thrushes, roast pork carved to reveal sausages and black puddings, and a hare with wings designed to resemble Pegasus.[18] Petronius raises the familiar issue of trickery in the presentation of food – a practice as old as cooking, and one that survives in parallel in the language of food (Bramble may call a sheep mutton, but we eat veal, pork, and beef, not calves, pigs and heifers).

Ostentation in reality could be taken a step further. An anonymous pamphleteer with a taste for skewering the more extravagant of London's revellers declared his surprise 'at the present luxurious and fantastical manner of Eating, which many of our People of Quality and false Taste are fallen into'.[19] He was particularly appalled at the cost of extravagant hospitality, noting that the money spent on 'a single Plate to please one of these foppish Gluttons' used to feed half a parish.[20] Fielding's comments on fish echo this sentiment. Although there is not a great deal of evidence to rely on, a call for simple and unostentatious food seems to amount to a call to remember the plight of the poor and to abandon the silly extravagance of showing off. The result, in the cookery books at least, is the slow development in England of a national cuisine that suits town and country tastes alike, characterised by robustness of texture and flavour, and in a way encouraging standardisation rather than regional variety and distinctiveness. Regional cuisines did begin to decline at the same time.

The characteristic flavours of this gradually emerging cuisine, on both sides of the English Channel, were the ones that had been established since at least the mid-seventeenth century: sherry, almonds, nutmeg, mace, pepper, cinnamon and, of course, sugar. It is an international sport to dismiss English cooking as bad, which is especially remarkable whenever the dismissal comes from the land of sodium-enriched ground meat steeped in hot beef tallow, but one part of the question of the pleasure of the English table is: what is English food? One part of the answer lies in the legacy of colonisation. In the eighteenth century, foods, dishes, and cooking methods were imported from the West Indies and from India, and adopted in English cooking practice. To take a few reasonably typical examples, English food included *escabeche* (raw fish marinated in lemon or lime juice and spices, then called *caveach*), which entered English cuisine with the capture of Jamaica in the mid-seventeenth century, and which fits quite nicely with the English love of pickled foods. Recipes for curried dishes in various guises started to appear in cookery books as soon as the English presence in India was established. Characteristic English blandness seems to have been the result of Victorian industrialisation and a growing urban proletariat. For those who could afford them, spices were abundant and were used with a fairly free hand. Spices, we are always told, were craved by Europeans as a means of making boring food interesting and of masking off flavours, but meat that has gone bad makes you sick, spices or no spices. I doubt that bulimia was one of the eighteenth century's gastronomic pleasures.

Overcooking, obviously difficult to document, appears also to be a mainly Victorian legacy, but a bane that Hannah Glasse addressed in 1747, as did John Farley in 1783 when he warned:

> Numbers of cooks spoil their garden stuffs by boiling them too much. All kinds of vegetables should have a little crispness; for if you boil them too much, you will deprive them both of their sweetness and beauty.[21]

His advice presupposes a reliable supply of vegetables of good quality. Some foods were clearly overcooked intentionally, such as the tomato, but the reason there was that it was thought to be potentially poisonous – with some justification, because it belongs to the nightshade family. Jane Austen, as far as I can tell, ate her tomatoes raw. And surely she recognised the truth of the Emperor Augustus's pet phrase 'as quick as boiled asparagus' when she had the hypochondriac Mr Woodhouse order asparagus to be boiled so long it would collapse into mush.[22] There would be no joke if overcooking was commonplace.

Lydia Fisher was one of the earliest authors to specify cooking times, although these are not especially helpful without temperatures. Even at 450°F, twelve to fifteen minutes per pound for mutton or pork would not result in a burnt offering, while a mere thirty minutes for a five-pound leg of lamb might confound today's critics of English food. Fisher recommended only forty-five minutes in total for a large fowl or a rabbit.[23] Fisher's cooking times seem to suggest that, if anything, roasted meats were served on the rare side. 'Bake until done' might be a common injunction in a recipe, but it means bake until your preference is satisfied, not bake until dry.

Some of these English cooking techniques, indeed some dishes, emerge in part from the least well known of all the eighteenth century's wars: the cooking wars between England and France. As Alice and Frank Prochaska rightly observe, it is not true that 'English cooks only learned to cook sauces from the French', and they point out that 'the flow of influence between the two countries was to some extent a two-way traffic, at least until the mid-eighteenth century'.[24] They cite Stephen Mennell's explanation of the increasing fashion for French food, together with a French attachment to 'the precise observance of personal customs and rituals, which included everything to do with food'.[25] Yet, *les îles flottantes,* in its eighteenth-century French manifestation, was an English trifle or a stale French brioche with fruit preserves served on a sea of sherry- or brandy-flavoured whipped cream and decorated with candied trees, animals, or anything else that would make dessert look like Robinson Crusoe's island. Today, it is meringue floating in a sea of *sauce anglaise.* It is practically impossible to determine whether this dish is English or French in origin, but it was enjoyed in both countries, more for its snob value in England, because it was thought French, and everywhere because of its attractive appearance. In England, food prepared according to French style and taste became an object of ridicule for its alleged fussiness and delicacy verging on the effeminate. Accordingly, Swift's directions to servants include this advice:

> If a Lump of Soot falls into the Soup, and you cannot conveniently get it out, scum it well, and it will give the Soup a high *French* Taste.[26]

Our anonymous pamphleteer tells a tale of meeting a French cook preparing dishes whose principal ingredients were unrecognisable: in the kitchen, the cook is pounding roast partridges 'in a Mortar, with all the Fat and the Inside of a Surloin of Beef; I ask'd him the Reason of this strange Havock, and he told me, it was to make a *Cullis* for a *Pupton*'.[27] This is the perfect example of cookery as trickery, but here with overtones of ostentation and Gallicism: 'Legerdemain . . . Affectation and Folly'.[28] This chef's bill of fare includes two soups, carp au court bouillon, pupton of partridge, beef à la tremblade, and cutlets à la maine; all this is followed by a fricasée of salamanders, huffle of chickens, pain perdu, oysters à la daube, blancmange (a tasty white sauce), and stewed lion.[29] Then comes a menu of supposedly 'natural' food: viper soup, stewed snails, roast hedgehog, fricassee of frogs, badger's ham and cauliflower.

Even an avowedly nationalist cookery book, as English as any other contemporary cookery book, contained a mixture of the French and the exotica. Patrick Lamb was aiming to provide recipes for '*Good Eating*', scorning 'those severer *Asceticks who keep* Lent *at* Christmas, *and weigh out their Diet by Drams and*

Scruples', and declining to offer '*an Art of Gluttony, or to teach the Rich and Lazy, how to grow fatter*'.[30] No, Lamb proposed '*to represent the Grandeur of the* English *Court and Nation*'. With such a declared purpose, it is all the more remarkable that most of Lamb's methods were visibly French and that he even acknowledged that '*many of the Receipts are of* French *Invention*'.[31] The truth is that the two-way traffic was easily concealed by nationalist rhetorical cant. English people clearly ate 'French' food if they pleased – and enjoyed it.

Recipes, like royal banquets, suggest that the well-to-do were overeaters. They were. Just as a four-bottle man would drink a whole bottle of claret with his dinner, followed by three more of port in an evening, he might expect to eat a pound of meat and a pound of poultry and a pie and a jelly and a few handfuls of nuts at his main meal of the day. George Cheyne, the Bath physician who was satirised for being a physician and for weighing 450 pounds at the acme of his obesity, knew the correlation between overindulgence and body weight, though the knowledge of which foods encouraged obesity was more empirical and a little less scientific than it is today. 'Fat People', wrote Dr Arbuthnot, 'ought to eat and sleep little, and use much Exercise, in which the Cure chiefly consists'.[32] Massive quantities and overindulgence did give pleasure, no doubt. I have found little information that might establish whether or not eighteenth-century anorexics derived pleasure from compulsive fasting.

Cookery books are the most useful guide we have to eating habits, yet they are inherently unreliable, because we have no sure way of determining whether or not they are prescriptive. And then there is the problem of plagiarism, which students of cookery books – especially eighteenth-century English ones – recognise as one of the reasons that we cannot be casual about the evidence. Cookery books frequently were prefaced with solemn disclaimers of authenticity, yet there are numerous cases of English books of the last quarter of the eithteenth century cheerfully repeating recipes that had already appeared in four or five generations of cookery books, each generation lifting the texts from the previous one. This may not tell us what people were eating in 1790, but it certainly does tell us that a tradition, if only a printing tradition, had been established. It seems most likely that the recipes that keep on being plagiarised are probably for the enduringly popular dishes. The cookery books should indicate which dishes were in demand, which ones the mistress of the household, middle-class and up, wished to have served to her family and guests, but the very lack of specifics in the recipes is probably a sign that it was up to the mistress and her cook to determine the details.

The overwhelming impression these books convey is a desire for meat. That England was a nation of carnivores was well established, for although there were vegetarians, they were frequently ridiculed.[33] Even the English appetite for meat had a political dimension: witness Hogarth's *Gates of Calais*, in which a spindleshanked Frenchman is incapable of even holding a good baron of beef. It was a commonplace that the English were hearty and healthy eaters of beef, which made them strong and hale, while the French liked their delicate sauces (virulently condemned by Hannah Glasse) but got so little nutrition from their diet that they were feeble and ridiculous. The French version of this was that the English were coarse, the French refined.

The cookery books have relatively little to say about vegetables, which might then be thought to have figured infrequently in the English diet. It is more likely that no one needed much advice on their preparation: in fact, the French usually complained that English cooks were unimaginative with vegetables, merely boiling turnips or cabbages and plopping them down on a plate with roast meat. One late edition of Hannah Glasse shows that the produce of the garden was used to garnish the table.[34]

Every middle-class dinner seems to have included what Jane Austen would call 'a comfortable soup'. The other English favourites were pies of all kinds, but especially those using fish and game birds. Obviously, the foods that people eat most are always going to be the foods that are frequently and regularly available, but what a cook does with them is a better guide to the way people like to have these foods prepared. Nor should we forget addictions. The astounding quantities of sugar consumed in eighteenth-century Britain are attributable to two addictions: to the mild narcotic first known as theine (the same as caffeine) in tea, and to sugar itself. The addiction to sugar was satisfied by tea-drinking, though a good sweet pudding never came amiss.[35] Tea and coffee were both fundamentally social drinks, as tea-tables and coffee-houses remind us. During his time in London, Swift frequently ate on his own but drank his tea or coffee or chocolate in company. Later in the century, Boswell shows us that a further pleasure of the table was the opportunity to turn meals into social occasions, as Swift would probably like to have done. Unlike Sir Fennystone Crutch, neither man would have snapped, 'Go away, can't you see I'm eating?'[36] For Boswell, breakfast, lunch and dinner were less pleasurable for the quality of the food than for the opportunity that meals offered to rub shoulders with the influential, or just to enjoy the company of friends. And, after all, no eighteenth-century recipe was ever designed to serve just one person.

4. Pleasures Engendered by Gender: Homosociality and the Club

MARIE MULVEY ROBERTS

Thus it appears these envied Clubs possess
No certain means of social Happiness:
Yet there's a good that flows from Scenes like these,
Man meets with Man at leisure and at ease;
We to our Neighbours and our Equals come,
And rub off pride that Man contracts at home;
For there, admitted Master, he is prone
To claim Attention and to talk alone.

George Crabbe

The famous jibe made by the brothers Goncourt during the nineteenth century, that if two Englishmen were to be cast upon an uninhabited island, their first consideration would be the formation of a club,[1] was not merely an observation of how post-Enlightenment England was viewed by the French, but also how English society had begun to view itself. The formation of clubs has become one of the enduring legacies of the eighteenth century, at a time when many were established to encapsulate various kinds of pleasure. From these we have inherited an invaluable record of social behaviour. How and why the rise of the club facilitated the pursuit of pleasure, particularly in regard to gender, are questions that tend to have been overlooked, even though they should be fundamental to our understanding of this period.

According to typologies of pleasure, there was a club in eighteenth-century London that corresponded to virtually every sort of pleasurable activity, real or imaginary.[2] For example, those who enjoyed the sensual appetites of the carnivorous, rather than of carnality could join the Sublime Society of Beefsteaks,[3] that had been founded in 1735, which nourished the image of a happy, hearty, meat-eating British bulldog. Another beefsteak club, predictably known as the Patriot Club, was the Liberty or Rump-Steak Club whose Bacchanalian revels were celebrated in a collection of verses entitled *The Toasts of the Patriots Club at London* in 1734. Founded by opponents of the Tory government, this Whig club satisfied both the stomach and the higher faculties. Clubs that accommodated the lower urges were legion and amongst the most notorious were the Hell-Fire clubs. These, along with bizarre clubs like the effeminate Mollies, the macho Roaring Boys or the rakish Mohocks were all part of the menagerie of the factual, fictional and fantastical clubs that mapped out the pleasures of eighteenth-century London.

The pleasure principle common to all was conviviality. Social enjoyment, enhanced by a glass of claret or good conversation, was the stock-in-trade of the numerous gentlemen's clubs that proliferated in London from the early 1700s onwards. These had grown out of the coffee houses of the seventeenth century, where men congregated to discuss business, politics or the latest poem or play, and to throw dice or play cards. By 1710, it was said that there were 2000 of these all-male coffee houses in London and Westminster for a population for the capital of about 800 000, and five million nation-wide.[4] The most well-known were Will's, from where the Grave Club and the Witty Club emerged; Button's, and White's that was a fashionable gambling club by 1730.[5] Resistance to the coffee houses as a masculine enclave that set up a rivalry between women and coffee, is suggested by a pamphlet called 'The Women's Petition against Coffee, representing to Public Consideration of the Grand Inconveniences according to their Sex from the Excessive Use of that Drying, Enfeebling Liquor' (1674). The implication that coffee drinking led to a deterioration of manhood may have been inspired less by cohorts of disappointed women than by the vintners and brewers, who were losing trade to the sellers of coffee.

While coffee houses and clubs were predominantly male, 'tea-tables' and salons modelled on those in pre-revolutionary France, tended to be mostly female. Although the salon was trivialised by some male *philosophes*, recent scholars have identified it as an institutionalised and politicised locus for Enlightenment thinking.[6] The dichotomy between the public and private spheres, and the gendering of these spaces, should not be seen simply as a forerunner to the more repressive gender roles of the nineteenth century. Rather, the clubs held out all kinds of possibilities for men and women and the eventual reinstatement of women within the domestic role was only one of many potential developments. Jürgen Habermas's model of the public sphere is one in which the clubs, coffee houses and salons occupy a zone that represents an alternative and even oppositional stance to the state and the family. He identifies the public sphere with the practice of rational discourse.[7] To infer from this that all-male clubs were bastions of rationality, would be misleading, when we consider how many were dedicated to such 'irrational' pursuits as drinking and gambling. The most visible women's clubs of the eighteenth century were devoted to rational conversation. Among these were the political salons in France and the Bluestocking circle in England, that had started out as a mixed-sex club. The club represented a site for either breaking down or reinforcing gender stereotypes such as the association between men and rationality and women with its converse.

Part of the appeal of homosociality, or socialising with the same sex, lies in its potential for transgressive behaviour. For example, it enables members to appropriate characteristics associated with the opposite sex even though the single-sex club valorises either the masculinity or femininity of its own particular members. At the same time, there was a desideratum for focusing upon the absent other. Instead of being in conflict, these attitudes towards gender were in concert with the eighteenth-century ideal of complementarity between the sexes. For example, men were more likely to adopt feminine characteristics in the absence of women, as in some rituals relating to the Masons and the Mollies, thereby enabling them to recover their own repressed female side. Some women's clubs modelled themselves upon a male counterpart or prototype. The most radical were the female French Freemasons who had been initiated into the higher degree, Amazonnerie Anglaise or the Order of the English Amazons, where they were instructed in a secret subversiveness which insisted that women assume the same power and rights as men.[8] The clubs of the French Revolution also initiated women into the Enlightenment ideals of Liberty, Equality and Fraternity that had usually been reserved for the opposite sex.[9] One reason why women's clubs flourished on the Continent more than in Britain around 1790 may have been because they enjoyed a greater social and political equality within a republican or revolutionary milieu.[10] None the less, all-female clubs were often in the firing line during a counter-revolutionary backlash. For instance, after 1793, 'Liberty, Equality and Fraternity' ceased to be applicable to both sexes when all the women's clubs were closed down by the Convention in Paris.

Female clubs have tended to nurture social and political transition rather than upholding the hegemonic. Traditionally, women have relied less upon the regimentation of a collective activity for confirmation of their gender identity. Instead, the social construction of femininity has been articulated from within certain designated female roles that have been mediated through the dominant patriarchal ideology. For men, it has been more socially acceptable to bond together for the purpose of confirming and enhancing masculinity. Single-sex or homosocial clubs provide an important focus for the way in which the relations between the sexes and gender-divisions have developed.

THE RISE OF THE CLUB

Various social and political developments during the seventeenth and eighteenth centuries had been marked by the emergence, first of the coffee houses, and then of the clubs. Of particular interest here is the way in which these social constructs may be viewed as a microcosm of society. Clubs cradled the development of a social sense of self that the Augustans believed to be fundamental to human nature.[11] As Joseph Addison notes, 'Man is said to be a Sociable Animal, and, as an Instance of it, we may observe, that we take all Occasions and Pretences of forming our selves into those little Nocturnal Assemblies, which are commonly known by the Name of *Clubs*'.[12] His Aristotelian observation makes light of the way in which clubs canalised the anti-social impulses of exclusivity, feuding and territorialism, which ought to have militated against the incoming spirit of the rational Enlightenment.

Following the civil and political upheavals of the seventeenth century, much of what passed as the so-called 'Peace of the Augustans'[13] actually thrived on the sublimated belligerence of club-warfare. Wits had become the new warriors of the age. While clubs were effective at containing feuds, they were just as efficient at causing them by institutionalising rivalry. Some clubs came into existence purely as antagonists to others, like the Gormogons, who were formed for the express purpose of ridiculing the Freemasons. In a poem entitled *The Moderator between the Freemasons and the Gormogons* (1729), Henry Carey draws attention to the absurdity of such competitiveness, saying,

> The Masons and the Gormogons
> Are laughing at one another,
> While all mankind are laughing at them;
> Then why do they make such a pother?[14]

An attempt made by the Gormogons to demystify the Freemasons is revealed in William Hogarth's 1724 engraving *The Mystery of the Freemasons brought to Light by the Gormogons* (Figure 4.1). Hogarth belonged to a number of Masonic lodges and also, not surprisingly, to the Artists' Club.

Clubs were at the forefront of the transition from an aristocratic to a bourgeois society. The introduction of coffee into England heralded the coffee houses through which public opinion percolated during the reign of Charles II. The advent of the coffee bean was regarded by many as emitting an aroma of impiety and treason. In 1675, the king issued a proclamation banning coffee houses for their involvement in the spreading of malicious rumours. They were, however, soon reinstated and became more well established than they had been before the reign of Queen Anne. Coffee drinkers were still treated with suspicion, during the first half of the eighteenth century, by writers such as Daniel Defoe, who exposed corruption in the judiciary in his play significantly entitled *The Coffee-House Politician* (1730). Mrs Delaney, in her criticism of White's Coffee House, whose members included the fashionable highwayman, James Macleane, complained: 'What a curse to nations is such a pit

Figure 4.1 William Hogarth, *The Mystery of the Freemasons Brought to Light by the Gormogons*, 1724 (reproduced by kind permission of the British Museum)

of destruction as White's. It is a sad thing that in a Christian country it should continue undemolished.'[15]

Once clubs started to gain ascendency over the coffee houses and encouraged the consumption of alcohol and gaming rather than of coffee and conversation, fears arose that an accelerated degeneracy would further erode the moral fabric of society. Worse still, some clubs were perceived as potentially, if not actually, politically subversive. The most blatant were the clubs of freethinkers, of which the most famous was the Robin Hood Society. The concerns regarding the political influence of such clubs are voiced in a verse from a collection entitled *Poems on the Affairs of State* (1707):

You meet in Clubs, and strong Cabals
To controvert Elections:
    But Party Interest there prevails,
Merit and Sense of Honour fails,
    And meets with no protection.[16]

Most threatening to the authorities was the existence of clubs whose members included radicals, revolutionaries and members of the middle as opposed to the ruling class. For example, members of the radical London Corresponding Society were accused of high treason in 1794. Such social and political 'subversives' had created for themselves a private space within which public opinion could be collected, considered and circulated.

While the exclusivity of a club invited privacy, it remained, at the same time, public. The life-style of a clubman permitted him to dine in his club, away from home. Lodges of Freemasons without a permanent residence brought their own lodge 'furniture' to their meetings when these were held in a hired room, usually at a local tavern. Such items as candlesticks, miniature pillars and even perhaps a coffin for ritual rebirthing constituted the 'furniture', which is a term more usually associated with the domestic space that was normally female-dominated. The exclusion of women and men of the wrong social class, or religious or political affiliation, was at odds with the principles of egalitarianism and openness that were upheld by many clubs. It is ironic to consider that while many clubs served as a refuge from the social hierarchies existing outside, they could also perpetuate discrimination and elitism of all kinds by restricting eligibility for membership. The exclusion of women was rationalised on the grounds that polite society would not tolerate the discussion of traditionally male subjects such as law and politics in the presence of ladies. In regard to the gender divide, Jane Austen's comment in *Emma* (1816), that 'one half of the world cannot understand the pleasures of the other',[17] is apt. The club as a primarily male phenomenon, whether it be imaginary or real, will be discussed below. In the next two sections the subject of women and their clubs, which represent 'the pleasures of the other', will be considered.

A COMPENDIUM OF CLUBS IN FACT AND FICTION

It was in 1775 that the word 'clubbable' was coined by Samuel Johnson, who defined a club in his *Dictionary* as 'an assembly of good fellows meeting under certain conditions.'[18] What constituted a club was invariably the name, regular meetings, a set of rules and sometimes a constitution. Since there was no permanent financial bond between the members, each member was liable only up to the time when he paid his 'score' after the meal. Few clubs remained static during the course of the century and several underwent considerable change in terms of their composition, constitution, agenda and activities. Confusion for the historian can be created by the co-existence of similar clubs. For example, there were four separate Beefsteak clubs founded during the first half of the eighteenth century, ranging from the Rabelaisian Club of Beefsteaks to the more thoughtfully masticatory Sublime Society of Beefsteaks.[19] Another complication is that clubs and societies were not always synonymous. Many societies, for instance, were keener to recruit than clubs, primarily because they were more willing to set up branches in different areas and maintain membership through correspondence. In some cases, societies and clubs were pitted against one another. For example, in 1802, a Society for the Suppression of Vice was formed that was associated with evangelicals such as Hannah More. That it had been founded on April Fools Day was an irony that would have escaped most of its members. In common with its predecessor, 'The Society to Effect the Enforcement of his Majesty's Proclamation against Vice and Immorality', this killjoy society was on a collision course with the hedonistic pursuit of pleasure that characterised so many clubs.

Far from suppressing vice, many clubs exulted in it, according to Grub Street. Members allegedly included a motley sprinkling of wits, debauchees, profligates and rakes, known as bucks and bloods. Pranks and hoaxes began to take over from the outright brutality and rioting carried out by rakes like the Mohocks. These aristocratic roisterers, who were sometimes known as Hawkubites, were reputed to terrorise the streets of London throughout the century. John Gay, in a farce called *A Wonderful Prophecy taken from the mouth of the spirit of a person who was barbarously slain by the Mohocks* (1712), claimed that the Mohocks tortured a porter by putting a hook in his mouth and dividing his nostrils before murdering him. Although 'half dead and speechless', he none the less managed to sing 'the following Ejaculation:'

From MOHOCK and from HAWKUBITE,
    Good Lord deliver me,
Who wander through the Street by Night,
    Committing Cruelty.

They slash our Sons with bloody Knives,
    And on our daughters fall,
And if they ravish not our Wives,
    We have good Luck withal.

Coaches and Chairs they overturn,
    Nay Carts most easily,
Therefore from GOG and eke MAGOG,
    Good Lord deliver me.[20]

In 1753, Edward Moore, in the periodical the *World* (no. 23), proposed that since the bucks and bloods already formed a club of lunatics, they ought to be committed to a well-equipped mad-house.

There is no better diagnostic tool for discovering the madness of mankind than the mock histories of Edward Ward's compendium of its club-life. His writings, such as the *Compleat and Humorous Account of Clubs* (1709), suggest that for every vice in existence, a club had been created in order to ensure its furtherance. That one should never go to Ward's satiric taxonomies for any accurate information regarding a club is signalled in the misogynistic lunacy of his dedicatory Epistle – 'To the Luciferous and Sublime Lunatick, the Emperor of the Moon: Governour of the Tides, Corrector of Female Constitutions.'[21] To classify the different kinds more accurately would require a Linnaeus rather than a Ward. It seems appropriate, in view of all this misinformation, that *The Gentleman's Magazine* contains details of another fictional club, called The Blundering Club, that was dedicated to the art of inaccuracy.[22] Yet, in view of this, it is ironic that the Lying Club, which encouraged tergiversation and expelled anyone for telling the truth was, itself, probably genuine. According to Ward, this club was the 'spring and fountain from whence all the rest have their very being.'[23] Many others are more likely to have been the product of Ward's mendacity. However much he deplored their continued existence and propagation, he was not averse to creating a few more himself. Of these, the most comical are the No Noses Club and the Big Noses Club, the Short Club and the Tall Club. Even though they are inventions, they do verify some eighteenth-century trends, namely the prevailing interest in physiognomy and the aesthetic pleasure derived from symmetrical relationships, which, in this case, underpin the balance between opposites. Furthermore, within Ward's baroque kaleidoscope of the grotesque, absurd, peculiar and eccentric, there is an underlying sense of Augustan order and a compulsion to classify.

Ward was by no means the only 'inventor' of clubs, as this form of invention was a popular pastime for many an enterprising wit and wag. Phantom, fictional and fictitious clubs are cited in broadsheets, novels and periodicals. All that existed as regards the Nonsense Club, for instance, was its anthem, which is printed in *The Gentleman's Magazine* for 1735 where an account, ascribed to Jonathan Swift, of the Swan Tripe Club, may also be found.[24] All that is known of the ludicrous Club of Fat Men, however, is that potential members were vetted by making them gain entrance literally through a narrow door:

> If a Candidate for this Corpulent Club could make his Entrance through the first, he was looked upon as unqualified; but if he stuck in the Passage, and could not force his Way through it, the Folding-Doors were immediately thrown open for his Reception and he was saluted as a Brother. I have heard that this Club, though it consisted but of fifteen persons, weighed above three Ton.[25]

With appropriate symmetry, the club in opposition to these bulky brothers consisted of a collection of Scare-crows and Skeletons.

Ward's histories of clubs expose the way in which human failings and absurdities could be ennobled and elevated through the authority of a club. The mock-eulogies he composed were for the express purpose of exposing 'the vanity of the whimsical'[26] clubs, particularly those that encouraged drunkenness and debauchery. The Dilettanti society must have caused him considerable rancour since its nominal entrance requirement was to have visited Italy but, according to Horace Walpole, the real qualification was to get drunk.[27] As Charles Darby indicates in his *Bacchanalia; or a Description of a Drunken Club* (1680), getting inebriated was a popular pastime for clubmen. Ward's objection to clubs would have made him a killjoy, had it not been for the voyeuristic and perverse delight that he took in their ridicule.

Ward's humour degenerates, from time to time, into a schoolboy bawdiness that is enshrined in his self-explanatory Farting Club. Another is the Surly Club, which is euphemistically described as encouraging its members, 'in the spirit of contradiction', 'to perfect one another in the art and misery of foul language', which he claims sets out to improve the vernacular of Billingsgate.[28] As Voltaire points out in *Candide* (1759), even misanthropy could be a perverse source of pleasure, as is Addison's all-male Humdrum Club who 'used to sit together, smoke their pipes, and say nothing till midnight.'[29]The clubbing together of those with irritating habits, like the Rattling clubs,[30] who interrupted church services, consolidated the anti-social. Indeed, many fictitious clubs were created in order to draw attention to the irregularities that permeated real clubs. Ward ridicules the degrees of absurdity that characterise so many initiation rites such as those practised by the Knights of the Order of the Golden Fleece, whom he dismisses as 'This fantastical Order of Dubb'd Fuddlecaps'.[31] Their leader, named Sir Timothy Turdpie, when about to 'take leave of his brotherhood and of his wits', is threatened with the punishment of 'worse company' or even 'the penitential conversation' of his own family.[32] This final rejoinder is a reminder that the club provided its members with a haven from their domestic and family responsibilities.

The activities of club-members provided Ward with scope for such nonsense as the weekly dancing club or Buttock Ball in St Giles. Here a motley collection of 'Bullies, Libertines and Strumpets' indulged in the 'shake-tail exercise.'[33] By invoking the carnivalesque, in terms of his descriptions of performance and display, Ward manages to capture more of the flavour of the circus than that of the zoo. These absurdities draw attention to the regressive nature of clubs, whose pleasures were found in a relentless exhibitionism and whose excesses were an affront to the Augustan ideals of moderation and restraint.

Every dubious human type, by having been entered into Ward's taxonomy, was rendered doubly dubious. Even learned clubs were not exempt from his satire, as in Chapter 17 of his *Secret History of Clubs* (1709), where the Quacks' Club is described as consisting of 'medicinal Coxcombs'. Scientists of the Royal Society are satirised in the Virtuosos' Club. Experiments being carried out include an attempt to turn sea brine into fresh water and a nuptial calendar which calculates how often a man has been cuckolded by his wife; 'to which is added, a very useful Table, by which he may discover, who, how, where and when, and all the other particulars of his wife's backslidings'.[34] This account bears comparison with Swift's satire of the Royal Society as in the Academy of Lagado in Book Three of *Gulliver's Travels* (1727). Indeed, any attempt to track down many of the clubs described by Ward would be as futile as trying to navigate a route to Lilliput or Brobdingnag. Like Swift, he was holding up a distorting mirror to London society within which usually only the sagacious could see their own reflection.

By decoding Ward's caricature, one can sometimes track down

a genuine society or a disruptive practice that had eventually been turned into someone else's hoax club. An example of the latter is 'The Man-Killing Club', which corresponds to Addison's Fire-Eaters' or Ardent Duellist club and Richard Steele's Club of Duellists. In *The Spectator* for 10 March 1711, Steele charts the brief existence of this club whose short-lived members died either by the sword or on the gallows. The reason behind the ridicule of these combatant clubs was to draw attention to the dangers of duelling. The 'Man-hunters' Club' is more likely to have been a reference to gangs like the Mohocks whose existence, was, alas, all too real for Londoners. Their members are described by Ward as constituting 'a juvenile society of mad libertines'.[35] All this violence, whether it was provoked by honour or hooliganism, would have been welcomed by the Club of Undertakers. This satiric club is mentioned in *A Trip through London* (1728), attributed to Erasmus Jones, where its members are depicted drinking toasts to 'The New Distemper' in the hope, presumably, of an ensuing epidemic.[36] An additional clientele for this funereal club could have been supplied by the Last Guinea Club. In 1755 the periodical *The Connoisseur*, portrays them as a sorrowful collection of desperate, impoverished rakes who, by virtue of having become 'broken gamesters', have pledged to die as gentlemen, now that their funds have expired. It proved fortunate for them that the Last Guinea Club was willing to accommodate their last wishes, since they were doubtless too poor to raise the entry fee for admission into a duelling club.

In another world where clubs proliferated, that of politics, duelling of another, no less belligerent sort, was commonplace. The most ludicrous was the Wet Paper Brigade, whose members allegedly read the newspapers, not hot off the press, but damp from the printers, before the ink had been given time to dry out. There were no keener clubmen than the Whigs, who patronised the Hanover Club, the Mug-House Club and the Green-Ribbon'd Club. Standing in opposition were the 150 Staunch Tories' Club, The Brothers' Club, the Saturday Club and the renowned October Club,[37] that outlived its splinter group, the March Club. Swift was a prominent Tory clubman who also patronised literary clubs, of which the most well-known was the Scriblerus Club. Fellow Scriblerians included Alexander

Pope, John Gay and John Arbuthnot. The Whig Club that was noted particularly for its connections in the world of literature and politics was the Kit-Cat Club. This was the creation of Christopher Cat, a cook who excelled in pork pies, more renowned for his culinary skills than for his literary talents. Another cabal with an emphasis on dining was the Calves' Head Club, whose annual banquet was dedicated to the unappetising memory of the beheading of King Charles. Even the name of the unsavoury Mohocks, mentioned earlier, had gastronomic nuances since they were called after a tribe of American Indians, who were reputed to be cannibals. According to John Gay's aforementioned farce, the candidates for admission were themselves called Cannibals.

What might be one man's dish of meat was another's flesh-pot, as the clubs devoted to debauchery suggest. The most notorious of these were the various Hell-Fire clubs, such as the Irish Blasters and the Dublin Hell-Fire Club, over which Peg Woffington, the actress and *travesti* performer, reputedly presided.[38] The earlier Club of the Hell-Fires, started by Sir Philip Wharton in about 1719, admitted ladies alongside gentlemen who dined on 'Holy Ghost Pie', 'Devil's Loins' and 'Breast of Venus'.[39] In April 1721 there was a royal edict condemning blasphemous clubs, which it defined as

> certain scandalous clubs or societies of young persons who meet together, and in the most impious and blasphemous manner insult the most sacred principles of our Holy Religion, affront to Almighty God himself, and corrupt the minds and morals of one another.[40]

The anonymous novel *The Accomplished Rake* (1727) describes how the rakish Sir John Galliard has to undergo an initiation ritual by drinking a toast to the devil on a tomb-stone in St Martin's church-yard at one o'clock in the morning.

Around the middle of the eighteenth century, Sir Francis Dashwood, the fifteenth Baron Le Despencer, allegedly founded the most infamous of these clubs. This was a diabolical Franciscan Brotherhood based at his family seat of Medmenham Abbey in West Wycombe, Buckinghamshire. The membership, who became known as the Medmenham Monks, was made up of the political, literary and licentious, most notably John Wilkes, George Selwyn, Charles Churchill, and George Bubb Dodington. They were alleged to cavort with 'nuns' in the nearby Hell-Fire caves that were really Dashwood's abandoned chalk-mines. It was in these tenebrous regions that the Black Mass was believed to have been celebrated by this satanic club. Serious doubt has been cast upon the existence of such a club by Dashwood's biographer, Betty Kemp. There is very little conclusive evidence. Even the composition of the club and whether any such organised body had ever existed is disputed. Were they merely a collection of house-guests who drew on the rituals of the Dilettanti Society or who had become associated with a portrait of Dashwood, dressed in the habit of St Francis, painted by George Knapton in 1742? It is more probable that the alleged debaucheries of the Hell-Fire Club had been devised in order to attack Dashwood in Parliament. But there is no doubt that the Medmenham Monks inspired the sensational novel by Charles Johnston entitled *Chrysal: or The Adventures of a Guinea* (1761), which stands as the only authority for the antics of the club. It is likely that this fictional work perpetuated, or even invented, the fiction of Dashwood's Medmenham Monks.

Reference is made to this Hell-Fire Club in John Hall-Stevenson's *Crazy Tales* (1772), which is based on a society called the Demoniacs that he founded at his ancestral home, Skelton Castle. Its most famous member was Laurence Sterne, who bases the character of Eugenius in *Tristram Shandy* (1759–67), upon Hall-Stevenson. In contrast, another novelist, Henry Fielding, had invented the Skull Club of 1740 for the purpose of attacking his enemies in the press along the lines of Daniel Defoe's Scandalous Club. The Gothic was in sufficient disrepute, during this period, to be used for the purposes of vilifying opponents. This was true of Dashwood's political enemies and Swift's fictional Club of Demoniacs, which was the name he gave to the Irish House of Commons.

Many fictional clubs were mercifully short-lived, such as the Everlasting Club, that brought about its own demise by insisting on sitting round the clock. Since everlastingness was its only appeal and ennui turned out to be its only 'pleasure', it soon closed down. Another failure was the Ace of Clubs, that never achieved the proverbial 'full house' because of its insistence on an unrealistically exclusive membership. It is likely that the Handsome Club had to turn away some hopefuls for admission, who might have been forced to retreat to Ward's Club of Ugly Faces or the Oxford Ugly Club, that was introduced to readers of *The Spectator* on 20 March 1711 by the aptly named Alexander Carbuncle.

Fictional clubs were normally devised as a way of attacking opponents in the world of letters, journalism or politics. However exotic and extraordinary they appeared to be, paradoxically, their existence cast a spurious uniformity upon the more outlandish elements within the public sphere. To a certain extent, the very nature of a club tends to iron out the idiosyncrasies of individuality. Clubs tended to reify the eighteenth-century's admiration of the generic and general. The Club of Originals was comprised ironically of a collection of imitators, similar to Abraham Gulliver who, we are told, had descended from Lemuel Gulliver. In view of this, one might expect to find the fictional Club of Eccentrics consisting of avowed conformists.

Amongst the most cloned club specimens were the gallants for whom there was no shortage of clubs. None the less, most of these clubs appear to have been nothing more than the fantasy of a libidinous imagination. The lovelorn and licentious need not suffer in silence, since they could club together in the Libertine Society for the Propagation of Sicilian Amorology, or The Schemers, which was a Society for the Advancement of Flirtation, allegedly founded by the Duke of Wharton. The fictitious No Noses Club was open to members of both sexes who, according to Ward, had sacrificed their noses to the God Priapus, possibly on the altar of syphilis, and whose subsequent disquiet is registered in the following lampoon:

Why then should not one mighty nose,
With patience bear the scoffs of those
Who hate to see a nose appear,
Because themselves have none to wear,
Since he is always made the jest,
That is the most unlike the rest.[41]

Languishing gallants formed themselves into clubs like the Beaus' Club subtitled by Ward as the Lady's Lapdog Club. Steele in

The Spectator draws attention to the Fringe-Glove Club whose members 'were persons of such moderate Intellects, even before they were impaired by their Passion', that they 'could express their Passion in nothing but their Dress'.[42] At Oxford, the Amorous Club met and are described by him as a 'set of sighers'[43] who separated themselves from other company so as to enjoy the pleasure of talking incoherently without appearing ridiculous to outsiders. The idea that a collective of gallants should share their romantic yearnings is a delightful absurdity. An example of a solitary romantic suffering the anguish of unrequited love, whose rehearsal for courtship is combined with a fantasy membership of a clandestine club, appears in Thomas Love Peacock's parodic *Nightmare Abbey* (1818). Here one of the most embarrassing moments in literature is described when Scythrop Glowry, believing himself to be alone, flings off his calico dressing-gown while imagining himself to have been elevated to the senior position of transcendental eleutherarch which enabled him to preside over the secret Bavarian illuminati. Inadvertently, he exposes his nakedness to the object of his passion, the indifferent Marionetta who is not prepared to humour the eleutherarch's 'new clothes'. This incident shows just how ridiculous the activities of clubs and secret societies can appear to outsiders, especially when there was only one member as in this case.

With the exception of Scythrop's secret society, ritual absurdity can mask a real threat, thus making secrecy an imperative. The real secret of many secret societies like the Illuminati, the Freemasons, and the Berlin-based Wednesday Society that was also known as Friends of the Enlightenment, lay in the cultivation of potentially subversive concepts such as reason and the process of enlightening.[44] Once these ideas had gained acceptance outside, then the rationale for the secrecy of the society was made redundant. What was left, however, tended to be a secrecy for its own sake and a greater dependence upon ritual and form, rather than on purposeful action and meaningful content.

In order to retain the identity of the club or society and enhance and consolidate its power, it was important to maintain a sense of adversity, even when it had become entirely redundant. The boundaries around an institution could be redrawn or upheld most effectively by excluding certain groups of people.

At the same time, homosocial clubs like the English Freemasons, who banned women, were incorporating the feminine into their rituals. What this meant was that the Masonic brotherhood, at the same time as valorising the masculinity of its members, could also signal its identification with the absent female in three major areas.

First, there is the Masons' enactment of female powerlessness through ritual humiliation and their oath of allegiance. For this, members were obliged to submit to the authority of the brotherhood that was embodied in the Master of the Lodge. The oath of obedience until death was not unlike that undertaken by a bride in her marriage vows. Indeed, the noose with which the neophyte was led around the lodge room has some of the symbolic resonance of the wedding ring. Secondly, Masonic metaphors relating to motherhood and initiation rites of rebirth enabled members to identify with the female experience of giving birth. Initiation involves the death of the old self and the resurrection of the new into the Mother Lodge. Finally, because of its cultivation of secrecy, Freemasonry may be seen as an attempt to recreate a male equivalent of the feminine mystique. The culture of masculinity endorsed by Freemasons enacted the sacred rites of passage into manhood as opposed to womanhood. But as the historian Margaret Jacob has shown, the exclusion of women from Masonic lodges was by no means universal. Her claim is based upon her discovery of the records of a lodge in Holland, called 'La Loge de Juste', that met in 1751 and admitted women on an equal basis.[45] The next section will look at instances of female Freemasonry in Ireland and on the Continent and the way in which the exclusion of women and the feminine was reinforced in England through masonic songs.

THE FEMININE AND THE MASONIC BROTHERHOOD

Stories of women who would conceal themselves in cupboards or clock cases, in order to spy on lodge meetings, circulated in England as warnings to Freemasons to maintain vigilance. One woman who supposedly infiltrated the Masonic brotherhood was Elizabeth St Leger who, in Ireland during 1710, hid in a cupboard where she overheard a lodge meeting, attended by her father, which was taking place in the family library. When the time came for the candidate due to be initiated to recite a blood-curdling oath, she screamed in terror. This attracted the attention of the family butler, who was doubling as the lodge guard or Tyler. That his greater allegiances were to the lodge is evident from his betrayal of his young mistress to the brotherhood, who then had to decide whether to execute or initiate her. Luckily for St Leger, they opted for the latter, thus allowing her to take her place in the ranks of the lodge, as well as in the apocryphal history of the craft. As Dorothy Ann Lipson points out, 'The frequent rehearsal of that single titillating exception powerfully reinforced male solidarity.'[46]

From the point of view of men on the proverbial Freemason's 'square', women tended to be regarded as the inquisitive daughters of Eve. In one Masonic version of the Fall of Mankind, Eve is not only punished for pursuing forbidden knowledge with expulsion from the Garden of Eden, shame over her nakedness, death and travail but is also banned from joining the Freemasons.

> How Adam look'd on her, as one struck with thunder!
> He view'd her from head to foot over with wonder!
> Then since you have done this thing, Madam, said he,
> For your sake no women free-masons shall be.[47]

In another variation, a more compassionate Adam takes pity on Eve's squirming nudity by providing her with no more suitable a garment with which to cover her than his mason's apron.

> And as she bewail'd in sorrowful ditty
> The good man beheld, and on her took pity:
> Free-masons are tender: so he to the dame
> Bestowed his white apron to cover her shame.[48]

The apron is quite an advance on the fig-leaf, though its presence in 'Genesis' is, of course, anachronistic. None the less, it is significant that in an earlier version of the verse above, Adam appropriates traditional female skills by 'making' Eve an apron.[49]

In the light of this reversal of gender roles, it seems appropriate to raise the question, not 'Who wears the trousers?', but 'Who wears the apron?'

Within Freemasonry, the postures of subordination demonstrate how the feminine can be appropriated for the purposes of ritual. The candidate for initiation, in being kept in a state of ignorance and physically confined in darkess and then blindfolded, is expected to adopt attitudes of submission, thereby simulating female powerlessness. The neophyte's formal ordeal includes being threatened by the point of a poniard, a symbol of phallic terror, which is ready to pierce him should he disobey. As an exaltation of masculinity which privileges the male, Freemasonry formalises male friendship, sealing it through ritual ordeals and terrifying initiation rites, which are a testing ground for manliness. The brethren are bound in a fierce loyalty gelled by a blood-curdling oath whose violence embodies a Masonic machismo. In this respect, such a brotherhood, with its accompanying ritual humiliations, held out little appeal or novelty for women, who were already familiar with positions of subordination. An exception can be found among the French aristocrats, who were able to enjoy, in secrecy, the novelty of the dangerous pre-revolutionary concept of equality. In being allowed to experience egalitarianism, they were being compensated within the lodge for their deprivations in the world outside.

One biological area to which men are denied access is that of motherhood. The 'Genesis' creation myth provides both consolation and compensation. Through the reversal of the biological facts of giving birth, the first parent is represented not as mortal and female but as divine and male. In the hierarchy of creation within Masonic cosmology, woman was said to have been created on the last day. This relegation rendered her even more of an after-thought of Adam's rib-cage than do most orthodox versions. Attempts to appropriate nurture and motherhood may be seen in Freemasonry through the matrix of the Mother Lodge and the rituals of rebirth. The rites of initiation, when the candidate is torn out of comforting darkness into the searing light of illumination by Mason midwives, simulates the moment of birth, only this time the candidate is being reborn into Masonry. The noose put around the neck of the neophyte, who is then paraded around the lodge room, has been interpreted symbolically by some Masonic historians as an umbilical cord.[50] All this may be interpreted as psychological and ritual compensation for the exclusion of men not only from actually giving birth but also from the procedures surrounding childbirth. It was not until the advent of the male midwife during the eighteenth century that they gained legitimate access to the mysteries of obstetrics.[51] But despite this triumph of the male medical scientist over female folk midwifery, men were still not able to encroach with any certitude upon the monopoly of the female over the mysterious and intangible aspects of reproduction and sexuality. Secrecy, as some of the bawdy Masonic songs to be discussed later suggest, contrived to create a masculine mystique relating to male reproductive potencies.

The Mollies, who were male-to-female cross-dressers, supposedly improved on the Freemasons through a simulated labour and child-birth. Ward, who dismisses the Mollies as 'Sodomitical wretches',[52] is the dubious source for this claim. But from the transactions of contemporary sodomy trials of 1726, one can surmise that these transvestites did enter, at the very least, into pretend marriages. As Alan Bray explains, the Mollies employed a heterosexual discourse to ironic ends:

> The room in a molly house where couples were able to have sexual relations was the 'chapel', and the act itself 'marrying' or a 'wedding night', similarly a 'husband' was a sexual partner.[53]

The Mollies were often synonymous with effeminate homosexual men and, as Randolph Trumbach insists, should not be confused with the heterosexual or bisexual sodomites. They were discredited by their opponents, such as the supporters of the Societies for the Reformation of Manners, as symptomatic of a social deterioration. A contemporary account of a drag ball conveys the feminised atmosphere within a 'Molly House':

> The men calling one another 'my dear' and hugging, kissing, and tickling each other as if they were a mixture of wanton males and females, and assuming effeminate voices and airs;

> some telling others thay they ought to be whipped for not coming to school more frequently.[...] Some were completely rigged in gowns, petticoats, headcloths, fine laced shoes, furbelowed scarves, and masks; some had riding hoods; some were dressed like milkmaids, others like shepherdesses with green hats, waistcoats, and petticoats; and others had their faces patched and painted and wore very extensive hoop petticoats, which had been very lately introduced.[54]

As this passage reveals, the Mollies were the extreme end of a process of feminisation seen more typically in the affected mannerisms of the fashion-conscious Macaronis and foppish Jessamies of 1765.

Since gender ambiguity could confuse admission into a homosocial club, the Freemasons screened the sex of neophytes by exposing the left breast, and placing upon it the point of a compass. In spite of these precautions, stories still circulated of female cross-dressers who had managed to fool the brethren into believing that they were men.

The most famous case of gender ambivalence was the Chevalier D'Eon, who became a member of the Lodge of Immortality in 1768. Ever the exhibitionist, the Chevalier attracted public attention when he fenced wearing women's clothing in front of large crowds at Bath, Brighton and Oxford (Figure 4.2). Dismissed by the *Public Ledger* for being 'an impertinent French female',[55] the Chevalier's real secret emerged after his death in 1810 when it was revealed that he was, in fact, a man. This must have come as a surprise in the wake of a legal hearing at which a doctor testified that he had treated him for women's ailments and had observed that his breasts were enlarged. These medical indicators had not unnaturally led the court to make a ruling that he was female. The judge's attempt to give a balanced summing up is conveyed in a poetic epistle based on the trial:

> Hail! thou production most uncommon
> Woman half-man and man half-woman.[56]

In the painting *The Discovery or Female Freemason* (1771), the Chevalier D'Eon is represented as a woman alongside two freak-

Mlle. de Beaumont, or The Chevalier D'Eon, Female, Minister Plenipotentiary, Captain of Dragoons, *British Museum.*

Figure 4.2 (a and b) Mademoiselle de Beaumont, or the Chevalier D'Eon, female minister plenipotentiary, Captain of Dragoons (reproduced by kind permission of the British Museum and the Grand Lodge)

show exhibits, Mary Tofts, who was rumoured to have given birth to rabbits, and a Hanoverian version of the incredible shrinking man, who drew large crowds eager to test out his claim that he could crawl inside a quart-sized bottle. The Freemasons were also ridiculed by the fabrication of a female membership, as in the satire ascribed to Jonathan Swift, *A Letter from the Grand Mistress of the Female Free-Masons to Mr Harding the Printer (1724) and the anonymous Sisterhood of Free Seamstresses* (1724), which is likely to have inspired it.

WOMEN'S CLUBS AND FEMALE FREEMASONS

Periodicals like *The Spectator* invented women's clubs such as the Chit-Chat Club for their own purposes. In the issue for 28 June 1714, a special concession is made to Mr Spectator, their guest speaker, who is allowed to speak for one minute in ten without interruption. The boisterous She-Romps Club is another that exists only within the pages of *The Spectator,* where it is recorded that Mr Spectator was 'much too delicate to endure the least Advance towards Romping'.[57] The *Tatler* had its own female club, which was a Basket Women's Club of Female Tatlers. Like the Spectator's Chit-Chat Club, the name implies that women are chatterboxes. Even the sub-title of Ben Jonson's play *Epicene: or The Silent Woman* (1609–10) is an oblique reference to this stereotyping. The plot turns on the challenge of finding a silent woman who once procured turns out to be a loquacious shrew. There is a number of strong female characters in the play, including the Collegiate Ladies who are a coterie of domineering women led by Lady Haughty and Captain Otter's Amazonian wife. A club dedicated to attacking both ladies and actors is mentioned in the anonymous verses 'On the Author of a Dialogue concerning Women, pretended to be writ in Defence of the Sex.'

> Near Covent-Garden theatre, where you know
> Poets their sense, players their shapes do shew,
> There is a club of critics of the pit,
> Who do themselves admire for men of wit;

And lo! an arbitrary power assume
On plays and ladies both to pass their doom;[58]

Although most imaginary women's clubs were invented by men, Lady Mary Wortley Montagu, who was nominated as a candidate for the Kit-Cat Club at the age of eight, went on to create her own fictional Widows' Club in *The Spectator.*[59] The idea of women freed from the restraints of marriage forming a club would have unsettled many men during this period. The roles are reversed in *The Female Tatler* where a society of baronets, called the Sweet-Meat Club, are described by Lady Scandal to Mrs Crackenthorpe:

> These *Baronets* it seems, have a Sweet-Meat Club at a Confectioners in *York Buildings,* where they meet three times a Week, to work a fine *Wastcoat* [*sic*] for a Brother *Beau's* Wedding, – Sir *Formal* did the *Border,* Sir *Tawdry* a *Sun-Flower,* Sir *Financial* a *Tulip,* Sir *Plump* an *Artichoke,* and Sir *Dapper* a *Primrose.* . . . They hugg'd themselves two Months with this mighty Secret, and thought themselves very Happy in making Business a Pleasure.[60]

The pleasure to be derived from an all-female club is conveyed by the novelist, journalist and playwright Delarivier Manley in her fictional *Secret Memoirs and Manners of Several Persons of Quality, of Both Sexes, from the New Atlantis, an Island in the Mediterranean* (1709). It is probable that, for this club, she was drawing upon an actual group of like-minded women. The most well-known of cabals that contained women was the Bluestocking group referred to earlier, which met around 1781 and whose most prominent members were Hannah More and Elizabeth Carter.

'Bluestocking' has been used as a metonym for the intellectual woman, even though blue stockings were an article of male attire. Likewise since Freemasonry has been treated as a metonym for male bonding, the notion of female Freemasonry in England was a contradiction in terms which serviced the male satirist and parodist with ammunition against both women and masons. Jane Elizabeth Moore in her poem of 1797, 'A Question to the Society of Freemasons',[61] challenges the anti-female assumptions of such ridicule. In a letter written by 'Sister Christophera Wren' which appeared in *The Free-Mason*, the advantages of masonic initiation are presented not only as improvements to the mind, but as a route to refining behaviour and preserving the face from the ravages of age. From time to time, Western culture sets itself the onerous task of correcting and improving the female body. The bogus lodge propaganda explained by Mrs Wren insists that knowledge of just proportions will assist self-improvement and lead to an aesthetic transformation. Her version of Masonry contains a guide to such body sculpture as the Five Orders of Architecture which are compared to the female body:

> Every Lady belongs to one of the *Five Orders*, and if she appears too *full or scanty* behind or before, too *broad* at bottom, or *narrow* at the Top of her Person, it is owing to one single and deplorable Defect, that she is not a *Free-mason.*[62]

Accounts of rituals for women's clubs on the Continent have survived. Whether these were actually practised is not altogether clear. Mixed clubs were usually concerned with courtly love and men appeared to have had little hesitation in joining the Maids and Dames of Truth. Rituals for men and women differed, and the symbolism was gendered so as to invoke either traditionally feminine or masculine virtues. In the Order of Felicity, which proved to be more felicitous for men than for women, the sisters made an imaginative voyage to the Isle of Felicity under the sail of the brothers, who also piloted them. Maritime motifs were employed for reinforcing female fidelity, as when the woman being initiated had to swear that she would never receive a foreign vessel in her port. Anxiety in regard to chastity inspired a number of societies devoted to the protection of virtue with such titles as the aptly named Order of the Ladies Slaves to Virtue, and the Dames of Mount Tabor, which was intended to offer relief to distressed woman of good character. Rising hopefuls set their sights on the Degree of Moral Mistress. To ensure female virtue, many of the female orders were founded and then controlled by men, as in Adoptive Masonry, where a male lodge would 'adopt' a women's equivalent. According to one of the rituals for 1765, there was a bizarre requirement following the reception of a female candidate that she sleep for the first night wearing a black leather garter upon which is inscribed the injunction: 'Virtue and Silence'. The insistence that she must never reveal the secret of this garter with its tantalising text and black ribbon attachment might have presented a challenge to a curious sexual partner. The eroticisation of female orders is apparent amongst those inaugurated by the charismatic Freemason, magician and charlatan Cagliostro, which effectively licensed the libertine. Much of the ritual homed in on the female body. In one mock manifesto, the oath, now refined and diluted, is no longer steeped in violent language and the secrecy it espouses is conveyed through the image of lips being anointed with a seal of discretion. The oath must be kept until the beauty of the lady Mason fades. This requirement suggests that the only way in which women are capable of grasping the passing of time is by counting their wrinkles. The duties of the female novitiate Freemasons are couched in the traditional female imperatives: to hear, obey, work and be silent.

Lodges of Adoption appear to have been founded between 1737 and 1747. Female lodges were popular among the upper classes and by 1744 they were granted official recognition by the Grand Orient, which was the ruling body of Freemasonry in France. Janet Burke suggests that, through these lodges women imbibed the ideals of the Rational Enlightenment and developed the kind of fraternal bonding that has been traditionally associated with men. She also argues that, in the higher degrees, their exposure to the Enlightenment concepts of Liberty and Equality led to an embryonic and specifically eighteenth-century form of feminism. For example, the higher degree of the Order of the Amazons, mentioned earlier, insisted that its members defy male authority and power. What this involved was a reversal of social and familial roles so that women would dominate in marriage, discriminate against their sons and educate their daughters. Women were exhorted to demand equal rights, to insist on power-sharing, to fight in war and to have equal educational opportunities. More subversive still, women were deemed to have an intellect equal to that of men and to be just as capable of excelling in such fields of knowledge as science and politics, while wealth was to be divided equally between men and women.[63]

WHY BELONG?

What the club-system offered was compensation for that which might be missing in everyday life. Even though the exclusion of women by many men's clubs could be seen as a reinforcement of woman as the proverbial 'other', the rituals practised could open up a means for accessing the otherness denied to men in life outside. The contradictory nature of the club for both men and women meant that it could be homosocial and yet appropriate the characteristics of the opposite sex. Although this was mainly true for men, for women the act of forming a club, in itself, was an encroachment upon a traditionally male territory. Among the many reasons why men excluded women was that their presence may have inhibited them from finding the female in themselves. This, combined with the privileging of male values, was used subsequently to separate men and women and to consolidate the formation of the distinctly gender-divided cultures of modern society. Another strategy for maintaining the exclusion of women was the introduction of bawdy drinking songs concomitant with the invention of female clubs, as a vehicle for male fantasy.

Paradoxically, clubs embraced democracy and equality and yet thrived on exclusivity and elitism. While they furthered the development of the social self and facilitated the ever-rising middle classes, they created a new social hierarchy with all its newly-found freedoms and attendant restrictions. In addition to the pleasure of wielding power and denying it to others, club members enjoyed the privacy to enter into make-believe worlds. Whether they wanted to play-act, carry out rituals, cross-dress, enjoy a sense of camaraderie, good fellowship, a simulacrum of social equality, or seek out same-sex company, what they shared was the pursuit of pleasure in the company of others. For some, the notion of a club might have provided a secular substitute for the church, while for others it opened up an escape route from taboos and fears such as that of death. At the end of his verses on 'Clubs and Social Meetings' which advance a teleological explanation for the impulse of individuals to run with the herd, George Crabbe warns that clubs may actually prevent us from coming to terms with our own mortality:

Griggs and *Gregorians* here their meeting hold,
Convivial Sects, and *Bucks* alert and bold;
A kind of Masons, but without their sign;
The bonds of union – pleasure, song, and wine.
Man, a gregarious creature, loves to fly
Where he the trackings of the herd can spy;
Still to be one with many he desires,
Although it leads him through the thorns and briers. . . .
  Men feel their weakness, and to numbers run,
Themselves to strengthen or themselves to shun;
But though to this our weakness may be prone,
Let's learn to live, for we must die, alone.[64]

5. 'The Luxury of Doing Good': Benevolence, Sensibility, and the Royal Humane Society

CAROLYN D. WILLIAMS

What is the most intense pleasure you can feel? In a book devoted to eighteenth-century concepts of pleasure, it seems sensible to consider what contemporary writers had to say on this matter. Ideas of what constituted a good time were many and various; most of them – particularly the more disreputable – are covered by other chapters in this book. But twentieth-century scholars tend to ignore one very important source of pleasure, despite the fact that, throughout the eighteenth century, it was recommended more frequently than any other: being good. Sermons, essays, conduct books, novels, plays, poems and philosophical treatises all drummed this lesson home. Even richer rewards could be reaped by those who had the resources not only to be good, but to *do* good to others, by exercising benevolence. The most exquisite raptures known to mankind were supposed to flow from the ability to feel for the suffering of others, and to relieve it by acts of unselfish courage and generosity. This belief was linked to the growing fashion for sensibility, which gave rise to the theory that, even if you could offer no practical assistance, the mere ability to feel for another's pain was a valuable characteristic, that somehow set you above the common, unfeeling herd – and was, in itself, a source of intense delight.

These attitudes have always been controversial, raising many philosophical, ethical and psychological problems. Eighteenth-century writers hotly disputed the true nature of benevolence and its appropriate rewards. Given the lavish benefits to be gained from this virtue, at what point did apparent benevolence turn out to be selfishness? Could *any* voluntary action, strictly speaking, be unselfish? Anybody who does anything must have *some* reason for choosing to do it. Today, philosophers often refer to this as 'the problem of altruism'. Twentieth-century critical and historical methods enable readers to adopt even more sophisticated, not to say cynical, approaches to the subject, by examining the language and social context of eighteenth-century statements on the joys of virtue. Some claims appear to be politically motivated. ('Politics', in this context, refers to any transaction involving the exercise of power.) Many of the writers who try to persuade readers that it is in their own interests to behave properly are trying, consciously or otherwise, to smother discontent, or even stifle justifiable resistance to oppression. After all, it is usually only the powerful who have the privilege of publishing their definitions of proper behaviour. Other claims look like the product of naivety and wishful thinking. Did virtue's advocates protest too much? If it was so enjoyable, why hadn't word got round through other channels? Nobody bothered to construct elaborate arguments proving that pleasure could be derived from eating, drinking, making love, or going to the opera. As for sensibility, that concept has always been regarded with suspicion. Even when it was at its most influential, many people condemned it as self-indulgent, useless and even harmful. Present-day scholars are continuing a debate that has been going on for over two hundred years. Both topics will be dealt with more fully in the first three sections of this chapter. After that, there will be an exploration of newer ground: a study of strategies by which charity fund-raisers managed to make benevolence pleasurable and sensibility useful, in ways that the most sceptical could not refuse to acknowledge.

I

To present-day readers, the most conspicuous element in the debate on benevolence is its patriarchal bias: in other words, it was largely concerned with upholding the power of men of high social status. 'Men', in this context, nearly always indicated adult males, rather than human beings in general. (Women, like children, were introduced only as special – and generally inferior – cases.) Actually or potentially benevolent men were generally envisaged as wealthy, well-educated members of the upper or middle classes, who exercised power in the public arenas of local or national politics. Furthermore, the most influential and widely read literature on benevolence was written by such men; all in all, it is easy to see why, despite differences in philosophical emphasis, most of it was designed to uphold the *status quo.*

For many upper-class men in eighteenth-century Britain, a high priority was preventing the religious fanaticism which had been a leading cause of the civil and international wars that had ravaged Europe in the previous century. As the Irish clergyman and satirist, Jonathan Swift (1667–1745), ruefully observed: 'We have just religion enough to make us *hate*, but not enough to make us *love* one another.'[1] It was widely believed that the interests of individuals and the state were best served by teaching people that Christianity was fully compatible with ease, comfort and happiness, and that they should devote themselves to cooperation and practical kindness, rather than theological speculation and intense spiritual introspection. A popular exponent of this doctrine was John Tillotson (1630–94), whose works were frequently reprinted in the eighteenth century. He survived the worst upheavals in seventeenth-century Britain, emerging from those dark days as a champion of tolerance and moderation, and became archbishop of Canterbury in 1691. His works expressed an attitude that was to become typical of many well-meaning, conscientious Britons in the following century.

Tillotson's principles were encapsulated in his eighteenth sermon, 'The Example of Jesus in doing Good.' He believed that benevolence was more enjoyable, as well as more meritorious than indulging in theological controversies whose main result was to foment sectarian strife: 'Were we but possessed with the true spirit of Christianity, these would be but dry and insipid and tasteless things to us, in comparison of the blessed employment of doing good in a more real and substantial way.' He offered six inducements to follow the example of Jesus, who 'went about doing good' (*Acts,* 10:38). Firstly, there was an appeal to self-esteem: 'it is an argument of a great and generous mind', since 'the noblest and most heavenly dispositions think themselves happiest when others share with their happiness'.[2] Secondly, benevolence was pleasurable in itself:

> To do good is the most pleasant enjoyment in the world. It is natural; and whatever is so is delightful. We do like ourselves whenever we relieve the wants and distresses of others. And therefore this virtue among all the other hath peculiarly entitled itself to the name of *humanity*. We answer our own nature, and obey our reason and show ourselves men, in showing mercy to the miserable.... There is no sensual pleasure in the world comparable to the delight and satisfaction that a good man takes in doing good.

Thirdly, the benefactor enjoyed superhuman status, becoming 'a good angel and a saviour and a god to men'.[3] Fourthly, 'this is one of the most substantial duties of religion'.[4] This incentive might not be so immediately appealing as the others, since the performance of duty did not, in itself, confer pleasure. Nevertheless, it was still worth serious consideration, because, without it, the last two benefits would be unattainable. For, fifthly, 'the conscience of well-doing will refresh our souls even under the very pangs of death. With what contentment does a good man then look upon the good he hath done in this life?' And, finally, goodness was rewarded, 'both in this world and the next'. On earth, grateful beneficiaries had been known to save their benefactors' lives, while 'prayers and blessings' helped to preserve the prosperity of benefactors' estates. All this, however, faded into infinite insignificance beside the bliss of heaven: 'But what is this to the endless and unspeakable happiness of the next life, where the returns of doing good will be vastly great, beyond what we can now expect or imagine?'[5]

As the upper classes consolidated their position in the eighteenth century, enjoying increased economic and political security, less stress was laid on the possibility that situations might arise in which the gratitude of beneficiaries might be a source of material benefit. Instead, the contemplation of this gratitude was recommended as a source of pleasure in itself. But all the other inducements offered in Tillotson's sermon were used repeatedly, throughout the eighteenth century, to recommend benevolence – though not necessarily all at once. This was where the controversy began. Some philosophers argued that those who recommended the full range of motives suggested by Tillotson were guilty of logical overkill. If the pleasures of benevolence were so great, why shouldn't they simply be their own reward? Could a man be considered truly virtuous, if he were motivated by hopes of happiness or fears of punishment, in this world or the next?

One of the most influential works to raise these questions was *Characteristics of Men, Manners, Opinions, Times* (1711) by Anthony Ashley Cooper, the Third Earl of Shaftesbury (1671–1713). In 'Concerning Virtue or Merit', he made 'public good'[6] the criterion of virtue. But public-spirited actions were not enough: 'to deserve the name of good or virtuous, a creature must have all his inclinations and affections, his dispositions of mind and temper, suitable, and agreeing with the good of his kind, or of that system in which he is included, and of which he constitutes a part. To stand thus well affected, and to have one's affections right and entire, not only in respect of oneself but of society and the public, this is rectitude, integrity, or virtue'.[7] Shaftesbury considered the possession of these feelings not only meritorious but pleasurable to the highest degree. He recommended the joy felt by a virtuous man when exercising the natural affections which inspired kindness towards others: 'there should methinks be little need of proving this to any one of human kind who has ever known the condition of the mind under a lively affection of love, gratitude, bounty, generosity, pity, succour, or whatever else is of a social or friendly sort. He who has ever so little knowledge of human nature is sensible what pleasure the mind perceives when it is touched in this generous way'.[8] According to Shaftesbury's description,

> The very outward features, the marks and signs which attend this sort of joy, are expressive of a more intense, clear, and undisturbed pleasure than those which attend the satisfaction of thirst, hunger, and other ardent appetites. But more particularly still may this superiority be known from the actual

> prevalence and ascendency of this sort of affection over all besides. Wherever it presents itself with any advantage, it silences and appeases every other motion of pleasure. No joy, merely of sense, can be a match for it. Whoever is judge of both the pleasures will ever give his preference to the former.

Why advertise such self-evident raptures? The problem was that not all men were competent judges. Shaftesbury continues,

> The honest man indeed can judge of sensual pleasure, and knows its utmost force. For neither is his taste or sense the duller; but, on the contrary, the more intense and clear on the account of his temperance and a moderate use of appetite. But the immoral and profligate man can by no means be allowed a good judge of social pleasure, to which he is so mere a stranger by his nature.[9]

Any reader who decided to take up virtue in order to enhance his sensual pleasures would be missing the point. Shaftesbury believed that acting from ulterior motives was not virtue, but base, slavish selfishness. Not even fear of hell and hope of heaven were acceptable. He drew an analogy between improper and proper notions of virtue, and the attitudes of servants and the master's children in an upper-class household:

> For slaves and mercenary servants, restrained and made orderly by punishment and the severity of their master, are not on this account made good and honest. Yet the same master of the family using proper rewards and gentle punishments towards his children, teaches them goodness, and by this help instructs them in a virtue which afterwards they practise upon other grounds, and without thinking of a penalty or a bribe. And this is what we call a liberal education and a liberal service; the contrary service and obedience, whether towards God or man, being illiberal and unworthy of any honour or commendation.

An exception, however, could be made if heaven were desired purely for the opportunities it provided for further virtuous action: 'the expectation or hope of this kind is so far from being derogatory to virtue, that it is an evidence of our loving it the more sincerely and for its own sake'.[10] In '*Sensus Communis*; An Essay on the Freedom of Wit and Humour', Shaftesbury showed even fiercer contempt of people who attempted to combine virtue with self-interest:

> the more vulgar of mankind often stand in need of such a rectifying object as the gallows before their eyes. Yet I have no belief that any man of a liberal education, or common honesty, ever needed to have recourse to this idea in his mind, the better to restrain him from playing the knave. And if a saint had no other virtue than what was raised in him by the same objects of reward and punishment, in a more distant state, I know not whose love or esteem he might gain besides, but for my own part I should never think him worthy of mine.[11]

For Shaftesbury, God was the supreme example of disinterested benevolence, and he claimed, in his 'Letter Concerning Enthusiasm', that the bigotry of humans had led them to underestimate divine generosity, as well as deny divine justice. What sort of ruler would act as God was commonly supposed to do, rewarding only those subjects who had the correct belief about him?

> But if it happened that of this number there should be some so ignorantly bred, and of so remote a province, as to have lain out of the hearing of our name and actions; or hearing of them should be so puzzled with odd and contrary stories told up and down concerning us, that they knew not what to think, whether there were really in the world any such person as ourself; should we not, in good truth, be ridiculous to take offence at this?[12]

Furthermore, Shaftesbury was dissatisfied with the common Christian assumption that God wanted eternal praise from the whole of creation, because this, too, was an ulterior motive:

> Does it really deserve praise to be thus concerned about it? Is the doing good for glory's sake so divine a thing? or is it

> not diviner to do good even where it might be thought inglorious, even to the ungrateful; and to those who are wholly insensible of the good they receive? How comes it then, that what is so divine in us, should lose its character in the divine Being? And that according as the Deity is represented to us, he should more resemble the weak, womanish, and impotent part of our nature, than the generous, manly, and divine?'[13]

Shaftesbury's God was much more broadminded and tolerant than the common run of Christian deities; his capacity for disinterested benevolence made the difference, and defined his nature.

A counterblast to Shaftesbury's aristocratic idealism came from Bernard Mandeville (1670–1733), a Dutch-born physician, who became notorious for a down-to earth realism that was often condemned as brutal cynicism. In *An Essay on Charity and Charity-Schools* (1723), he defined charity as 'that Virtue by which part of that sincere Love we have for ourselves is transferred pure and unmixed to others,'[14] and found it very rare. He claimed that, on examination, acts of apparent unselfishness often turned out to be a form of self-advertisement, carefully disguised self-interest, or moral cowardice: 'thousands give money to beggars from the same motive as they pay their corn-cutter, to walk easy'.[15] In his 'Enquiry into the Origin of Moral Virtue' (1714), he argued that an element of self-regard could be detected, even in cases where men 'from no other motive than their love to goodness, perform a worthy action in silence'. For 'the humblest man alive must confess that the reward of virtuous action, which is the satisfaction that ensues upon it, consists in a certain pleasure he procures to himself by contemplating on his own worth'.[16] In other words, virtue sprang from pride – which, according to traditional Christian doctrine, was the first deadly sin. Mandeville's critics found his views particularly alarming because they so closely resembled the philosophy of Thomas Hobbes (1588–1679), who had argued that selfishness, not benevolence, was the most basic human impulse. Perhaps both writers would have been more readily forgiven if supporting evidence for their claims had not been so distressingly easy to find.

Although Mandeville's claims were hotly disputed, nobody denied the importance of pleasure as a motive to action. The philosopher David Hume (1711–76) was typical of his age. In his *Treatise of Human Nature* (1739–40), he frankly acknowledged that 'The chief spring or actuating principle of the human mind is pleasure or pain'.[17] He believed this was perfectly consistent with goodness: in his 'Enquiry concerning the Principles of Morals' (1777), he maintained that virtue 'declares that her sole purpose is to make her votaries and all mankind, during every instant of their existence, if possible, cheerful and happy; nor does she ever willingly part with any pleasure but in hopes of ample compensation in some other period of their lives'.[18] Conscientiously sceptical, Hume avoided the question of whether this period might begin after death. He also argued that, to the truly virtuous man, further compensation would be unnecessary, since virtue always guaranteed

> Inward peace of mind, consciousness of integrity, a satisfactory review of our own conduct; these are circumstances, very requisite to happiness, and will be cherished and cultivated by every honest man, who feels the importance of them.[19]

But what did virtue offer to those who failed to appreciate her charms? Advocates of a specifically Christian approach to morality believed that men were corrupted by original sin and needed strong controls to prevent them from acting accordingly. John Brown (1715–66), Doctor of Divinity and Vicar of Newcastle, wrote a celebrated critique of Shaftesbury, entitled *Essay on the Characteristics* (1751). He argued that disinterested benevolence could coexist both with earthly happiness and the hope of heaven: 'Hope is the most universal source of happiness: and that man is never so sincerely and heartily benevolent, as when he is truly happy in himself.'[20] This mood was not only an effect but a cause of virtue, since the good man felt 'tranquillity and joy, which will naturally diffuse itself in acts of sincere benevolence to all his fellow-creatures, whom he looks upon as his companions in this race of glory'.[21] William Paley (1743–1805), Archdeacon of Carlisle, attacked Hume in his *Principles of Moral and Political Philosophy* (1785). He invited readers of Hume's *Enquiry* to

> consider, whether any motives there proposed are likely to be found sufficient, to withhold men from the gratification of lust, revenge, envy, ambition, avarice, or prevent the existence of these passions. Unless they rise up from this celebrated essay, with very different impressions upon their minds than it ever left upon mine, they will acknowledge the necessity of additional sanctions.[22]

Paley defined virtue as 'the doing good to mankind, in obedience to the will of God, and for the sake of everlasting happiness'.[23] Christians might also enjoy happiness in this life; Paley's God displayed infinite benevolence and ingenuity in spreading pleasure throughout his creation:

> When we are in perfect health and spirits, we feel in ourselves a happiness independent of any particular outward gratification whatever, and of which we can give no account. This is an enjoyment which the deity has annexed to life; and probably constitutes, in a great measure, the happiness of infants and brutes, especially of the lower and sedentary orders of animals, as oysters, periwinkles, and the like; for which I have sometimes been at a loss to find out amusement.[24]

Thus pleasure became not only an incentive to good conduct, but a proof of the benignity – and perhaps even the existence – of God. It was a concept which no eighteenth-century moralist, Christian or otherwise, could ignore.

II

Eighteenth-century philosophers tried hard to discover how people recognised virtue in the first place, and what mechanisms enabled them to enjoy doing good. Here, too, pleasure provided an answer. In 'Concerning Virtue and Merit', Shaftesbury claimed that, just as the eye and ear could distinguish between different sights and sounds, so the mind had an inborn ability to respond to good and evil:

> It feels the soft and harsh, the agreeable and disagreeable in

> the affections; and finds a foul and fair, a harmonious and a dissonant, as really and truly here as in any musical numbers or in the outward forms or representations of sensible [perceptible] things. Nor can it withhold its admiration and ecstasy, its aversion and scorn, any more in what relates to one than the other of these subjects.[25]

This ethical connoisseurship appealed to every human heart: 'However false or corrupt it be within itself, it finds the difference, as to beauty and comeliness, between one heart and another, one turn of affection, one behaviour, one sentiment and another.'[26] Francis Hutcheson (1694–1746) named this faculty the 'moral sense', claiming that God had implanted it in mankind to direct our actions, 'so that while we are only intending the good of others, we undesignedly promote our own greatest private good,'[27] and that 'it gives us more pleasure and pain than all our other feelings'.[28] David Hume made this sense the only criterion for judging the ethical value of any action, asserting that 'moral distinctions depend entirely on certain peculiar sentiments of pain and pleasure, and that whatever mental quality in ourselves or others gives us a satisfaction, by the survey or reflexion, is of course virtuous; as every thing of this nature, that gives uneasiness, is vicious'.[29] Although this method of ethical assessment might seem very unsystematic and unreliable, Hume believed that all the pleasurable qualities had something very important in common: 'their tendency to the good of man'.[30]

How could individuals be so profoundly influenced by contemplating the good of others? For philosophers who believed in the moral sense, there could be only one answer: sympathy. In the *Dictionary of the English Language* (1755–73) compiled by Samuel Johnson (1709–84), 'sympathy' was defined as 'Fellow-feeling; mutual sensibility; the quality of being affected by the affection of another.' The connection between sympathy and sensibility was crucial: sensibilility was the emotional sensitivity that enabled its possessors to feel sympathy with each other. Shaftesbury believed that anyone who was 'not exceedingly ill-natured' would realise

> how many the pleasures are of sharing contentment and

> delight with others; of receiving it in fellowship and company; and gathering it, in a minute manner, from the pleased and happy states of those around us, from accounts and relations of such happinesses, from the very countenances, gestures, voices and sounds, even of creatures foreign to ourselves, whose signs of joy and contentment we can anyway discern. So insinuating are the pleasures of sympathy, and so widely diffused through our whole lives, that there is hardly such a thing as satisfaction or contentment of which they make not an essential part.[31]

It was even necessary for a satisfactory sex life:

> The courtesans, and even the commonest of women, who live by prostitution, know very well how necessary it is that every one whom they entertain with their beauty should believe there are satisfactions reciprocal, and that pleasures are no less given than received. And were this imagination to be wholly taken away, there would be hardly any of the grosser sort of mankind who would not perceive their remaining pleasure to be of slender estimation.[32]

The capacity to feel another's pain was equally important. For Hutcheson, it proved the existence of disinterested kindness: 'we are excited directly to desire the relief of the miserable, without any imagination that this relief is a private good to ourselves'.[33] Hume saw sympathy as a principle that took us 'out of ourselves'.[34] Thus sympathy, and the sensibility from which it took its rise, kept society going, by inspiring individuals with a desire to help their fellow-creatures.

But there was no guarantee that sensibility and sympathy would be channelled into useful action. In '*Sensus Communis*', Shaftesbury celebrated the 'moral magic' which made observers respond to 'the beauty of sentiment, the grace of actions, the turn of characters, and the proportions and features of a human mind'. The language of ethics and of aesthetics became indistinguishable, as morality merged with good taste. It is not surprising that Shaftesbury should continue by claiming that this happened even when the characters under inspection were fictitious:

> This lesson of philosophy, even a romance, a poem, or a play may teach us; whilst the fabulous author leads us with such pleasure through the labyrinth of the affections, and interests us, whether we will or no, in the passions of his heroes and heroines.[35]

'Interest', in contexts such as this, meant 'emotional involvement'. Hutcheson, too, believed that pleasurable sympathy could be aroused both by reality and by fictitious representations: 'People are hurry'd by a natural, kind Instinct, to see Objects of Compassion,'[36] which accounted equally well for the popularity of public executions and tragedies. Was there a risk, ignored by the philosophers, that romance-readers and theatre-goers, instead of learning moral lessons they could apply to daily life, would retreat into an imaginary world, undisturbed by sordid realities?

Bernard Mandeville regarded the growing taste for compassion with suspicion:

> The weakest minds have generally the greatest share of it, for which reason none are more compassionate than women and children. It must be owned, that of all our weaknesses it is the most amiable, and bears the greatest resemblance to virtue; nay, without a considerable mixture of it the society could hardly subsist: but as it is an impulse of nature, that consults neither the public interest not our own reason, it may produce evil as well as good. It has helped to destroy the honour of virgins, and corrupted the integrity of judges; and whoever acts from it as a principle, what good soever he may bring to the society, has nothing to boast of but that he has indulged a passion that has happened to be beneficial to the public.[37]

Adam Smith (1723–90) addressed this vexed question in his *Theory of Moral Sentiments* (1759–90), first published while he was Professor of Moral Philosophy at the University of Glasgow. He believed that the most admirable man combined perfect control of his own selfish urges with exquisite sensitivity to the feelings of others, but that in most cases, compassion was the result of weak and womanish self-indulgence:

> Humanity is the virtue of a woman, generosity of a man. The fair sex, who have commonly much more tenderness than ours, have seldom so much generosity. That women rarely make considerable donations, is an observation of the civil law. Humanity consists merely in the exquisite fellow-feeling which the spectator entertains with the sentiments of the persons principally concerned, so as to grieve for their sufferings, to resent their injuries, and to rejoice at their good fortune. The most humane actions require no self-denial, no self-command, no great exertion of the sense of propriety. They consist only in doing what this exquisite sympathy would of its own accord prompt us to do. But it is otherwise with generosity.[38]

The romantic poet, Samuel Taylor Coleridge (1772–1834), summed up the case against sensibility in *The Watchman* of 25 March 1796: 'Sensibility is not Benevolence. Nay, by making us tremblingly alive to trifling misfortunes, it frequently prevents it and induces effeminate and cowardly selfishness.'[39] Yet for Shaftesbury, Hutcheson and Hume, as for Tillotson, the capacity to feel the pains and pleasures of sympathy was either a cause or an effect of virtue – perhaps virtue itself. These diverging opinions point to contradictions inherent in the concept of sensibility; not surprisingly, they were reflected in society at large.

III

The object of this section is to show how ideas about sensibility, sympathy and the pleasures of benevolence affected the thoughts and behaviour of the middle and upper classes in eighteenth-century Britain. Much evidence has been drawn from *The Gentleman's Magazine* (GM), a periodical which started in 1731 and continued well into the nineteenth century. It was a miscellany of news, current affairs, original contributions and selections from other publications, rather like today's *Reader's Digest.* It faithfully reflected the ambiguity of contemporary attitudes to sensibility. When people were invited to stop and think about it, they had their doubts as to its value. These doubts were well expressed in 'A Prize Poem by Mrs King. Whether Sensibility be conducive to Happiness.' She decided that it was, since 'The heart can ne'er a transport know,/That never felt a pain,' (ll, 1–2), but concluded with a plea for moderation: 'Who feels too *little* is a fool,/Who feels too *much* runs mad; (ll, 31–32; *GM*, LXVIII, 1798, 519). But when sensibility itself was not the point at issue, many writings indicated an automatic assumption that it was a good thing. In the poetry section, sensibility was often listed among sexually attractive feminine characteristics. Thus the anonymous 'Panegyric on the Forbury, at Reading' – a park where ladies and gentlemen could meet for walks and flirtations – enumerated the charms of various girls, singling out Miss Deane because 'Another's woe thy tender bosom feels,/While down thy cheek the tear of pity steals' (ll, 63–68; *GM*, XXXIV, 1764, 596). Writing under the pseudonym of 'Philalethes', the author of 'Lines Addressed to a Lady' clearly believed that women liked to be told they possessed this quality in heaping measure: 'None other of thy sex can rival thee,/For thou art meekness, love, and sensibility' (ll, 7–8; *GM*, LXVII, 1798, 519).

Even the warmest admirers of sensibility, however, realised it could be something of a liability. John Mullan, in his illuminating study *Sentiment and Sociability* (1988), observes that 'sensibility can be considered as the sign of a privileged susceptibility – to pain and pleasure'; eighteenth-century authorities on the subject believed that it characterised the socially and intellectually superior, who were more vulnerable to physical and mental illness.[40] This led to an obnoxious combination of social and emotional snobbery, which found complacent expression in 'An Essay; by a young Lady not sixteen':

> The innumerable accidents and infirmities to which human life is continually exposed, will deeply wound those hearts that 'Bleed and agonize at every pore,' while they hardly ruffle vulgar minds, void of such delicate sensations; yet these fine feelings, however painful to the possessor, are the parents of compassion and benevolence, which humanise the heart, and are the best bonds of society. (*GM*, LXVI, 1766, 535)

How society could be held together by the possession of feelings whose very existence marked a barrier between refined and 'vulgar' minds was a problem which the young authoress ignored. In some tragic cases, sensibility was held responsible for provoking the ultimate withdrawal, not only from society, but life itself. For example, the obituary section records the death of Miss Halifax, aged twenty-three: 'one of the most distinguishing traits in her character was her filial affection; and it was the recent loss of an amiable and beloved parent which, preying on her exquisite sensibility, probably hastened her to an early grave' (*GM,* LIX, 1789, 1052). Such statements attempted to persuade the reader that dying of a broken heart was, somehow, an admirable achievement. In the circumstances, they are quite understandable, and it would be equally stupid and callous to condemn them. Who could be grudge the smallest crumb of comfort to mourners caught up in the hideous reality of eighteenth-century mortality rates? But it is legitimate to cultivate a more detached view of developments in art.

The cult of sensibility favoured the growth of sentimentality. Praise was lavished on works which moved tears by their 'pathetic' style. A sentimental aesthetic developed, emphasising the nuclear family, the virtue and simplicity of country life, the innocent vulnerability of children, the capacity of women to feel agonies of grief and terror, and the godlike sensations experienced by those who relieved the woes of others. Since the heart's impulses were valued more than reason, speech was regarded as a less reliable means of communication than actions, gestures and physiological processes: blushing, trembling, fainting and, above all, weeping. The hallmark of sensibility was the tear of pity. This grand old cliché shows every sign of surviving into the third millennium: it is distinctly visible on Spock's cheek in *Star Trek – The Motion Picture* (1979). A typical sentimental ploy was the creation of 'affecting scenes', described in novels and narrative poems, and made visible in plays and pictures. As Janet Todd points out, sentimental drama was full of carefully contrived 'familial tableaux', composed of 'father and son and of husband and wife, caught in an ecstasy of weeping and kneeling'.[41] Yet even creative artists in the sentimental mode felt the need to appease their critics by denouncing sentimentality, with highly ambiguous results. As Janet Todd observes,

'Clear sentimentalists degrade sentiment, and sentimental novelists claim not to be writing sentimental novels.'[42] Readers would be invited, in the most touching style, to weep for the misfortunes of a heroine who came to grief through excessive sensibility.

Twentieth-century critics like to leave sensibility balanced on a knife-edge of paradox. This provides much intellectual satisfaction, but distracts attention from the question of how a large number of eighteenth-century people managed to live their lives without either rejecting sensibility completely, or succumbing to total paralysis. The following section offers one of the answers.

IV

Eighteenth-century fund-raisers were practical men, determined to make the most of prevailing conditions. They resolved the paradox of sensibility by using sentimental techniques to encourage generous donations. Organised charities provided the perfect context for turning tender feeling into helpful action. An excellent example is the Humane Society, which was founded in London by two medical men, Dr William Hawes (1736–1808) and Dr Thomas Cogan (1736–1818) in 1774. It acquired the prefix 'Royal' in 1787. Its original aim was to promote the resuscitation of people who were no longer breathing, but who might be revived with proper treatment. It took as its model a society founded in Amsterdam in 1767, which already had several imitators in Europe. Later on, as similar societies proliferated in Britain, America and Europe, the London society took the credit for spreading the gospel of resuscitation. Most of the Humane Society's early beneficiaries were victims of drowning; it offered rewards to people who attempted resuscitation according to its directions, whether or not they were successful. Its activities rapidly extended to rewarding those who rescued other people from drowning, or attempted to do so. Members of the lower classes received money, while their social superiors received medals. Treatment was also given to those who had hanged themselves, or been suffocated by noxious vapours; the resuscitation of stillborn babies was another area of growing interest. At any moment, anybody might be faced with a situation in which the society's precepts could make the difference between life and death. By the end of the eighteenth century, it was encouraging medical research, spreading information on resuscitation techniques, providing apparatus for the rescue and treatment of casualties, and equipping and building receiving houses: these were forerunners of today's casualty wards, resuscitation units and intensive care facilities. They also recruited medical assistants to attend at emergencies: physicians and surgeons, who gave their services for nothing, but were rewarded with plenty of free publicity. (This could be valuable at a time when many medical men were short of work.)[43] Methods recommended included warming the body (often by placing it in bed with a naked person of the same sex), friction (ideally with flannel cloths soaked in warm brandy), bloodletting, inflation of the lungs through mouth or nostrils (using the mouth or bellows), and blowing air, tobacco smoke or other fumes into the anus (fumigators, which looked like bicycle pumps, were designed for the purpose, but other equipment that might be used in an emergency included bellows, pipe-stems, and a dagger-sheath with the end cut off). Although some of these techniques might appear ineffectual, or even counter-productive, by present-day standards, it should be remembered that these standards are based on traditions of research established by this very society. Another feature of the society which might seem odd today, but which was quite in keeping with its historical context, was the exclusively masculine composition of its organising and executive bodies. Women were allowed to become members, and the society was very conscious of the publicity value to be gained from the support of the Princess of Wales, but its official business was perceived as men's business. This was an age when women were not supposed to be willing or able to take part in corporate management of any kind.

Until now, little attention has been paid to the Royal Humane Society; social historians have preferred to concentrate on charities that drew a firmer line between upper-class benefactors and lower-class beneficiaries. Yet it would certainly repay more extensive investigation: it is still flourishing today, and it has kept its archives intact since 1774. For the present purpose, it is an ideal subject, because the breadth and complexity of its activities gives the best possible scope for showing how powerful emotions were exploited for the common good throughout society. Something in the nature of the project tended to raise the emotional temperature. This appears in the language of the first article on mouth-to-mouth resuscitation to appear in Britain's most august scientific periodical, *The Philosophical Transactions of the Royal Society*. Written by the Quaker physician John Fothergill (1712–80), himself a notable philanthropist, it refers to the procedure as a 'charitable experiment' and expresses a wish that anyone who tries it will be prompted by 'humanity' to 'favour the public with an account of their success'.[44] Furthermore, the sensational nature of the daring rescues and apparently miraculous resuscitations recorded by the society inspired artists and writers to depict its triumphs in works which provided further gratification to the public – and, incidentally, contributed to the good work by providing yet more publicity. Examination of ways in which theoretical links between virtue and pleasure were exploited in practice offers fresh insights into a neglected aspect of eighteenth-century life.

As might be expected, the rescue and resuscitation of helpless victims was presented as a source of intense pleasure for benevolent members of the upper classes. A typical story appears in the society's report for 1778, describing what happened when Dr Rogers, one of its medical assistants, was crossing Blackfriars Bridge and observed a swimmer in difficulties. 'The doctor immediately called aloud to a waterman that was near the spot, who put off his boat and rowed to the spot, and catching hold of the lad's hair just as he was sinking, dragged him into the boat; and thus providentially saved his life. The doctor recommended him to the treasurer, who made him a suitable recompense. The doctor humanely adds that, respecting himself, he was richly paid by the pleasing reflection of the happy consequences of an evening's walk' (p. 16). If sensibility was the prerogative of high rank, it was only natural that royalty should feel the delights of resuscitation. Prince Ernest (1771–1851), one of George III's many sons, was awarded the society's gold medal 'for his exalted philanthropy in the restoration of an unfortunate, desponding suicide'. He declared 'that he should be at all times happy to render the same assistance on a similar occasion, from the particular pleasure he had experienced in the present instance' (*GM*, LXVIII, 1798, 719). Similar sentiments were expressed by Alexander I, Czar of Russia (1777–1825), who was awarded the society's gold medal for organising the resuscitation of a drowned Polish peasant. In a letter to the society, cited in its report for 1808, he declared, 'It is impossible to deny myself the satisfaction of being enrolled among the members of a society, of which the objects and the zeal are so interesting to humanity, and so congenial to the dearest feelings of my heart' (p. 12).

The society's genteel and aristocratic members realised they were heavily dependent on the cooperation of the lower orders. Since the processes involved were not only time-consuming but strenuous, it was customary to delegate them to members of the working class, while their enlightened social superiors superintended operations. Sometimes it took four strong men, working for several hours, to revive a victim. The society's cash rewards were designed partly as compensation for missing a large part of a day's work, partly as motivation to those whose vulgar minds might be deficient in natural compassion. Members who discovered that the working classes were not uniformly callous, selfish and apathetic believed their own efforts were responsible. The report for 1776 claimed that, within two years of the society's foundation, its generous initiatives had led to an increase of cooperation, and even humane feeling, among their inferiors. Landlords of public houses were a shining example; the society offered rewards to those who agreed to accommodate victims on their premises:

> The cheerfulness and alacrity with which publicans receive the objects, and administer every assistance in their power, cannot be too much commended. This temper is become so general, that the man who rejects an application of such a nature, is now deemed by the whole neighbourhood as a monster of inhumanity. A stigma which begins to operate very powerfully on some who would not be actuated by other or better motives! (pp. 88–9)

William Hawes, an indefatigable publiciser, argued that the society's activities encouraged the development of sensibility and benevolence throughout the nation. He put his case in an article over the initials 'C. A.' – cunningly adopted to give an impression of impartiality. He described the society as

> an admirable institution for strengthening all the finer feelings and affections of the human mind, for drawing closer those delicate links and chains that unite mankind together in the various relations of husband and wife, of parent and child, of brother and sister.

It had 'a manifest tendency to improve the morals, at the same time that it preserves the lives, of the human species'. It was necessary for national stability: 'no government, at least no free government, could ever be long supported where the morals of the people are become thoroughly depraved' (*GM*, LX, 1790, 684).[45] This article was part of Hawes' campaign to get government funding for the society – it failed. Nevertheless, it is noteworthy that so shrewd an operator as Hawes should choose an appeal to sensibility when he wished to achieve maximum political impact.

The finer feelings were also fostered by the sermons, dinners and other fund-raising functions organised by the society. At the religious services, every attempt was made to arouse the emotions of the congregation. When the Bishop of Norwich preached a benefit sermon for the society, his efforts were supplemented by the performance of 'three sublime and beautiful hymns, written for the occasion by Mr John Taylor' (*GM*, LXIX, 1799, 1185). The sermons themselves might be praised for their 'pathetic' qualities (*GM*, LXVIII, 1798, 781). Since no paraphrase or description can do them justice, two extracts have been selected. The first is from a sermon preached in 1776 by William Dodd, Doctor of Divinity (1729–77). The latter date has an ironic significance in this context: he was hanged for forgery, and clandestine efforts by his friends in the society to resuscitate him were unsuccessful. A tearjerking style reflected the histrionic character of this shifty, self-publicising, but frequently well-intentioned performer, as in the following imaginative account of a successful resuscitation:

> In agonies of joy the almost frantic wife perceives a sign of life! she hears, and for the first time with transport hears, a

> deep groan from his heart. She sinks, o'erpowered with the mighty efforts of affectionate anxiety; she sinks on his recovering frame – She bathes with tears of love his reanimating face – she sees at length, she sees! – support her, God of nature, in the mighty struggle! she sees the lamp of life relumined in his countenance! He lives, – he lives! – and she no more laments herself a widow, and her children fatherless![46]

The wife's antics are in the best traditions of sensibility: the sheer intensity of her love for her husband makes her incapable of helping him. All she can do is watch, and hinder, the efforts of others: the high-flown emotionalism of this passage enabled Dodd to gloss over the fact that restoring respiration and circulation is much easier if a weeping woman does not insist on lying on top of the casualty. But it was a good money-raiser: Dodd's benefit sermons were famous. Furthermore, this particular example, coming very early in the society's history, set valuable precedents: its tone, structure, and subject matter were imitated in many later publications associated with the society, though they never acknowledged the embarrassing origin of their legacy.

The second extract is from the less inspired, but more respectable, Colin Milne (1743/4–1815). He chose the same text as John Tillotson (Section I, above), and asked his congregation to consider what emotions they felt when they followed the example of Jesus, who 'went about, doing good':

> What were the sentiments which a reflection of your conduct excited within your breast? Were they not those of self-complacence, self-congratulation, and self-applause? Felt you not a certain glowing, a certain expression of the soul – a something which proclaimed your high original, which told you, that you were indeed but a little lower than the angels – an undescribable somewhat – an emotion, in fine, for which expression is inadequate? – You did, and you exult in owning it. You felt yourselves great, and you *were* great. You felt yourselves noble, and you *were* noble. You were above youselves. You were superior to mere humanity. Ye were angelic. Ye were godlike and divine: for the source of excellence, and

> standard of perfection, we never so completely resemble, as when, like him, we are benevolent, compassionate and merciful.[47]

To twentieth-century readers, this mode of oratory must always be tainted by the satirical tradition which began with Charles Dickens' brilliant portraits of pontificating clergymen. It can no longer be read with a straight face. To Milne's original congregation, listening with more innocent ears, this sermon spoke eloquently of authentic joys.

One method of attracting publicity was to make a public exhibition of the beneficiaries. Some of these occasions, like the concerts performed by the Charity Children of London and Westminster, or the inmates of the Magdalen House for the Reception of Penitent Prostitutes, were eagerly attended by large and discriminating audiences. The Royal Humane Society was no exception. As well as food, drink, music and a chance to meet the cream of society, it offered processions of the grateful resuscitated. The 1789 anniversary festival seems to have been a particularly riotous occasion:

> The Earl of Fife presided, and was supported by the Bishop of St. David's and the Lord Viscount Grimston; and by 4 o'clock nearly 400 persons, many of them of great eminence, were assembled at the festival board, which was plentifully served, and succeeded by many loyal toasts. The *Non Nobis* was admirably performed by the gentlemen of St. Paul's choir; some of whom sang 'God save the King' in a capital style, the whole company joining heartily in chorus; some excellent glees were also sung. After dinner a large number of men, women, and children, whom the society had rescued from premature graves, walked round the tables. The procession chiefly consisted of beautiful and promising children, whom their sports had led to the water, and who would have become early victims but for the humane interference of this society. A subscription of more than £300 was made by the company; and the day was spent with that warm and exhilarating mirth which philanthropy is always sure to bestow.
>
> (*GM*, LIX, 1789, 273)

Apparently, a good time was had by all, with the possible exception of the beneficiaries, whose subordinate status was indicated by the fact that they were not actually invited to the dinner, which was reserved for members of the society. The high proportion of children does not reflect the rescue statistics in the annual reports, but suggests that the processions were composed of people who were easy to control.

An anonymous poem describing such a display raises disturbing possibilities:

> With conscious gratitude their bosoms burn,
> Their timid step and glowing cheek declare; –
> No language can their grateful thanks return,
> 'Tis seen perspicuous in their modest air.
> (ll. 6–8, *GM*, LXIII, 1793, 324)

This is such a full description of exactly what a conventional disciple of sensibility would expect to see, that the poet might not have been present at all. But if it is an accurate eyewitness account, there is a strong chance that the beneficiaries' wordless blushes were less expressive of modest gratitude than of overwhelming embarrassment. It is not the least humane of the Royal Humane Society's present policies that it never names victims.

The language describing the emotions which members felt, or were supposed to feel, when contemplating resuscitated victims suggests that a certain amount of depersonalisation was taking place: 'To behold these living monuments of the national utility of this Institution' was depicted as 'a treat for Britons and Philanthropists' (*GM*, LXV, 1795, 251). Since a monument is an inanimate structure, often associated with death, the idea of 'living monuments' is a deliberate contradiction in terms, designed to startle the reader into realising just how wonderful the society's achievements are. So turning the victims into 'monuments' is not necessarily to treat them as objects. But the invitation to 'behold' them, combined with the statement that this provides a 'treat' for the beholders, implies a measure of exploitation. An even clearer example of this tendency to turn human beings into gratifying spectacles occurs in a sermon preached in 1778 by Robert Poole Finch (1724–1803):

> If we are struck with admiration at the productions of genius, in which the artist captivates us by an imitation of nature, and teaches canvas or marble to resemble animation, with what rapture must enlarged and benevolent minds view the corporeal faculties actually restored, the cheeks again blooming with undiminished lustre, and the countenance replete with gratitude to those who have been the happy instruments of resuscitation! (*GM*, LVIII, 1788, 730)

In this case, the chief difference between revived victims and works of art is that the latter are incapable of displaying gratitude towards those whose actions are responsible for their existence. As the ethics of benevolent sensibility merge yet again with the aesthetics of sentimentality, it seems apropriate to examine some more obvious ways in which the Royal Humane Society impinged upon the realms of literary, visual and performance art.

V

Up to now, works on the link between sensibility and literature have ignored the mass of verse generated by charitable organisations in the late eighteenth century. Its overall quality is not particularly distinguished, but it does have the merit of demonstrating the sentimental style in its purest form, unadulterated by any suspicion of wit or irony. An example which provides illuminating insights into the psychology of eighteenth-century life-saving is recorded in the society's report for 1797. It is 'An Occasional Address', originally recited at a meeting at Jones's Royal Circus, St George's Fields, on Friday 22 July 1796. The opening, with its depiction of rescuers weeping both before and during the rescue, is a long way from the impersonal efficiency and disinterested courage commonly believed to prevail today:

> 'Sweet is the balm which Friendship's aid bestows,
> To lighten grief and mitigate our woes;'
> Sweet the big tear which moistens Pity's eye,

The lucid gem of fair Philanthropy!
That tear you've shed, when hurried down the wave
Some victim seemed to court a watery grave;
That balm bestow'd, when, snatching from the flood,
You felt the luxury of doing good:
See Life restor'd, clouds yield to skies serene;
Yourselves blest actors in the godlike scene!
Your proud reward in this pleas'd group is view'd,
The 'living monuments' of Gratitude!
(ll. 1–12, p. 49)

Any reader who compared this poem with the society's reports of actual rescues would soon realise that this account was unrealistic: however hysterical the behaviour of relatives and other onlookers, rescuers were never described as weeping. It is a fair assumption that they were too busy, at the time, to indulge their feelings in this manner. But the difference in tone between factual reports on the one hand, and sermons and poems on the other, suggests that, once in the sentimental mode, readers were in no condition to make cross-references. Besides, the organisers of benefit meetings always wanted to pull out every available emotional stop, since getting the patrons' tears to flow was believed to be the most effective way to loosen their purse-strings.

Pictures had their part to play, as well as words. The society's most widespread visual propaganda took the form of illustrations in its reports, but it instigated the creation of other works, notably a pair of oil paintings which it commissioned from Robert Smirke (1752–1845). The first depicts a pleasant rural scene, with a river in the foreground, and a cottage in the distance. A young man is being recovered from the water, apparently dead, by four stalwart companions. His anxious father watches; his aged mother faints in the arms of a bystander; his children cling in alarm to their unconscious grandmother. The second painting shows the victim sitting up in bed, supported by Dr Hawes, while two of his rescuers stand attentively by. His father kneels in prayer; his mother and children (who have been excluded from the scene of operations up to now) are ushered in by Dr John Coakley Lettsom (1744–1815), another prominent member of the society. In 1787 Robert Pollard (1755–1838) made engravings of the pictures, entitled 'The Young

Man Restored to Life'. Although the relevance of these pictures to medical history has been examined by John P. Griffin,[48] little has been done so far to set them in their appropriate artistic context. In themselves, they are anthologies of sentimental iconography: feminine weakness, the vulnerability of childhood, idealised depictions of cottage life and the English countryside, unfeigned rustic piety, the enlightened philanthropy of the benevolent gentry and the supreme emotional value of family ties are all evoked by these affecting scenes.

These pictures have a strong, though hitherto undetected, link with the literature of the subject; they were probably designed to meet the specifications laid down by Thomas Francklin (1721–84) in a benefit sermon preached in 1779. He invited his congregation to imagine a series of scenes. First, 'At a little distance from you behold a busy bustling crowd of industrious labourers encircling the body of their hapless companion, whom they have taken, at the hazard of their own lives, out of the neighbouring river, and dragged to the shore without sense or motion.'[49] Then the victim is brought home, and surrounded by his wife, his dependent mother, and his children, all rendered helpless by the double bind of excessive sensibility:

> They who would most gladly take upon them the task of restoring him are most unable to perform it; their faculties are all absorbed in grief, their limbs petrified with despair, and all the precious moments which should have been employed in the means of his recovery, are lost in fruitless tears and useless lamentation. (p. 18)

The situation is transformed by the arrival of a member of the society – presumably a medical assistant:

> he flies, like the good Samaritan, to the chamber of sorrow, he stops the retreating multitude, the idle sons of curiosity who had assembled but to gaze on and desert him, calls on the most vigorous and active amongst them to assist him, applies with zeal and alacrity those plain and simple means which reason dictates, as the most proper to reanimate, if possible, the lifeless mass, and pursues them with ceaseless toil and unwearied assiduity. (p. 19)

Finally, the victim recovers: 'What follows is not within the power of language to describe; imagination alone can suggest to you the delightful scene of wonder and astonishment, of mutual joy, transport and felicity' (p. 20). Francklin himself said that 'The little imperfect narrative here given might, I think, furnish matter to some of our eminent artists for an excellent picture' (pp. 16–17, n). The recommendation was brought to the attention of a wider public when it was repeated in a review of the sermon (*GM*, XLIX, 1779, 554). Apart from the omission of the victim's wife and the substitution of his father, Smirke's paintings are a faithful representation of the events recounted in Francklin's words. (*Two* fainting women might have looked monotonous.) So it is a fair assumption that Francklin's benefit sermon gave the society the idea of commissioning the pictures.

The last work to be discussed in this chapter is a play by the popular and prolific German sentimental dramatist, August von Kotzebue (1761–1819). *Der Opfer-Tod* (*The Suicide*) first appeared in 1798; in 1799 an English translation was published, entitled *Self Immolation; or, the Sacrifice of Love.*[50] The play is set in London. The main characters are: 'Robert Maxwell, a decayed merchant', whose 'decay', or financial ruin, has been brought about by the fraud of a wicked partner; Arabella Maxwell, his devoted and virtuous wife; Walwyn, a rich and amiable man who was Arabella's former suitor, and is still in love with her; and Harrington, a rich wine merchant, and member of the Royal Humane Society.[51] On the point of starvation, Maxwell seeks honest work that will enable him to earn enough to feed himself, his wife, his son and his blind mother. He is still too virtuous to turn to crime, and too proud to accept handouts. One of the people who withholds the help he requires is Harrington, who refuses to pity Maxwell because, in his opinion, Maxwell is better off than himself. He feels bitter because, on the day before, he had seen his own son drowned whilst bathing; by the time he was brought to shore, he was dead.

Maxwell: And, was there no means to save him? –
Harrington: None.
Maxwell: The Humane Society – ?
Harrington: Could –

Maxwell: Have not hundreds been recovered by the means of this benevolent institution?

Harrington: True. I am myself a member of the society. I have known the joy of restoring a husband to his wife, a son to his mother. I may say, in truth, that I was ever one of the most active members. My associates eagerly flew to attempt the recovery of my son. No means was left untried. For hours I hung over his breathless body, pressed his pallid lips with mine, and employed every conceivable aid to rekindle the flame of life, – in vain. I kneeled till my knees were stiffened: till my voice was hoarse, I called on the God of mercy. God heard me not. No, he heard me not. I have lost my all. . . . You have made me to open my lips to complain; – and I had resolved not to complain. You have brought burning tears into my eyes; – and I had determined not to weep. No, my grief shall suffocate me in silence. . . .

Maxwell: He wrongs me, cruelly wrongs me. But his heart is full. All his sensibilities are absorbed in the contemplation of his own griefs. But it is, surely, less miserable to see one's darling child lie dead before you, – than to behold that child pine away by inches, and perish for hunger. Time passes. Once I could feel for the sufferings of others. The tale now whistles by my ears, but cannot touch my writhing heart.

(II, iv, pp. 33–4)

Any reader or spectator of proper sensibility would view with concern the failure of these men to feel sympathy for each other. It indicates that things are terribly wrong.

As in the literature produced by the Royal Humane Society, there seems to be an intimate connection between the proper circulation of air, feeling, and money. By Act II of *Self Immolation*, all three have become disastrously impeded. Maxwell then hits upon an apparent solution to his problems which will only make matters worse. Somebody offers him a job overseas, which will support him, but not his family. He decides to take this opportunity, and separate himself from Arabella, handing her over, along with his other family obligations, to the eternally devoted Walwyn. Walwyn, realising that Maxwell is temporarily insane, agrees to the scheme, but without intending to go through with it. Unfortunately, his action brings about the very crisis he was trying to avoid. Maxwell tells Arabella of the proposed arrangement, before Walwyn has had a chance to explain his true intentions to her. Arabella is a good woman: at the beginning of Act III, Scene i she declares that she feels the joy of virtue: 'It refuses not to reside in the house of want. It even now cheers my bosom!' (p. 43). Consequently, she is too chaste and dutiful a wife to accept Maxwell's proposition. Seeking the only possible means to free Arabella from her marital obligations, Maxwell drowns himself in the Thames. His body is retrieved by a porter called John Hartopp, who describes the subsequent events:

> I can't say, after all, that it was I who saved him. For, when I laid him on the bank, he was as dead as a herring. But, there is a Society in London, do you see, who will not let a brave fellow drown himself, without a struggle to save him. Some of them were quite at hand. Great gentlemen! God knows who! – They instantly seized the body, and continued rubbing, warming, and blowing, till they opened his eyes.' (III, xi, p. 58)

A leading part in the resuscitiation was played by Harrington, who joins Walwyn, Hartopp and the Maxwells in the touching final scene, where the succession of familial tableaux has a far greater impact than the dialogue:

(*Act III, scene xii. Enter Maxwell, Walwyn and Harrington*)

Maxwell: (*Still of a death-like paleness in his countenance, hair hanging down in disorder, his looks downcast, is led by Walwyn to Arabella*)

Arabella: (*Attempting to rise, is unable, but sinks back, and holds out her arms*)

Maxwell: (*Kneels before her, and with involuntary feebleness, lays his head in her lap*)

Arabella: (*Bends sobbing over him*)

Hartopp: (*Wipes his eyes with his fingers awkwardly*)

Harrington: (*Stands lost in deep thought; and now and then casts a look on the reunited pair*)

Maxwell: (*Lifts up his head, and looks on Arabella with an expression of anguish*)

Arabella: (*Clasps his neck, and joins her cheek to his*)

Walwyn: (*Beholds them with strong emotion*)

Hartopp: By my soul, this is the man, who this morning tried my load. He perhaps carried heaveir than I.

Harrington: Are you not the same person, who this morning asked my assisance in the tea-garden?

Maxwell: I am.

Harrington: I am, then, perhaps, in part, the author of your despair. I have much to atone for. (*Taking Walwyn aside*) Sir, I know you to be an honest man. May I entirely confide in the truth of what you just now mentioned?

Walwyn: You may, upon my honour! –

Harrington: (*To Maxwell, after a short pause*) Sir, my son was yesterday drowned in bathing. I have this day saved your life. Today, then, God restored to me a son. You, sir, must supply the place of my lost child. I adopt you as mine.

Maxwell: (*Turns to him, kneels, and with ardent emotions of gratitude, stretches out his hands*)

Harrington: I understand – no words – there is no need – your excellent wife, – will she not be my daughter?

Arabella: (*Folds her hands and smiles*)

Harrington: I understand – it is settled – I am not childless – God forgive me my murmurs.

Arabella: (*Sinks on her knees beside her husband, clasps him in her arms, and presses him to her heart*)

Hartopp: Ha! the next load I shall have to carry, will be as light as a feather! (*The curtain falls*). (pp. 59–60)

This play is not a completely accurate depiction of the society's procedures. In real life, men like Harrington contented themselves with giving money, and did not join in the actual resuscitations: they left such matters to the medical assistants. But it is true to the society's aims, depicting not merely the restoration of breathing and circulation to a drowning man, but his reintegration into the communities of friendship and family life, as well as the larger, but less emotionally significant, world of business. And no connoisseur of sentimentality could deny that this play provides a classic display of the methods used by the society to arouse the audience's emotions. It is a supreme example of the eighteenth-century theory that, for those equipped with the proper sensibility, the practice and contemplation of benevolence in all its forms made a major contribution to the pursuit of happiness.

6. The Seductions of Conduct: Pleasure and Conduct Literature

VIVIEN JONES

> *Chastity is a suppression of all irregular desires, voluntary pollutions, sinful concupiscence, and of an immoderate use of all sensual, or carnal pleasures. . . . If wanton dreams be remembered with pleasure, that, which before was involuntary, and therefore innocent, becomes a voluntary and sinful transgression of this virtue. Chastity is so essential and natural to your sex, that every declination from it is a proportionable receding from womanhood. An immodest woman is a kind of monster, distorted from its proper form.*

This is the Reverend Mr Wetenhall Wilkes in *A Letter of Genteel and Moral Advice to a Young Lady*, a popular mid-eighteenth century conduct book.[1] In its explicit rejection of female pleasure, its stress on asexual 'modesty', the passage seems to epitomise our sense of 'conduct books' as inculcators of feminine propriety, instruments of repression and confinement. Over recent years, conduct literature has become a familiar source of evidence within feminist histories of modern sexuality and gender construction since it describes, or at least prescribes, a particularly unambiguous and, it is argued, increasingly dominant, definition of femininity as docile, domestic, asexual. It articulates a bourgeois programme of self-discipline and self-improvement which is anti-pleasure, where pleasure is identified with aristocratic sexual licence and consumerist excess. But Wilkes's moral discourse of chaste conduct evokes precisely the desires and fantasies it claims to police. Chastity is defined through the psychosexual language of Gothic melodrama and monstrosity, turning its readers into (guilty) fantasists. In this context, the relationship between conduct literature and pleasure becomes more problematic – and potentially more productive – and in this essay I want to disrupt monologic accounts of the genre as straightforwardly repressive, and to argue that even these most recalcitrant of texts offer possibilities for pleasure – and for resistance.

I don't want to defend or recuperate conduct books themselves as radical or progressive, but I do want to suggest that they are both more interesting and more varied than is sometimes implied. It's useful to remember that the homogenising label 'conduct literature' was not an eighteenth-century term. When Sarah Pennington gives her selection of recommended reading in *An Unfortunate Mother's Advice to her Absent Daughters*, for example, she includes 'religious and instructive' as well as 'entertaining books', but it would be difficult for a modern reader to decide which texts on her list are intended to fit into each category. Those which we would now confidently think of as 'conduct books' are dispersed across other generic groupings: sermons, letters, histories, fictions. And when Mary Wollstonecraft offers her devastating 'Animadversions on Some of the Writers Who Have Rendered Women Objects of Pity, Bordering on Contempt' in *Vindication of the Rights of Woman*, she introduces her chosen texts under the very general heading of 'some modern publications on the female character and education'. Again, the list includes two 'conduct books' – James Fordyce's *Sermons to Young Women* (1766) and John Gregory's *A Father's Legacy to his Daughters* (1774) – but, not surprisingly since Fordyce writes sermons and Gregory uses the epistolary form, they are not discussed in terms of a common generic identity.[2] The Wollstonecraft example, particularly, tends to support the modern feminist recognition that a dominant ideology of ideal femininity is pervasive across a wide range of eighteenth-century texts. My point, however, is that in isolating that 'conduct-book' ideal, and in reading it teleologically in terms of the nineteenth-century 'angel in the house', we lose sight of the textuality of eighteenth-century 'conduct books'. We underplay, in other words, those aspects of conduct books which might suggest that their ideological effects were rather more precarious and mixed: the differences between individual texts; the ways in which they draw on a variety of, potentially contradictory, generic motifs; and the fluid and various context of a newly burgeoning print culture within which they were produced, and within which, even more importantly, they were actively consumed.

I

Recent feminist work on conduct and instructional literature for women during the eighteenth century has focused on its instrumental role in the production of a gendered class identity. In doing so, it has tended to stress its repressive, or its disciplinary, effects on female subjectivity. A familiar version of women's history traces consumer capitalism's gradual exclusion of middle-class women from productive labour and the public sphere – and therefore from significant cultural identity. Margaret George, for example, sums up this view in an important early article: 'That the fundamental "bourgeois personality" was male, that individual man was both subject and object of the new society, is the primary point of contact with a changing woman's world.'[3] In her influential Marxist–feminist study, *The Proper Lady and the Woman Writer* (1984), Mary Poovey uses conduct literature as important evidence of the ideological apparatuses through which women were persuaded into this culturally devalued role. And she goes on to argue that women's writing at the end of the eighteenth century is inevitably marked, disfigured even, by the powerful ideal of the bourgeois 'proper lady' – domestic, chaste and self-effacing. In Poovey's account, the ideology of femininity can only be disempowering; it is 'full of the most debilitating contradictions', and repressive in its effects: 'Equating chastity with value . . . required a woman to suppress or sublimate her sexual and emotional appetites.' As in Gilbert and Gubar's then recently published *The Madwoman in the Attic*, women writers are presented as able to express their 'true' desires only through strategies of indirection.[4] Readers, we assume, were even more thoroughly subject to the 'proper lady's' repressive domination.

In her preface, Poovey makes a far-reaching observation about the way in which gender cuts across social differences: 'The ideals disseminated by conduct books and periodicals . . . helped,

I think, make women of different beliefs and slightly different social positions more nearly of one faith and one class than their fathers or brothers were' (pp. xi–xii). In the work of Nancy Armstrong, this recognition of a feminine class identity, generated by the ideology of domestic conduct and cutting across masculine signs of class difference, becomes the basis for the challenging contention that: 'it was the new domestic woman rather than her counterpart, the new economic man, who first encroached upon aristocratic culture and seized authority from it'. Using a Foucauldian model of power as a productive rather than a repressive mechanism, Armstrong rethinks the old 'repressive hypothesis' about women's cultural identity. In direct opposition to the view represented by Margaret George, Armstrong's excitingly corrective (if ultimately over-extravagant) claim is that, 'the modern individual was first and foremost a female'.[5] Armstrong narrates the emergence of a coherent bourgeois identity as a function primarily of 'private' and domestic rather than professional and economic aspirations; the domestic woman, generated by advice literature, becomes a figure of authority rather than disempowerment as conduct books and novels produce her as 'what men were supposed to desire in women, and what women, in turn, were supposed to desire to be'.[6] For Armstrong, then, conduct ideology produces desire in a particular (restricted) form, rather than distorting desires which are pre-existent.

Working alongside histories of the family, these exciting studies provide an importantly corrective account of the kinds of material that must be considered as 'evidence' in analyses of the relationship between histories of class and of literary forms – particularly, of course, in the story of 'the rise of the novel'. Domestic manuals, periodicals, sermons and letters to young women – the long-ignored female-directed products of the new print culture – are foregrounded and given an explanatory status which has significantly changed ways of thinking about the construction of modern subjectivities.[7] Indeed the tendency has been, perhaps, to overstate their explanatory and instrumental power, with conduct books in feminist analyses taking the place held by philosophical and polemical texts in old-style 'history of ideas' criticism.[8] In the work of both Poovey and Armstrong, conduct books implicitly attain a kind of truth-bearing status: they are the comparatively static and monologic 'context' for the 'literary' texts which, it is suggested, tackle the complexities conduct literature cannot reach.[9] The conduct books themselves are reduced to manifest content; they are not treated as *readable* in the same way. For Poovey, as I have already suggested, they are agents of repression. For Armstrong, similarly, they are primarily a stable and efficient disciplinary mechanism, rather than subject, like any other text, to a process of active consumption. Historical readers are thus reduced to a single implied reader, a predictably submissive textual effect.

But in what circumstances were 'conduct books' actually read? Alone and in private, or collectively? silently or aloud? by whom and to whom? What other texts were being read alongside them? How were the 'conduct books' we think of as generically similar categorised at the time, and how did that affect their possible meanings? What unexpected, transgressive readings might their contemporary audience have produced? I write on behalf of numerous historical readers who, I want to believe, read conduct books more actively and unpredictably, more resistantly, than the texts themselves – and some modern accounts of them – seem to assume. And my interest in possibilities for resistant reading in the past comes out of a present commitment to resistance and change; out of a desire to tell the history of femininity as more contested, various and, again, unpredictable than repeated narratives of repression and containment sometimes imply. In making histories of the present, we are necessarily involved in a process of interpretation, of selecting among historical particularities in order to tell a certain story. I want to contribute to a feminist history which acknowledges the ideological power of the 'proper lady', but resists accepting that figure as monolithic, or wholly explanatory. The will to read conduct books contentiously in the present is itself part, then, of my argument for the existence of comparable, but largely irrecoverable, readings in the past.

Young women read conduct literature in an atmosphere of changing social practices and impassioned debate about what were the most correct, the most advantageous, the most desirable, forms of courtship and marriage for the monied and propertied classes. Central to that debate was the issue of parental authority, the question of the extent to which parents had the right to choose their children's marriage partner. The controversy brought questions of liberty and property into particularly sharp focus: claims to individual freedom, personal happiness, even romantic love, were variously seen as supporting, or dangerously threatening, the preservation of property, the circulation of wealth, and the maintenance of proper familial and social hierarchies. The debate climaxed with the passing in 1753 of 'Hardwicke's Marriage Act'.[10] Marriage without parental consent for those under the age of twenty-one, and marriage without the reading of banns or a bishop's licence, were made illegal. The aim was to put an end to 'clandestine' marriages which, since they were more often the result of financial opportunism than of thwarted love, were generally agreed among the propertied classes to be a threat to social and economic stability. But debate didn't end with the passing of the Act: it was seen by many as an endorsement of parental tyranny, or as inhibiting marriage altogether. In 1781, for example, an amendment which lowered the ages of consent to sixteen for women and eighteen for men was passed in the Commons, but rejected by the House of Lords.

Historians disagree about what the Marriage Act, and its surrounding commentary and court cases, tell us about actual day-to-day practices and assumptions. What is very clear is that a discourse of romantic love (variously defined, and subject to various degrees of mistrust) is mobilised as an alternative to financial self-interest. The context might be morally conservative, as in James Fordyce's *Sermons to Young Women* (1766):

> The times in which we live are in no danger of adopting a system of romantic virtue. The parents of the present generation, what with selling their sons and daughters in marriage, and what with teaching them by every possible means the glorious principles of Avarice, have contrived pretty effectually to bring down from its former flights that idle, youthful, unprofitable passion, which has for its object personal attractions, in preference to all the wealth of the world. With the successful endeavours of those profoundly politic parents, the levity of dissipation, the vanity of parade, and the fury of gaming, now so prevalent, have concurred to cure completely

> in the fashionable of both sexes any tendency to mutual fondness.[11]

Fordyce is here contrasting 'romantic virtue', the principle of chivalric honour which motivated 'Old Romance', with 'loose and luscious' scenes in modern novels. But his rhetoric against the culture of fashion and conspicuous display puts him in the strange position of encouraging 'idle, youthful, unprofitable passion'. And it brings his ideal of 'mutual fondness' into close touch with the more liberal and pragmatic position of, for example, William Buchan, who deals with the question of parental consent in a footnote to the chapter 'Of the Passions' in his home medical manual:

> Even the conduct of parents themselves in the disposal of their children in marriage is often very blameable. An advantageous match is the constant aim of parents; while their children often suffer a real martyrdom betwixt their own inclinations and the duty which they think they owe to their parents. The first thing which parents ought to consult, in disposing of their children in marriage is certainly their own inclinations. Were due regard always paid to these, there would be fewer unhappy couples; and parents would not have so often cause to repent the severity of their conduct, after a ruined constitution, or a distracted mind, has shewn them their mistake.[12]

My point is that, read against this atmosphere of active debate, the passive and asexual proper lady looks much less secure. Together with the plots of countless novels, and in the light of changing social practices, such comments give us access to a more complex structure of feeling which takes 'inclinations' seriously, and within which female choice is a significant factor. In what follows, I shall be speculatively suggesting resistant readings of conduct literature which might have emerged from, and contributed to, that atmosphere of family negotiation and public debate around issues of desire, pleasure, duty and property.

'Resistance' and 'pleasure' are not, of course, necessarily the same thing. For feminists, 'resistance' necessarily evokes Judith

Fetterley's concept of the 'resisting reader', her call for a process of conscious 're-vision' which will mean that books 'will lose their power to bind us unknowingly to their designs'.[13] Since 1978, when Fetterley's ground-breaking book was written, a greater awareness of the complexity of the reading process has made us less comfortable with a notion of texts as conspiratorially 'binding' readers to their 'designs', or with an idea of opposition to those designs as dependent simply on an autonomous act of will. Recent theories of textual reception, and particularly those focusing on women's consumption of popular culture, discuss reading as an active process of negotiation; they warn against a view of the reader/text relationship as mindless subjection, a form of false consciousness; and they refuse to categorise texts – or readings – according to an imprisoning binary choice between the 'repressive' and the 'liberating'. Instead, they document women's sceptical, ironic, or simply unexpected, reading responses; using psychoanalytic theory, they point out that fantasy offers multiple, potentially contradictory, positions of identification; and they stress the ways in which meanings and pleasures shift across different reading contexts. But they also warn, importantly, against conflating pleasure and transgression with progression.[14] Whilst not wanting to lose touch entirely, then, with Fetterley's call to oppositional reading, my use of 'resistant' invokes a more plural model of reading as negotiation. It is a model which draws on Foucault's account of resistance as a function of, but as not necessarily contained or predicted by, power relations and cultural constraints:

> there is a plurality of resistances, each of them a special case: resistances that are possible, necessary, improbable; others that are spontaneous, savage, solitary . . .; still others that are quick to compromise, interested, or sacrificial; by definition, they can only exist in the strategic field of power relations. But this does not mean that they are only a reaction or a rebound.[15]

For Foucault, it is also true that 'power induces pleasure',[16] and the relationship between resistance and pleasure will be similarly 'plural', needing careful analysis in individual instances.

Pleasure is a slippery and much-debated term – more easily

recognised, perhaps, than satisfactorily theorised – and it can take all sorts of, potentially contradictory, forms.[17] There is pleasure, for example, precisely in non-resistance, in the comforting plenitude of acceptance and approval gained by conforming to an expected role. However impossible and contradictory the feminine ideal might be in practice, its imagined achievement is undoubtedly one of the most important satisfactions offered by conduct books: like all advice literature, they are in that sense 'a species of romance'.[18] But, as I have suggested, this isn't the kind of pleasure I'm interested in here, since my concern is with readings made against rather than with the grain of these texts.

In current usage, as within the moral scheme of advice literature itself, pleasure most frequently means sexual pleasure; it is conflated with active sexuality, or with fantasy.[19] Again following Foucault's recognition that sexual identities and pleasures are not 'natural' or inherent, but are produced through discourse, I shall suggest that, far from repressing sexual pleasure, the effect of conduct books' insistence on an ideal of chastity is to open up spaces of fantasy and female desire which are potentially transgressive. But the identification of pleasure, or at least transgression, simply with active sexuality is problematic for women and for feminism, since it tends to reproduce a view of women as primarily, or exclusively, sexual beings. We need to be open to the possibility that the powerful discourse of chaste femininity might also produce pleasures less easily recognised as such in a modern context of 'sexual liberation'. So in the third part of the essay, I want to move beyond a too-narrowly sexualised definition of pleasure, and to explore ways in which the discourse of conduct might also, unexpectedly, foster these different pleasures and resistances: what Mary Wollstonecraft would call 'independence of mind'.[20]

I shall explore first the possibilities for active female desire and fantasy in readings of courtship advice, and the stress here will be on the continuities between 'conduct literature' and fiction. I shall then go on to consider a much less obvious manifestation of women's 'inclinations', the choice of refusal, and look at an ideal of female independence which emerges from conduct texts' negotiation of the risks of marriage. The most obvious generic parallels here are with educational and polemical writings, but there are also connections to be made with a specifically female appropriation of the pastoral ideal of retirement. In both cases, representations of masculinity provide a useful starting-point.

II

Courtship advice is haunted, and fascinated, by predatory aristocratic masculinity in the form of the rake. At the level of manifest content, it abounds with warnings against 'the ridiculous opinion, "A reformed libertine makes the best husband"' – as Sarah Pennington put it in 1761.[21] At the same time, however, it assures young women of their reformative power: 'conscious virtue . . . is able to awe the most shameless and abandoned of men'.[22] It is, of course, novels that are held responsible for that 'ridiculous opinion' about the reformable rake, and conduct books distinguish themselves absolutely, but unconvincingly, from fiction's tendency 'to give a romantic turn to the mind, which is often productive of great errors in judgment, and of fatal mistakes in conduct' (Pennington, 1761, p. 88). Like novels, conduct manuals represent courtship as a vertiginous exercise in reading masculinity; and like novels, they work within the heterosexual seduction narrative of threat, resistance and transformation which casts the young marriageable woman as simultaneously vulnerable and unassailable, sexually susceptible and naturally chaste. This young marriageable woman, with her equivocal right to a degree of marital choice, is the heroine who defines and facilitates an emergent class identity just as much as Armstrong's domestic female.

The seduction plot, in which vulnerable femininity is betrayed into ruin by socially superior masculinity, is a founding bourgeois myth. In warning against that tragic story, against 'the snares of a seducer', as told in the novels of Eliza Haywood for example, conduct literature also evokes its comedic opposite: the upward trajectory of Richardson's heroine in *Pamela*, who withstands Mr B's threats, to achieve spectacular social success.[23] This sexual narrative imagines the possibility of taming, and so controlling, the social and economic power represented by the morally reprehensible libertine. In a recent article, Michael McKeon usefully describes this ambivalent inter-class dynamic:

> from the beginning the ideology of the middle class has been defined in part by the self-canceling impulse to assimilate upward. Indeed, in its oscillation between the will to assimilate and the will to supersede the aristocracy, the middle class has displayed the ambivalence – the intertwined attraction and repulsion – that we have come to associate with modern critique of homosexuality.[24]

McKeon's point here concerns the class-based construction of the male homosexual 'molly' culture, but a comparable dynamic of 'attraction and repulsion' also structures the representation of heterosexual relations – through which, of course, in the institutionalised form of marriage, class differences were both cemented and redrawn. Like Lovelace in Richardson's *Clarissa,* the predatory libertine figure must be dangerous, but also sexually and aesthetically fascinating: aristocratic masculinity is both threat, and object of (illicit) desire. Upward social mobility is thus motivated and legitimated through female sexual fantasy. At a moment of transition from, in Foucault's terms 'the deployment of alliance' to 'the deployment of sexuality',[25] bourgeois hegemony needs the sanctioned transgression of (imagined) seduction.

Advice literature maps that shift from 'alliance' to 'sexuality' through a growing willingness to accommodate female desire: the representation of marriage within conduct books moves from making the best of an arranged marriage to suggesting that an appropriately decorous version of romantic love is a legitimate expectation. Writing at the beginning of the period, and from within the aristocracy, the Marquis of Halifax regrets that: 'It is one of the *Disadvantages* belonging to your *Sex,* that young Women are seldom permitted to make their own *Choice*. . . . In this case there remaineth nothing for them to do, but to endeavour to make that easie which falleth to their *Lot*'. Halifax's *Advice to a Daughter* was reprinted throughout the eighteenth century, and versions of this view recur in other advice manuals, but they are increasingly in tension with the image of the bourgeois couple who 'have chosen each other, out of all the species, with a design to be each other's mutual comfort and entertainment'.[26] Hence the hints on how young women might distinguish acceptable from unacceptable forms of masculinity.

One of the most interesting aspects of this kind of advice is its disingenuous collusion with what became the *Pamela* narrative, with the idea that women's role might be to create, rather than simply to choose, desirable masculinity. This is Foucault again:

> One of [the bourgeoisie's] primary concerns was to provide itself with a body and a sexuality – to ensure the strength, endurance, and secular proliferation of that body through the organization of a deployment of sexuality. . . . It converted the blue blood of the nobles into a sound organism and a healthy sexuality.[27]

The seductive fantasy of conduct-book heroinism is to effect that conversion by transforming the 'blue blood' of the libertine into the 'healthy sexuality' of the man of feeling. This is Wetenhall Wilkes again, from his 'Advice in the Time of Courtship'; the *Letter of Genteel and Moral Advice* was published in 1740 – the same year as *Pamela*:

> If it be agreeable to see craft repelled by cunning: it must be much more so, to behold the snares of a seducer defeated by the management of innocence.[28]

Far from encouraging female readers to have nothing to do with the rake, Wilkes's inflammatory warnings against 'the snares of a seducer' invite a fantasy of female sexual power. 'The management of innocence', with all the contradictory self-consciousness that the phrase implies, is precisely what Henry Fielding and others found so threatening about *Pamela*.[29] We are familiar with the idea that novels dramatise the material of advice literature, but the reverse is also true. Courtship advice works through the sexual narratives which also structure fiction: in this case, the story of aggressive masculinity revealed as 'manageable', which would become the standard paradigm of popular romance.[30]

I shall come back to Wilkes, but I want first to look at a text where the boundaries between fiction and advice literature are even less clear. Elizabeth Singer Rowe's *Letters Moral and Entertaining, in Prose and Verse* is a collection of short first-person narratives. Published in three volumes between 1728 and 1732, the *Letters* are contemporary with the first phase of Eliza Haywood's writing career, and, like Haywood's novels, they represent the transition from the heroic to the bourgeois romance. Where Haywood was pilloried for her sexually explicit fictions, however, Rowe became the type of the virtuous female writer: James Fordyce described her as 'that female angel'; and in John Duncombe's *Feminiad* in praise of female writers, she is a shining example of 'the modest Muse'.[31] The *Letters* are incomplete narratives, about characters with romance names, and set in vague, moralised landscapes; from within this idiom of 'Old Romance', they attack arranged marriages, Otway's heroic plays, and libertine scepticism as the dangerously corrupting conventions of an aristocratic culture; and they play rather static variations on standard moral themes: the corruptions of city consumerism, the pleasures of retirement, and, overwhelmingly, the threat of early death – both arbitrary and self-inflicted – as the great leveller of passion and pleasure.

But in doing so, these relentlessly sublimatory narratives necessarily reveal points of continuity with Haywood's transgressive fictions. They reproduce, perhaps consciously imitate, motifs from the novel of seduction – which also, of course, made claims for itself as a moral vehicle. (Haywood claimed, for example, that her 'Design' was 'only to remind the unthinking Part of the World, how dangerous it is to give way to Passion'.[32]) The following seduction scene is from Haywood's second novel, *The British Recluse.* Belinda is recounting to Cleomira, the recluse of the title, the moment when she was almost seduced by Courtal (the libertine who is also, it transpires, responsible for Cleomira's ruin):

> Never was a Night more delectable, more aiding to a Lover's Wishes! The arching Trees form'd a Canopy over our Heads, while through the gently shaking Boughs soft Breezes play'd in lulling Murmurings, and fann'd us with delicious Gales; . . . every Thing was soothing – every Thing inspiring! the very Soul of Love seem'd to inform the Place, and reign throughout

> the whole. . . . My Soul dissolv'd, its Faculties o'erpower'd – and Reason, Pride, and Shame, and Fear, and every Foe to soft Desire, charm'd to Forgetfulness, my trembling Limbs refus'd to oppose the lovely Tyrant's Will![33]

The following passage is from Rowe's letter '*To Mrs.* —— *from AMORET, giving an account of her criminal passion for SEBASTIAN* '. The situation is again one of confessional restrospect. Amoret failed to spot the predatory male, and was betrayed by 'that disguise of honour, which the false *Sebastian* always avow'd':

> Time and place, the evening gloom and verdant shade, every circumstance conspired to my undoing. The whispering gales, the falling fountains, the green retreats and flow'ry scenes, heighten'd the soft temptation: All nature seem'd to sooth the tender passion, and gave my charming seducer new advantages, his form, his aspect acquir'd unusual graces, and his language was all enchantment. . . .
>
> Whither is my imagination wandering? Ye powers of chastity assist me![34]

Rowe's version is more consistently moralised – 'conspired'; 'undoing'; 'temptation' – but its closeness to Haywood's idiom of heightened sexual sensibility, and its willingness to acknowledge female desire for 'the charming seducer', are very clear. The speaker's anguished guilt barely contains the eroticism of the seduction scene: as in Haywood's evocation of helpless 'Forgetfulness', the reader is drawn, with Amoret, into the dangerous pleasure of imaginative re-enactment. Like Richardson's Clarissa, unable to write her name immediately after her rape,[35] and like Wilkes's 'monstrous' female quoted earlier, Amoret's guilt is expressed in terms of a loss of identity: 'I am at variance with my self' (p. 107). Haywood's heroines are similarly given to bewailing their 'Deformity', their loss of 'Fame, . . . Virtue, and . . . Peace of Mind . . . those Beauties, which Guilt and Shame had utterly defac'd' (Haywood, 1722 p. 49). And, unlike their faithless seducers, the women in Haywood's fictions remain constant in love. In Rowe's *Letters,* too, protagonists rhapsodise, like the heroines of heroic epistles, on the exquisite agony of unrequited love: 'There is a pleasure in our very sorrows, when they flow for a worthy object: You can give me that pleasure, and justify me to myself' (Rowe, 1740, p. 320). Death becomes an eroticised alternative to forbidden or frustrated passion. Amoret, for example, at the end of the letter quoted above, lovingly imagines her death scene: 'in the languishments of love divine / [I] Resign my breath, and wake in endless joy.' And in another letter a male character proves his desirability when a letter found after his death shows him to be capable of the most refined feeling: 'the soft affections of my soul will be perfectly refined into a noble and seraphic ardour' (pp. 109, 156). The languages of earthly and spiritual passion are almost indistinguishable: Rowe's moral narratives seduce their readers into emotionalist fantasies, making ideal love the focus of female existence. No less than Haywood's fictions, they are fixated on the pleasures and dangers of desire.

One of the most significant differences between Rowe and Haywood is their representation of masculinity. A striking number of the *Letters* are written by male protagonists, who are almost invariably recounting their conversion from libertinism to virtue. The hero of one letter even describes himself as 'an example of the reformation of manners' (p. 167), perhaps consciously alluding to the campaigning society of that name.[36] Precisely because of its commitment to the efficacy of virtue, Rowe's anti-heroic moral text has to convert desire into romance, the libertine into the man of feeling. Haywood, paradoxically, is more consistently radical in her warnings against the rake as deeply desirable, but utterly untrustworthy – and certainly not reformable. Thus, again, the instructional text opens up the space of fantasy, justifying female desire on the promise of masculine reformability.

I want now to return to Wilkes's *Letter of Genteel and Moral Advice to a Young Lady*, and particularly to his contradictory representation of masculinity. The contradictions emerge as he develops that image, already quoted, of the seducer defeated by 'the management of innocence':

> It is as much the province of a licentious rake to betray the young, the rich, the beautiful, or gay female; as it is the

> quality of a fox to prey upon poultry.... An honest man, with a moderate share of good sense, may as easily convince a lady of his designs being honourable and intended for her welfare, as the best master of address and rhetoric....
>
> Be careful how you give way to what many ladies call 'an innocent liberty'; for her civility may be taken for an invitation. The double temptation of vanity, and desire, is so prevalent in our sex, that we are apt to interpret every obliging look, gesture, smile, or sentence, of a female we like, to the hopeful side. Therefore, let your deportment forbid without rudeness, and oblige without invitation....
>
> Opportunities should be avoided as much as possible. Great is the danger, that a female incurs, let her imagine her simplicity and innocence to be ever so invincible, by too much familiarity with a male companion.... Whoever is made of flesh and blood, is subject to human frailties. (Wilkes, pp. 31–2)

Like many male conduct writers, Wilkes offers his female readers a tantalising glimpse into masculinity. One effect of that privileged access to a male point of view is the familiar mechanism by which the woman imagines herself as a set of signs for male consumption; as object, rather than subject, in a narrative driven by men's susceptibility to the 'double temptation'. Wilkes's prurient anxiety about young women's vulnerability thus saturates not just the female body, but all her social exchanges, with sexuality – and danger. In a situation where the woman must be constantly checking whether this is or is not an 'opportunity', whether she is or is not behaving with 'too much familiarity', sex is always on the agenda. Courtship advice of this kind is inescapably collusive with the popular fictional narratives it claims to oppose. The discourse of innocence, modesty and propriety necessarily encourages women to focus obsessively on the possibility of sexual transgression, whether that takes the form of the seduction scenarios lovingly described in Haywood's popular fictions, or of the deferred pleasure of reforming the rake.

The protective boundaries of class and gender begin to break down in Wilkes's text, as the distinctions between libertinism and respectability, between active and passive sexual roles, become increasingly uncertain. In order to effect 'the management of innocence', the woman is also allowed to look and to appraise; she is reciprocally engaged in reading men for signs of libertine masculinity. And Wilkes's fatherly advice takes on a more seductive tone, as it plays across the boundaries of innocence and knowledge, passivity and activity: 'forbid without rudeness, oblige without invitation'. His overt message is that innocence can be preserved because men differ: women should have no difficulty in distinguishing mere rhetoric from 'honourable' designs and in making a firm choice between the 'licentious rake' and the 'honest man'. But Wilkes's own dubious fascination with feminine innocence, and his confession that 'the double temptation of vanity, and desire, is so prevalent in our sex', expose the possibility that 'ev'ry *Man* is at Heart a rake'.[37] The *Pamela* narrative's transformation of the rake into the man of feeling is, it would seem, all too easily reversible, and the proper lady's power to make a correctly passionless choice begins to look increasingly precarious. Wilkes's libidinised advice releases possibilities for fantasy which disrupt any claim that 'chastity is . . . essential and natural to your sex'. More sinisterly, from a post-Freudian perspective, it reveals desire at the heart of the bourgeois family itself.

III

The problem with such a reading, eager to put female desire and sexual fantasy back into conduct literature, is that it evaluates eighteenth-century texts in terms of a modern preoccupation with sexuality and the importance of sexual expression. And, to use Mary Wollstonecraft's phrase, it is in danger of reproducing the reduction of women to 'a sexual character'. In *Vindication of the Rights of Woman,* Wollstonecraft attacks James Fordyce's *Sermons to Young Women* as 'most sentimental rant'. Fordyce's mixture of protectiveness and prurience is very similar to that of Wilkes, and Wollstonecraft was quick to recognise that the attentive voice of the man of feeling – what she called his 'love-like phrases of pumped-up passion' – is ultimately indistinguishable from the lascivious gaze of the libertine. 'In sermons or novels', she asserts, 'voluptuousness is always true to its text'. And:

> till women are led to exercise their understandings, they should not be satirized for their attachment to rakes; or even for being rakes at heart, when it appears to be the inevitable consequence of their education.[38]

Wollstonecraft's *Rights of Woman* is itself, of course, a kind of conduct book. But, as this comment reminds us, it represents that aspect of advice literature which connects with the urgent eighteenth-century debate on the nature and function of women's education, as much as with the questions of courtship, marriage and masculinity, which associate conduct books more closely with fictional texts. Wollstonecraft's first sole-authored publication was *Thoughts on the Education of Daughters* (1787), and in the chapter of *Rights of Woman* in which she criticises Fordyce and Gregory, she registers her respect for Hester Chapone's *Letters on the Improvement of the Mind* (1773), an often-reprinted advice book on women's education, and she praises Catherine Macaulay Graham's more radical *Letters on Education* (1790).[39] Wollstonecraft's response to 'sentimental rant' was to refuse the power of masculine definition. Citing John Gregory's warning, in *A Father's Legacy to his Daughters*, that 'Many a girl dancing in the gaiety and innocence of her heart, is thought to discover a spirit she little dreams of', Wollstonecraft retorts, 'Let the libertine draw what inference he pleases'; and to the 'artificial grace' inculcated by Fordyce, she opposes the 'true grace [which] arises from some kind of independence of mind'.[40] It is this Wollstonecraftian inheritance, the pleasures of 'independence', which I want to explore now. Questions of marital choice, unacceptable masculinity, and female education combine within conduct literature, I want to argue, to produce the possibility for more radically resistant readings.

Wilkes's unwitting conflation of the rake with the man of feeling is more explicitly acknowledged in a popular female-authored conduct book: Sarah Pennington's *Unfortunate Mother's Advice to her Absent Daughters*, first published in 1761. Pennington gives instruction on distinguishing between the 'quality of Good-Nature' and mere 'Good-Humour' in men, since 'no two principles of action are more essentially different'.[41] But she is far less sanguine than Wilkes about the possibility of distinguishing successfully:

> A man by this specious appearance has often acquired that appellation [of 'Good-Humour'], who, in all the actions of his private life, has been a morose, cruel, revengeful, sullen, haughty tyrant. (p.99)

Personal experience gives such passages an authority which threatens to undermine the surface orthodoxy of Pennington's text. *An Unfortunate Mother's Advice* is framed by veiled references to the story of Pennington's own marital difficulties, and of her fight to recover her good name after her estrangement from her husband. In choosing to publish a book of advice, Pennington defines herself against the overtly transgressive femininity of the 'scandalous memoirists'.[42] By tantalisingly refusing to give a full account of her marital history, she presents herself as heroinically maintaining a much more conformist identity in the face of personal abuse and financial difficulty. But from her precarious position on the margins of respectability, Pennington's text opens up a less spectacular, but perhaps ultimately more productive, space for transgression and resistance. She instructs her daughters in the self-effacing skills of orthodox domesticity, and asserts that marriage can be 'the highest satisfaction of human life' (p. 116). But it gradually becomes all too apparent that marriage is more likely to be a damage-limitation exercise, staving off 'absolute misery' rather than embodying the romantic ideal of 'true happiness' (p. 115):

> so great is the hazard, so disproportioned the chances, that I could almost wish the dangerous die was never to be thrown for any of you. (p. 96)

This moment of anxiety about her daughters' possible fate within the marriage market briefly suggests the possibility of refusing marriage altogether. It mobilises an ideal of independence which is embodied in the text by Pennington herself: her own narrative ends happily, in a life of 'constant rational composure' and independent retirement which gives 'more real satisfaction . . .

than the gayest scenes of festive mirth ever afforded me' (p. 127).

Pennington's anxieties about marriage, and her use of the retirement ideal, should (and would) be read in the context of similar motifs, both in other advice books, and in other kinds of writing. Parental anxiety about the realities of marriage for women is a common feature of some of the most popular and frequently reprinted conduct books: it goes back to Halifax's *Advice to a Daughter.* In his introduction, Halifax admits that he has '*Visions* of your being Happy in the World, that are better suited to my partial *Wishes,* than to my reasonable *Hopes* for you. . . . when my *Fears* prevail, I shrink as if I was struck, at the Prospect of *Danger,* to which a young Woman must be expos'd'. And John Gregory, in *A Father's Legacy,* prays that his daughters need never 'relinquish the ease and independence of a single life, to become the slaves of a fool or tyrant', and promises to leave them 'in such independent circumstances as may lay you under no temptation to do from necessity what you would never do from choice'.[43] Though we might scorn the counsel of appeasement and self-effacement which often follows from this kind of paternal concern, it is too easy to dismiss such sentiments as no more than cynical strategies to keep women subservient. They are articulations, sometimes even quite moving articulations, of ideology's impact on personal experience; precisely because of their orthodoxy, they give access to the tensions involved in living through the ideological contradictions of a marriage system which is simultaneously romantic and financial, 'companionate' and hierarchical. Implicitly, they raise doubts about the system itself, and questions as to possible alternatives.

These hints of dissension within conduct books gain resonance when they are read in conjunction with, for example, the critiques of marriage which are a significant feature of women's poetry – a genre rarely discussed in connection with advice literature. The anti-marriage strain is particularly marked in the first half of the century: in Mary Chudleigh's 'To the Ladies' (1703), for example:

> Wife and servant are the same,
> But only differ in the name: . . .
> Then shun, oh! shun that wretched state . . .;

in Mary Leapor's 'An Essay on Woman' (published 1751):

> . . . mighty Hymen lifts his sceptred rod,
> And sinks her [Woman's] glories with a fatal nod,
> Dissolves her triumphs, sweeps her charms away,
> And turns the goddess to her native clay.

Or in Lady Mary Wortley Montagu's witty and erotic romantic fantasy, 'The Lover: A Ballad' (published 1747):

> And that my delight may be solidly fixed,
> Let the friend and the lover be handsomely mixed;
> In whose tender bosom my soul might confide,
> Whose kindness can soothe me, whose counsel could guide. . . .
> But till this astonishing creature I know,
> As I long have lived chaste, I will keep myself so.[44]

Chastity here is a regrettable but necessary retreat from the forms of masculinity represented as actually available: the 'lewd rake' or the 'dressed fopling'. In Leapor's poem, domestic independence and female friendship are the alternatives to the phallic power of 'mighty Hymen': 'Still give me pleasing indolence and ease / A fire to warm me and a friend to please' (p.208). Through her characteristic use of a Popeian satiric idiom, Leapor creates a female version of the Horatian pastoral ideal of retirement, and reiterates, for example, Anne Finch's combination of retirement with female friendship in her 'Petition for an Absolute Retreat': 'Let a Friend be still convey'd / Thro' those Windings, and that Shade!'.[45] Though first published in the first half of the century, the work of Chudleigh, Finch, Montagu and Leapor (including 'To the Ladies' and 'The Lover') remained available later in the century in Colman and Thornton's popular anthology *Poems by Eminent Ladies.*[46]

This pastoral retirement motif recurs, in various forms, in women's poetry as well as in fiction, and it is this tradition, often set up as an explicit alternative to marriage or to sexual relationships, which informs Pennington's self-image at the end of *An Unfortunate Mother's Advice.* For women, it can carry overtones of punishment. At the end of Haywood's *British Recluse,* for example, the heroines' 'Resolutions of abandoning the World' can be interpreted as a just punishment for their sexual transgression, or as an excessive willingness to accept the judgment of conventional morality; but the ending can also be read as the potentially radical choice of an alternative female community: 'happy in the real Friendship of each other'. Clarissa's readiness to retreat to 'my grandfather's late house' rather than give in to her family's insistence that she marry the odious Solmes echoes Rowe's *Letters Moral and Entertaining*, with its commitment to children's right of refusal, and celebration of rural retirement. And in Sarah Scott's *Millenium Hall*, a member of the ideal female community asserts, 'I would not change my present happy situation for the uncertainties of wedlock'.[47] My point in adducing these various examples (there are, of course, many others) is not to suggest that they carry identical meanings in relation to marriage (some retirement ideals include a heterosexual partner), but to establish a sense of a reading context within which the milder refusals of conduct literature might become sites of possible resistance.

At the beginning of the period, the work of Mary Astell radically combines retirement with female education as an explicit alternative to marriage. In *A Serious Proposal to the Ladies*, Astell's planned female seminary is, among other things, a refuge 'where Heiresses and Persons of Fortune may be kept secure from the rude attempts of designing Men'. Astell's works were not reprinted beyond her lifetime: as Ruth Perry has demonstrated, her radical influence survived into the later part of the century only, if at all, by word of mouth in bluestocking circles.[48] But a less radical version of Astell's rationalist independence survived at a more popular level throughout the century in conduct-book form. The Marchioness de Lambert's *Advice of a Mother to her Daughter*, for example, which was regularly reprinted after the publication of the first English translation in 1727, opens with the challenging contention that: 'The world has in all ages been very negligent in the education of daughters . . . as if the women were a distinct species.' This implicit claim to intellectual equality is based on the same female appropriation of Cartesian rationalism which underpins Astell's feminism. Like Halifax, Lambert writes from an aristocratic class position in which an arranged marriage is inevitable and, like Pennington, she advocates an outward acceptance of an orthodox feminine role; but within those constraints, a rational education becomes a vital means of escape: 'secure yourself a retreat and place of refuge in your own breast; you can always return thither, and be sure to find yourself again'; 'the greatest science is to know how to be independent'.[49]

The first meaning of 'independence' when applied to women in the period is economic – as John Gregory recognised when he promised to leave his daughters in 'such independent circumstances' as would give them the freedom to make an independent marital choice. In her important article on the Marriage Act, Erica Harth condemns Astell's ideal of mental freedom as 'no more . . . revolutionary than the men who would restrain her'.[50] This seems to me a dangerously doctrinaire rejection of a discourse of independence which, surviving into advice and education literature, maintains the presence, the possibility, of an alternative feminine identity, an imagined place outside the realities of dependency. Commenting on Astell's outspoken rejection of marriage as tyranny, Betty Rizzo has recently argued that, 'Direct critiques of marriage by women by no means disappear, but after midcentury they tend to appear more in private letters than in published works.' And, like so many commentators, she uses 'the prescriptions of the conduct books' (represented by Gregory) to establish a submissive feminine ideal.[51] Critiques of marriage also survive, I would suggest, in the less demonstrable arena of women's reading practices – and even in resistant readings of the conduct books themselves. The commitment to 'know how to be independent' maintains a muted presence until the revolutionary moment of the 1790s turned Wollstonecraft's *Thoughts on the Education of Daughters* into *A Vindication of the Rights of Woman.*

IV

Let me end with a moment from Jane Austen's *Pride and Prejudice.* Soon after his arrival at Longbourn, Mr Collins is invited to read aloud to his cousins:

> a book was produced; but on beholding it, (for every thing

> announced it to be from a circulating library,) he started back, and begging pardon, protested that he never read novels. – Kitty stared at him, and Lydia exclaimed. – Other books were produced, and after some deliberation he chose Fordyce's Sermons. Lydia gaped as he opened the volume, and before he had, with very monotonous solemnity, read three pages, she interrupted him. . . .
>
> Mr Collins, much offended, laid aside his book, and said, 'I have often observed how little young ladies are interested by books of a serious stamp, though written solely for their benefit. It amazes me, I confess; – for certainly, there can be nothing so advantageous to them as instruction.'[52]

Austen's text doesn't overtly endorse Lydia and Kitty's rudeness but, given his refusal even to read novels and the pompous inaccuracy with which he holds forth about female behaviour elsewhere in the novel, still less does it endorse Mr Collins's account of 'serious' reading matter for 'young ladies'. The episode plays with the familiar generic opposition: between fiction's dangerous pleasures, and the irreproachable programme of self-improvement provided by sermons and other forms of advice literature. In texts like Fordyce's *Sermons*, women were warned against novels; here, in response to such attacks, fiction is implicitly allowed to get the better of the contest.

But, characteristically, Austen's comedy goes beyond a simple binary choice between pleasure and instruction – or even between fiction and advice literature. Instead, it assumes knowledge of both genres, and turns that intertextual expertise into a source of critical pleasure. Fordyce's *Sermons to Young Women* was still frequently reprinted in the period when Austen was writing *Pride and Prejudice*. One of its distinguishing features is an almost frenzied vehemence about the corrupting effects of most novels:

> What shall we say of certain books, which we are assured (for we have not read them) are in their nature so shameful, in their tendency so pestiferous, and contain such rank treason against the royalty of Virtue, such horrible violation of all decorum, that she who can bear to peruse them must in her soul be a prostitute, let her reputation in life be what it will.[53]

Typically of conduct discourse, Fordyce's moral outburst makes femininity and fiction into sites of transgressive desire: one effect of his apparently absolute distinction between respectable and 'treasonous' femininity is to fuel fantasy (and guilt) by casting women as always already 'prostitutes'. The effect of Austen's intertextual play, however, is to displace such sexually saturated categories. Knowledge of Fordyce's text reveals the full force of the joke against Mr Collins, and it turns out to be a joke about, precisely, knowledge, about 'instruction' and its 'advantages'. Fordyce's virulence is based on ignorance – as is Mr Collins's rejection of the novel from the circulating library. 'Young ladies' on the other hand who, contrary to Mr Collins's claim, have read not only novels but also books 'of a serious stamp', are by implication far better informed than their male instructors. (In the case of *Pride and Prejudice*, this would describe Elizabeth and Jane – and Austen's implied reader – rather than Kitty and Lydia.) Austen's text undermines both Mr Collins's model of women as passive, grateful recipients of 'advantageous' instruction, and Fordyce's hysterical condemnation of novel readers as prostitutes. Instead, Austen defines female reading in terms of wit and knowledge; 'young ladies' are revealed as actively using and interpreting, rather than being used and defined by, the books they read. It is that possibility which I hope to have demonstrated in this essay.

7. 'Strains of New Beauty': Handel and the Pleasures of Italian Opera, 1711–28

DEREK ALSOP

I doubt operas will not survive longer than this winter, they are now at their last gasp; . . . harmony is almost out of fashion.[1]

So wrote Mrs Pendarves, a devoted follower of Italian opera, and an admirer of Handel since childhood, on 25 November 1727. Two months later John Gay's *Beggar's Opera*, which was to become the greatest stage success of the eighteenth (and any other) century, opened with the first of a record-breaking sixty-two first run performances. Gay's work, a bathetic satire on the lives of fence and thief-taker Peachum, his family, and his low-life criminal acquaintances such as the notorious highwayman Macheath, had a variety of targets, not least of which was Walpole and his political allies and methods. But it also offered a thorough travesty of Italian opera, with its sixty-nine English airs on mock-heroic subjects set to popular tunes. On 29 January Mrs Pendarves wrote again to her sister:

> Yesterday I was at the rehearsal of the new opera composed by Handel: I like it extremely, but the taste of the town is so depraved, that nothing will be approved of but the burlesque. The Beggars' Opera entirely triumphs over the Italian one.[2]

By March the 'last gasp' was nearly exhausted, prompting an attack in the *London Journal*:

> As there is nothing which surprizes all true Lovers of Music more, than the Neglect into which the *Italian* Operas are at present fallen; so I cannot but think it a very extraordinary Instance of the fickle and inconstant Temper of the *English* Nation.[3]

'Fickle and inconstant' because the public was shifting its allegiance from the art-form which for the last seventeen years had, in London at least, swept all before it.

The rise of Italian opera in London had been as rapid a development in the early eighteenth century as its demise now seemed in 1728. Before 1705, music on the English stage had generally been at most no more than an equal partner to the spoken word. Even when Purcell's great English opera *Dido and Aeneas* had been partly revived in 1700 and 1704 it had served only as a musical interlude in a spoken drama.[4] And though, as Dean and Knapp note, 'Italian music other than opera had been familiar in London well before the end of the seventeenth century'[5] it was not until the first decade of the eighteenth century that the influence of Italian opera itself was directly felt. But, in 1705, there were two developments of crucial consequence for the future of London opera. On 16 January Christopher Rich, the manager of the famous Drury Lane Theatre, opened a production of the opera *Arsinoe, Queen of Cyprus* with music by Thomas Clayton (both libretto and tunes being borrowed from Italian sources, though the piece was in English). Its Preface proudly announced its design as 'being to Introduce the *Italian* manner of Musick on the *English* Stage, which has not Been before attempted'.[6] The limitations of both drama and music in this work did not prevent a most remarkable success. 'It is a measure,' notes Jonathan Keates, 'of the naivety of London audiences that anything so woefully inadequate . . . should have had the success it did'.[7] *Arsinoe* enjoyed a first run of no fewer than twenty-four performances and began a craze for Italianate opera that was very soon to educate audiences to admire finer music than Clayton was capable of. Three months later, in April, the new Queen's Theatre was opened in the Haymarket. Built by Vanbrugh, its cost provided by private subscriptions, it was a building designed for music, though its first incumbents were Thomas Betterton's drama company. There followed a fierce period of musical competition between the two theatres – Drury Lane and Queen's. At first it seemed that Drury Lane would triumph. Following the success of *Arsinoe* came a staging of *Camilla* to music by one of the leading Italian composers of the period, Giovanni Bononcini (who was later to become Handel's main opera rival). This opera, with music incomparably finer than Clayton's, sung in a mixture of Italian and English, was to achieve an astonishing sixty-four performances between 1706 and 1709, and could lay claim to being the first complete Italian opera to be adapted for a London stage. But Vanbrugh, at the Queen's Theatre, had influence in high places:

> On the last day of 1707, at the direct instigation of Vanbrugh, the Lord Chamberlain . . . stirred the broth, transferring the actors to Drury Lane and the musicians (together with *Camilla* . . .) to the Haymarket, which thus became London's first opera-house, a role it was to retain for nearly a century.[8]

Later to become the King's Theatre (after the death of Queen Anne), this was to be the site of Handel's opera career and the future home of the Royal Academy of Music. Now, after 1707, the Italian language increasingly replaced the English in opera, and the Italian singers, led by the great castrato Nicolini, charmed the ears and captivated the imaginations of the London audiences. By the time Handel arrived the Italian form of 'opera seria' (in which he already excelled) had been fully established.

Opera seria (literally 'serious' opera) takes as its material heroic, mythological and idealised historical subjects and treats them with a musical formality befitting their grandeur. Its two main units of composition are the aria and the recitative. Broadly speaking, recitative is sung speech conveying the main actions and developments of plot through soliloquy or exchanges between characters. It can be supported merely by a line of 'continuo' (a simple bass line usually played alone on the harpsichord) known as *secco* ('dry') recitative, or by a more elaborate orchestration known as *accompagnato* ('accompanied') recitative. The recitative links together the arias ('airs' or 'songs') whose form is equally standardised. In an aria the first section of singing (the 'A' section), introduced by an orchestral *ritornello*, is followed by a contrasting or complementary development (the 'B' section), which returns *da capo* to the beginning and repeats the 'A' section (where the singer can show off tastefully by improvised variation). As with any standardised forms, their mastery allows variation, and Handel was never a slave to the conventions when dramatic effect deserved a departure from the normal structures.

By the time Mrs Pendarves writes of her fears for Italian opera, in 1727, Handel has explored the full potential of the basic opera seria forms, meeting the various expressive and dramatic demands of all aspects of human emotion. To Mrs Pendarves and others mainly interested in music, reasonably, the innovations of *The Beggar's Opera* were trivial in comparison with the musical innovations every season to be witnessed at the King's Theatre.

The demise of Italian opera and the simultaneous success of *The Beggar's Opera* is more than coincidence, though Mrs Pendarves' first letter shows that Gay's work cannot be taken as the cause of all the Royal Academy's problems. It did, though, not only drain more of the audience away from the King's Theatre, Haymarket, and its opera seria, but also ridiculed its activities. Its competition was both practical and ideological. Only a year previously Handel's opera *Admeto* had proved a great success, as Francis Colman's *Opera Register* recorded:

> Apr. 4 Easter Tuesday, Admetus again, & was declared for Satturday, but Signa Faustina being taken very ill – no Opera was perform'd – during all this time the House filled every night fuller than ever was known at any Opera for so long together – 16 times.[9]

But now, on 1 June 1728, a revival of this production brought an end not only to the season, but also to the Royal Academy of Music which had made possible all such productions. 'It was,' to use Robbins Landon's clichéd, but apt, formula, 'the end of an era'.[10] At the end of 1729, the Italian venture was revived, but, despite some of Handel's greatest operas in the 1730s, it was never again to have the remarkable success of the period 1711–28.

There were three main elements to Gay's parody of Italian

opera: an attack against its set pieces and the subject matter of its arias; a mockery of its plots with their fortuitous and illogical dénouements; and a satire on the petulant rivalries of its star singers. In considering the previous successes of Italian opera it is worth conceding that all three targets were, to an extent, fair ones. But if we take, as a comparative example, the success of Handel's *Ottone* (1723), we will also see that the apparent failings rather than making the opera a laughing stock at the time, actually contributed to its pleasures.

The 'Preface' to *The Beggar's Opera* promises 'the similies that are all in your celebrated operas: the swallow, the moth, the bee, the ship, the flower, etc.'.[11] Thus begins Gay's travesty of the 'simile aria', the typical vehicle for vocal display and, structurally, an excuse for characters to exit, usually at the end of a scene or act (after describing their present state by way of a metaphorical conceit). Gay's promise is fulfilled. Here is Polly Peachum, whose parents seem to have accepted and forgiven her betrothal to the dashing highwayman Macheath:

I, like a ship in storms, was tossed;
Yet afraid to put in to land;
For seized in the port the vessel's lost,
Whose treasure is contreband.
The waves are laid,
My duty's paid.
O joy beyond expression!
Thus, safe ashore,
I ask no more,
My all is in my possession.[12]

This is an apt parody of the typical, clichéd, material of the simile aria. Indeed its subject coincides with the first such aria to be heard by London opera-goers, in 1705:

Thus sinking Mariners,
In sight of Land are lost;
Dash'd on the Rocks
And cannot reach the Coast.[13]

Closer to Gay's text, though, are two arias in *Ottone*: the first is from the wicked Gismonda, the second, later in the opera, from the hero Ottone:

Gismonda:

La speranza è giunta in Porto,	[All my Hope is safely landed,
Ne sa più di che temere,	And will now no longer fear,
Se tranquillo vede il mar;	The treacherous Seas tempestuous Wave.
Sol mancava al mio conforto	This was the only Pleasure
Questa sorte di piacere	Wanting to compleat my Bliss:
Ora più non so bramar.	All I wanted, now I have.[14]]

Ottone:

Dell' onda a i fieri moti	[After a dreadful Storm,
Sottratto in Porto il legno,	When the Sailor safely Anchors
Scioglie il Nocchiero i voti	In his long-wish'd for Harbour,
A qualche Deità.	Then he pays his Vows to some Deity.
Cosi tornato il Regno	Just so, my Kingdom
In sen di bella calma	being now in Peace,
All' amor suo quest' alma I voti scioglierà.	I will pay mine to my Love.[15]]

In Handel's opera neither aria is *merely* metaphor; both have an associative relationship with the plot. Ottone has been engaged in a sea-battle which has delayed his return to Rome, allowing Gismonda to disguise her son, Adelberto, *as* Ottone and promote him to power; her calm seas *are* Ottone's stormy ones and her hopes ironically *depend* on Ottone's failure to reach port. But Ottone soon wins his battle, and turns his attention to Adelberto. By the end of Act 1 he has defeated his usurper and, having 'turned the tide', sings his 'ship' aria reversing the direction of the simile. Gay's parody lacks this metonymic significance (as *he* is concerned to pervert the metaphor with the bathetic language of trading and dealing), but it does suggest the commonplace nature of this kind of analogy. For the opera audience, though, such typicality is not a problem. The arias can be enjoyed all the more for their conventional subjects, and the score and its virtuosic performance can bring pleasure without the encumbrance of plot information (in Italian). The musical *treatment* of such material need not be *as* conventional as the subject (and in Handel's hands rarely is: he does for instance, play imitative tricks with the movement of stormy seas). Boats reach port, and we, like the singers, can take a rest from machinations. But the simile aria also dramatises the natural shift in opera seria from actions and events to states of mind and emotions, and can thus contribute to the whole process of characterisation. We need not, though, defend *Ottone*'s similes with such justifications. Charles Burney, the celebrated eighteenth-century historian of music, noted of *Ottone*:

> The number of songs in this opera that became national favourites, is perhaps greater than in any other that was ever performed in England. . . . Indeed, there is scarce a song in the opera, that did not become a general favourite, either vocally or instrumentally.[16]

Dean and Knapp, who, from a late twentieth-century perspective, see glaring weaknesses in the plot of *Ottone* conclude that Burney 'was not concerned with character or dramatic unity'.[17] But this is not necessarily true for our two simile arias, which rather contribute to both. They *are,* though, standard repertoire, and this is the point of Gay's attack.

Gay's mockery of plot is also relevant to *Ottone.* After three full acts of devious and gloating conspiracy against Ottone and his allies, Gismonda and Adelberto suddenly repent and are reconciled, duteously, to those they have tried to ruin (Gismonda's last words are: 'E l'odio cangia in amor Gismonda' – 'And Gismonda's hatred turns to love'). Adelberto is reprieved from the dagger with the same kind of suddenness that rescues Macheath from the gallows ('for an opera must end happily').[18]

But surely the dénouement, however absurd, is as pleasurable in *Ottone* as it is in *The Beggar's Opera.* Gay's ludicrous ending, whilst *happily* reprieving one of the audience's heroes, Macheath, is also rescued from banality by its coherent place in the strategy of self-conscious satiric artifice. But does this mean that opera audiences should have demanded motivational realism in the most manifestly artificial of all art-forms – Italian opera itself? And if Gay's work excuses itself by satiric convention, so *Ottone* does by heroic convention. The heroic code *often* demands the reprieve of villains; the more sudden and unmotivated the reprieve the greater the measure of the hero's grace. (It ought to be noted that, elsewhere, Handel's operas can show a mastery of other conventions – the tragic, as in the death scene of Bajazet in *Tamerlano* (1724); and the satiric, as in the subversion of heroic codes in *Flavio* (1723).)

Ottone also offers a fitting focus for Gay's mockery of the prima donnas, as it introduced to the English stage one of the greatest of them all, Francesca Cuzzoni. Later, in 1727, her undignified and scandalous rivalry with the period's other great soprano, Faustina Bordoni, during a performance of Bononcini's opera *Astianatte* was described by the *British Journal* in its edition of 10 June:

> On Tuesday-night last [the 6th], a great Disturbance happened at the Opera, occasioned by the Partisans of the Two Celebrated Rival Ladies, Cuzzoni and Faustina. The Contention at first was only carried on by Hissing on one Side, and Clapping on the other; but proceeded at length to Catcalls, and other great Indecencies: And notwithstanding the Princess Caroline was present, no Regards were of Force to restrain the Rudeness of the Opponents.[19]

The two singers actually came to blows on the stage, and Gay was to have great fun in imitating the episode by setting up the rivalry between Polly Peachum and Lucy Lockit (as in their duet: 'Why how now, Madam Flirt? . . . Why how now, saucy jade?').[20]

No sooner had Cuzzoni arrived than she began to establish her reputation for spoilt behaviour. She refused, at rehearsal, to sing 'Falsa imagine', the aria from *Ottone* that Handel had intended for her introduction (though new research by C. Steven LaRue suggests the aria was originally composed for Margherita Durastanti) – at which point, in French (for he was a fluent linguist) Handel famously threatened to defenestrate her:

> Having one day some words with CUZZONI on her refusing to sing *Falsa imagine* in OTTONE; Oh! Madame, (said he) je sçais bien que Vous êtes une veritable Diablesse: mais je Vous ferai sçavoir, moi, que je suis Beelzebub le *Chéf* des Diables. With this he took her up by the waist, and, if she made any more words, swore that he would fling her out of the window.[21]

Such behaviour may have provided Gay with some of his best material, but it certainly contributed to the public's enjoyment of Italian opera. Here, in England, were the most famous, most glamorous singers of the age, giving London the right to proclaim itself the musical capital of the world. Here, and it is not stretching the comparison, was the origin of a celebrity system we, in the late twentieth century, understand perfectly. We demand that our stars live larger than life; Cuzzoni did not disappoint. A Frenchman in London at the time, noted the excitement of Cuzzoni's début in *Ottone*:

> In the end the famous Cozzuna not merely arrived but even sang in a new opera by Hendell, called Othon – the same subject as the one at Dresden – with enormous success; the house was full to over-flowing. Today is the second performance and there is such a run on it that tickets are already being sold at 2 and 3 guineas which are ordinarily half a guinea, so that it is like another Mississippi or South Sea Bubble.[22]

So standard simile arias it may have had; sudden, happy, and unmotivated endings certainly; and its great singers may have behaved with impropriety, but the criticisms of *The Beggar's Opera* do not actually challenge *the pleasures* of the opera in the period that preceded it. The popularity of Gay's work may be explained perhaps by the English 'singability' of its songs. But it would be absurd therefore to argue that the far richer, incomparably profound music of Handel was not one of the main pleasures of the great period of Italian opera in London.

Cuzzoni made a sensational impact in the opera we have been discussing, particularly in her 'Falsa imagine'; Handel had judged the piece with typical insight and was right to insist on the aria. It provides a good example of Handel's skill in handling emotions. In *Ottone* Teofane, played by Cuzzoni, has been promised in marriage to Ottone, King of Germany, and has cherished a portrait of him. Now, though, Adelberto courts her in the guise of her betrothed, whom she has never seen in the flesh. She is, to say the least, disappointed, and upbraids the portrait with deception: 'False image [Falsa imagine] you have deceived me.' Jonathan Keates describes the aria's 'nonchalant artistry', yet explains why Cuzzoni had been so mistaken in wishing not to sing it:

> Constructed in the old-fangled Venetian manner with the string ritornello at the end and the vocal line strung over a slow dotted bass, 'Falsa imagine' is a mere 28 bars.[23]

Hardly flattering, thought Cuzzoni, who would have expected a lavish introduction (the ritornello) and then a long aria with dazzling accompaniment. She hadn't realised that the simplicity of the setting was the perfect opportunity for her most eloquent lament to shine (see Example 1).[24]

Keates notes the 'sense of Teofane's baffled disappointment... wonderfully conveyed by pitting the blank simplicity of the opening melody, to the words 'False image, you have deceived me, you showed me a lovely face', against the ornate dotted semiquavers of the subsequent 'and that face attracted me', ending with a melisma on the word 'allettò' ('attracted')'.[25] (A 'melisma' is the sustaining of a syllable over a number of notes – Keates's point is that the 'attraction' of Ottone's portrait was seductive and deceiving, hence the ornate and artificial sustentation of the word.)

However successful the songs in *The Beggar's Opera,* if one's pleasure (and knowledge) is primarily musical it is easy to understand, considering music like this, the frustration of Mrs Pendarves and the critic of the *London Journal* faced with the fall of Italian opera and the rise of the burlesque. Pepusch, Gay's composer, though a musical figure of some stature and skill, did

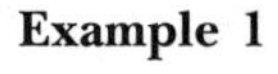

Example 1

not, after all, admire Handel. According to Burney he treated most music 'in which there was fancy or invention with sovereign contempt'.[26]

Gay and Pepusch's explicit inclusion of Handel's march from *Rinaldo* in the parodic context of *The Beggar's Opera*[27] is a reminder that Handel's opera career in London, which began with *Rinaldo* in 1711, began, as it ended, in mockery.

The 'stage' had been set as early as 1706 with John Dennis's ludicrous and xenophobic attack against Italian opera: '*a Diversion of more pernicious consequence, than the most licentious Play that ever has appear'd upon the Stage*'.[28] His arguments are absurd, but certainly express a rich vein of anti-culture typical of the worst kind of provincial Englishness. '*Pleasure of Sense*,' argues Dennis, '*being too much indulged, makes Reason cease to be a Pleasure, and by consequence is contrary both to publick and private Duty*.'[29] The pleasures of Italian opera are too great for Dennis, offering, particularly, a threat to all young ladies, in its celebration of love and all its arts. French music is less a danger as it is '*by no means so meltingly moving as the Italian*'.[30] It's ironically amusing that such a silly and vituperative polemic should so manifestly reveal the intensity of the sensuous pleasures of Italian opera. But Dennis's real grouse seems to be that Italian opera is *effeminate* and *foreign*: '*the Reigning Luxury of* Modern Italy, *is that soft and effeminate Musick which abounds in the* Italian Opera'.[31] And the English, of all people, should least appreciate such entertainments:

> What must those Strangers say, when they behold Englishmen applaud an Italian for Singing, or a Frenchman for Dancing, and the very Moment afterwards explode an Englishman for the very same things? What must they say, unless they have Candour enough to interpret it this way, that an Englishman is deservedly scorned by Englishmen, when he descends so far beneath himself, as to Sing or to Dance in publick, because by doing so he practises Arts which Nature has bestow'd upon effeminate Nations, but denied to him, as below the Dignity of his Country, and the Majesty of the British Genius.[32]

Actually, at least one of Dennis's objections should have been met by Handel's arrival ('But yet this must be allow'd, that tho' the Opera in *Italy* is a Monster, 'tis a beautiful harmonious Monster, but here in *England* 'tis an ugly howling one').[33] But Handel's enterprise, in 1711, had more formidable literary arguments to overcome than from this raving nonsense. *Rinaldo,* like the operas which immediately preceded it, was attacked in the influential *Spectator* by Richard Steele and Joseph Addison. Alexander Pope, who named both Dennis *and* Addison as his satiric targets, could dispense with Dennis as a mere dunce, but, in the very midst of attack had to acknowledge Addison's literary skills. However, there may have been an element of hubris in the *Spectator*'s attacks, especially in Addison's emphasis on the absurdities of the *Italian* elements of the opera. Addison himself was the *English* librettist of the failed opera *Rosamund,* composed by the dire musician of *Arsinoe,* Thomas Clayton, and staged in 1707. Only two years after *Arsinoe,* London opera audiences had learnt to expect more, and the production was dropped after a dismal three performances.

The *Spectator*'s pillory was certainly a concerted attempt to discredit the Italian operas. Five issues (Nos 5, 13, 14, 18, and 29) gave over their space to the ridicule of the increasingly popular new form, over a period of less than one month from 6 March to 3 April 1711. And though the sophistication of the critique offered here is not comparable with Dennis's clumsy, ill-conceived onslaught, there is still the condescending assumption that the English should have higher pleasures than the mere continentals:

> If the *Italians* have a Genius for Musick above the *English*, the *English* have a Genius for other Performances of a much higher Nature, and capable of giving the Mind a much nobler Entertainment.[34]

The criticism of the use of Italian sources is interesting, as it reveals, aptly, the absurdities of the period preceding Handel's *Rinaldo*. As Dean and Knapp note: 'All the operas between *Rosamund* and *Rinaldo* were pasticcios processed locally from Italian materials.'[35] Some of these were sung in Italian but others were productions in both languages. The *Spectator* ridicules the absurdities of translation from the Italian which does not match the music:

> I have known the Word *And* pursu'd through the whole Gamut, have been entertain'd with many a melodious *The*, and have heard the most beautiful Graces, Quavers and Divisions bestow'd upon *Then*, *For*, and *From*; to the eternal Honour of our *English* Particles.[36]

The macaronic use of both languages in the same opera was a manifestly unsatisfactory compromise, allowing Addison many further strokes of wit: 'The King or Hero of the Play generally spoke in *Italian*, and his Slaves answer'd him in *English*.'[37] There are two possible answers to Addison's critique of linguistic impropriety: either operas should be sung wholly in Italian, or librettos *conceived* in English should be sung in English. Despite the failure of the wholly English *Rosamund* (which also should have proved to Addison that the music is more important than the words), the former possibility was (illogically) seen to be an even *greater* impropriety:

> At length the Audience grew tir'd of understanding Half the Opera, and therefore to ease themselves intirely of the Fatigue of Thinking, have so order'd it at Present that the whole Opera is perform'd in an unknown Tongue.[38]

'An unknown tongue'! – even allowing for satiric exaggeration this is a ridiculous claim. It is right to suppose that the majority of the audiences could not speak Italian, but this comment puts it in the same category as an Asian or African language. Anyway, for the Italian productions of Handel's period the audience was supplied with word books, giving fuller translations than are usually available to a modern opera audience. And the singers the audiences wanted to hear (like the great castrato Nicolini, whom even Addison admires) were Italians, so the impropriety of having them sing in English operas would have been considerable. There is an odd contradiction in a literary culture which expects the educated to have at least *some* classical Latin, but then assumes that none (despite the increasing popularity of European tours) has any modern Italian. The parochialism of the *Spectator* has often been echoed since. When Roger Fiske, writing in 1986, acknowledges that the 'appeal of Italian Opera to intellectuals was fully justified', adding that 'Handel's music was of superb quality', his comments act as an unsuccessful apology for the following:

> As in more recent years, it affected only a coterie of society people and intellectuals; the middle and lower class theatregoer inevitably preferred the playhouses where he could understand the words. But opera in a foreign tongue has always had a strong snob appeal for those who wish to be thought cleverer than they are.[39]

This is a helpful comment, because we, if we enjoy Wagner or Puccini, but do not wish to fall into the category of those 'intellectuals', can feel some of the insult that our fellow music lovers might have experienced reading Addison. Moreover, the assumption behind the linguistic criticisms is a false one: they imply that if we *hear* opera in our own tongue we immediately have a true *understanding*. Actually the opera lover who enjoys, for instance, *Peter Grimes* cannot fully follow the text or its plot *as sung*. We must either know the opera beforehand, or study the libretto whilst listening. Handel's audiences had at least the advantage that the material for many of the operas is derived from well-known sources, and often forms the subject for a number of operas in the period (hence the contemporary comment already quoted praising *Ottone* refers to another production of the same material). The stories of Amadigi, Ottone, Rinaldo, Caesar, Tamburlaine and most of the other heroes and heroines of this period of Italian opera are already broadly familiar, so the problem of comprehension is less than might be imagined. The English critical reaction to Italian opera misses the point in yearning, as it sometimes does, for an English national opera in the early eighteenth century. The Italians (Nicolini was followed by the sensational success of Senesino; and we have already touched on the popularity of Cuzzoni and Faustina) and their language were exotic, sensuous, and glamorous: they did not inhibit the pleasures of the music – they made them possible. Even if one admits that for some there is a delusive sense of social elevation in the enjoyment of things foreign, one has to ask whether this is not attractive in comparison with the stultifying xenophobic nationalism of Dennis, or the inverse snobbery of English anti-intellectualism.

The second focus for the *Spectator*'s attack was the spectacle of the new operas; again an attack which ironically helps us to focus on the *pleasures* of such productions. The *Spectator* had great fun with the famous lion that appeared on stage in productions of Francesco Mancini's opera *Idaspe* (generally known as *Hydaspes*) from May 1710. The hero, played by Nicolini, was supposed to grapple with this costume lion, and Addison plays charmingly with the dramatic postures of the different wearers of the costume. But Addison understands, at least, that his wit is pointless – the lion was a great success; there are even comments about the propriety of its performance:

> In the evening we went to the opera 'Hidaspis'. . . . The opera was very lovely in all respects, in composition, music and representation. . . . In especial the representation of the lion with which Hidaspes has to fight was incomparably fine. The fellow who played him was not only wrapped in a lion-skin, but, moreover, nothing could be seen of his feet.[40]

Really, then, the *Spectator* is ridiculing the *taste* of opera audiences; its pleasures are seen to be trivial and laughable. With Handel's *Rinaldo*, though, as with *Teseo* (1713) and *Amadigi* (1715), his other 'magic operas' (so called because they both have a sorceress who conjures up all kinds of visions and monsters) the opera audiences could enjoy state of the art special effects, *both* in the production *and* in the music. *Rinaldo* calls for two chariots, one drawn by white horses and blackamoors, the other drawn by two dragons issuing fire and smoke; furies and dreadful monsters (more fire and smoke); a delightful grove with singing birds in the trees; singing and dancing mermaids; a dreadful mountain prospect; an enchanted palace; a magician's cave; ugly enchanted spirits; and plentiful supplies of thunder, lightning and 'amazing noises'. Not all this was possible – Steele notes that the horses drawing the chariot never appeared – but as much as *was* possible was done. Addison ridiculed the whole enterprise in the issue of 6 March. Especially ludicrous to him seemed the provision of real birds for the delightful grove:

> As I was walking in the Streets about a Fortnight ago, I saw an ordinary Fellow carrying a Cage full of little Birds upon his Shoulder; and, as I was wondering with my self what Use he would put them to, he was met very luckily by an Acquaintance, who had the same Curiosity. Upon his asking him what he had upon his Shoulder, he told him, that he had been buying Sparrows for the Opera. Sparrows for the Opera, says his Friend, licking his Lips, what are they to be roasted? No, no, says the other, they are to enter towards the end of the first Act, and to fly about the Stage.[41]

For all Addison's humour here and elsewhere, his descriptions *do* suggest the excitement of these productions: '*Rinaldo* is filled with Thunder and Lightning, Illuminations, and Fireworks.'[42] Some self-appointed proprietors of eighteenth-century taste may have scorned such entertainments but the opera public loved them. *Rinaldo* was one of the greatest successes of the period. The publication of its songs alone was reputed to have made their publisher fifteen hundred pounds. As Christopher Hogwood notes, *Rinaldo* 'can be said to have settled the course of Handel's career and the future of opera in England'.[43] In a sense the number of issues devoted by the *Spectator* to the mockery of Italian opera is a testament to the futility of its arguments. The thirst for Italian opera was already established before the *Spectator*'s first issue. Handel, after the famous opera successes of *Rodrigo* (1707) and *Agrippina* (1710) in Italy, visited a London already predisposed to the success of *Rinaldo*. In Italy, Cardinal Pamphili, patron of music and the arts, had written a cantata in praise of Handel (originally in Italian):

> Sing all and raise each voice
> To strains of new beauty,
> And let your fingers play
> To this new Orpheus' tune.[44]

So now London repeated the legendary phrase: Addison noted that the preface to *Rinaldo* referred to 'Minheer *Hendel*' as 'the *Orpheus* of our Age'.[45] Handel did not disappoint, despite Addison's idea that this is merely florid Italian overstatement. Typical of the 'strains of new beauty' was the sublime aria 'Lascia ch'io pianga' where 'Handel obtains an intensely emotional effect from a simple tune and accompaniment in a major key'.[46] Dean and Knapp, notable for their close reading of the scores, go on simply to comment 'this perfection is scarcely susceptible of analysis'.[47] In 1712 Handel returned to Hanover but was back the next season with *Teseo*. His *Amadigi di Gaula* (1715) was a further testimony to the attractions of spectacular production and fine music. Burney noted: 'There is more enchantment and machinery in this opera than I have ever found to be announced in any other musical drama performed in England.' But he, unlike Addison, was primarily interested in the music, and went on to describe the work as 'a production in which there is more invention, variety, and good composition, than in any one of the musical dramas of Handel which I have yet carefully and critically examined'.[48] Again, to get the full sense of the pleasures of such an opera we need to consider the music (an obvious point which rather seems to have eluded the contemporary detractors). At the beginning of Act II, amongst its many exotic scenes, *Amadigi* calls for an enchanted garden with magnificent palace, and in the midst of the scene a Fountain of True Love: already the scene is spectacular. But now Amadigi, separated from his true love Oriana, sings a complaint of sublime beauty – 'Sussurate, onde vezzose' ('Murmur pleasing streams'). Of this aria Burney wrote:

> *Sussurate, onde vezzose* is an admirable *cavatina*, accompanied by two common flutes [what we would call 'recorders'], two violins, tenor, and base. The bright and brilliant tones of the violins playing in octaves, from which so many pleasing effects have lately been produced, seems to have been first discovered by Handel in the accompaniment to this song, which must have delighted and astonished every hearer.[49]

This 'largo' piece is the perfect expression of a lover's sweet melancholy. The recorder phrase, supported by the first violin, trills its imitation of the gentle fountain while the other strings murmur below. The water moves in overlapping crotchets, quavers, and semi-quavers, against which the sustained opening note of 'sussurate' breaths Amadigi's longing into the scene, its repetition allowing a melisma which then imitates the instrumental play of the stream. There is a perfect consonance of word and music here, as Amadigi hopes for consolation (see Example 2).[50]

Amadigi, not surprisingly with its *combination* of musical and stage attractions, was a great success and was regularly revived. This fountain scene was so popular that its reappearance in another opera (not by Handel) was advertised three months later.[51]

Handel was by now an established figure in England. He had already received a pension from Queen Anne, and had found welcoming lodgings with the Duke of Chandos and with the greatest patron of the period, the Earl of Burlington. Burlington kept an open house for a wide circle of artists, and Gay himself, in his 'Trivia: or the Art of Walking the Streets of London' noted his acquaintance with Handel in 1716:

> There *Hendel* strikes the Strings, the melting Strain
> Transports the Soul, and thrills through ev'ry Vein;
> There oft' I enter (but with cleaner Shoes)
> For *Burlington*'s belov'd by ev'ry Muse.[52]

Example 2

Largo.
Flauto I.II.
Violino I.
Violino II.
Viola.
AMADIGI.
Bassi.
unis.

There, at Burlington House, Handel would have met Pope and Arbuthnot, who perhaps *did* have the conversation reported by Mainwaring:

> The Poet one day asked his friend Dr. ARBUTHNOT, of whose knowledge in Music he had a high idea, What was his real opinion in regard to HANDEL as a Master of that Science? The Doctor immediately replied, 'Conceive the highest that you can of his abilities, and they are much beyond any thing that you *can* conceive.'[53]

But Handel's familiarity with the Burlington scene was to prove double edged. On the one side Gay was to provide (with the help, perhaps, of Pope) the libretto for Handel's English masterpiece *Acis and Galatea.* On the other side Gay's formative association with the literary satire and pastiche of the Scriblerian circle headed by Pope was to lead, ultimately, to the writing of *The Beggar's Opera.* And whilst Burlington was an invaluable sponsor, he himself was later to champion the cause of Handel's greatest rival, Bononcini.

However, before such competition became significant, and with the Hanoverian Succession complete, Handel found not only the support of earls and dukes, but of his own German patron, the Elector of Hanover, now King George I. The right patronage was therefore available for the most remarkable venture in English opera history. As Mainwaring notes:

> A project was formed by the Nobility for erecting an academy at the Haymarket. The intention of this musical Society, was to secure to themselves a constant supply of Operas to be composed by HANDEL, and performed under his direction.[54]

In an unprecedented expression of artistic venture capital (with little promise of return, considering the enormous cost of opera productions) £10 000 of stock in the new company was bought by an elite group of investors, the King allowing an annual £1000 to support the scheme. So began the period of the Royal Academy of Music in the early months of 1719. On 21 February the *Original Weekly Journal* announced that:

> Mr. Hendel, a famous Master of Musick, is gone beyond Sea, by Order of his Majesty, to Collect a Company of the choicest Singers in Europe, for the Opera in the Hay-Market.[55]

So exciting was news of the venture that this journal had actually anticipated Handel's departure by three months. Italian opera was now a cosmopolitan enterprise and Handel went not to Italy but to Dresden where the Elector of Saxony had gathered one of the finest opera companies in Europe. Handel returned having secured the services of the famous soprano Margherita Durastanti and other signings soon followed. But the Academy had to wait until the end of 1720 to secure its star attraction, the castrato Senesino, with an astonishing fee of £3000. The Royal Academy's first season opened with Giovanni Porta's opera *Numitore* on 2 April 1720, little more than an appetizer for Handel's first Academy production – his masterpiece *Radamisto*. Senesino hadn't arrived yet, but the fervour of anticipation was none the less for that. The first night, on 27 April, according to Mainwaring, was a night to remember:

> In the year 1720, he obtained leave to perform his Opera of RADAMISTO. If persons who are now living, and who were present at that performance may be credited, the applause it received was almost as extravagant as his AGRIPPINA had excited: the crowds and tumults of the house at Venice were hardly equal to those at LONDON. In so splendid and fashionable an assembly of ladies (to the excellence of their taste we must impute it) there was no shadow of form, or ceremony, scarce indeed any appearance of order or regularity, politeness or decency. Many, who had forc'd their way into the house with an impetuosity but ill suited to their rank and sex, actually fainted through the excessive heat and closeness of it. Several gentlemen were turned back, who had offered forty shillings for a seat in the gallery, after having despaired of getting any in the pit or boxes.[56]

The opera was a magnificent début. Not only did Handel reveal a complete mastery of the high heroic mode of opera seria, but he also revealed his profoundest capacity to move. The most famous aria in the opera was (and remains) Radamisto's

'Ombra cara', another aria that leaves the loquacious acuity of Dean and Knapp almost silent: 'Of "Ombra cara" it is difficult to write in measured terms.'[57] In this they agree with eighteenth-century commentators. Burney noted:

> Indeed, too much praise cannot be given to that song. . . . I remember Reginelli sing this air at the opera in 1747, among some light Italian songs of that period, and it seemed the language of philosophy and science, and the rest the frivolous jargon of fops and triflers.[58]

But Handel treats even minor roles with a musical mastery of emotion, as in Polissena's aria 'Tu vuoi ch'io parta'. Polissena is the loving and duteous wife of Tiridate, the belligerent King of Armenia. He has a reputation for infidelity, and has just besieged the citadel of Farasmane (Polissena's father) in the hope of seizing Zenobia (Polissena's sister in law) for the exercise of his lust. Pleading mercy for her father and brother, Polissena is abruptly and disrespectfully dismissed by her husband, prompting an aria of tragic regret ('You wish me to go, I go') (see Example 3).[59]

The unaffected simple accompaniment here expresses Polissena's artless integrity. There can be no introductory ritornello, as she sings directly, spontaneously, from the heart. The upward yearning of the opening phrase abruptly ends with a long rest, before the disappointed, resigned 'io parto' ('I go'), with its falling sadness. This is followed (after another rest – the rests indicating the hopelessness of her situation: she has so many contradictory feelings they keep stopping her short) by an eloquent expression of unrewarded love: 'idolo del mio cor'. Then, *without a rest where we would most expect one*, 'mà', the 'but' brilliantly capturing the apparent futility of having such a husband for the idol of your heart! The 'but' hovers over the rests, lingering with its uncertainties, until completed by the 'senza core'. An English translation that gives *this* as 'unwillingly' (as in a recent recording) is inept. She leaves the love of her heart, *without heart*: and the *music* captures perfectly the painful ambiguity.

The title role in *Radamisto*, on 28 December 1720, was to give Senesino his first Handel part on the London stage. It's

Example 3

Adagio.
Traversiere, e Violino I.
Violino II.
Viola.
Polissena.
Bassi.
la prima parte colle Traversiere.
Tu vuoi ch'io par_ta, io par_to, i _ do _ lo del mio cor, mà sen_za co _ re; tu vuoi ch'io par_ta,
H. W. 63.
io par_to, i _ do_lo del mio cor, mà sen_za co _ re; io
par_to, io par_to, i _ do _ lo del mio cor, mà sen_za co _ re.
(Fine.)

worth pausing, for a moment, to consider the added pleasures of the castrato role for the audiences of eighteenth-century opera. Ours is an age, with its celebration of sexual ambiguity, polymorphism, and trans-sexuality, which can particularly imagine the strange appeal of these sensuous emasculated figures playing heroic, romantic roles. We do not need to condone the cruelty that gave the castrati their voices, to imagine the voyeuristic fascination (and often violently partisan loyalties) they inspired in their audiences. They belonged to a stage where travesty was a normal rule rather than a perverse exception. It was normal for female sopranos to be cast as men when no castrato was available, and it is a frequent device of opera plots that women disguise themselves *as* men. The permutations for sexual transgression were not lost on the period, as Angus Heriot's fascinating book *The Castrati in Opera* records. Here we find castrati masquerading as women playing the roles of men disguised on stage as women. Such indeterminacy fascinates a postmodern age. Indeed, one anecdote noted in Heriot's book concerns the French sculptor Sarassin who, convinced that the travestied castrato Zambinella was a woman, pursued her as an object of desire 'until the singer's protector, Cardinal Cicognara, had the importunate Frenchman assassinated'.[60] Heriot notes that this incident inspired Balzac to write *Sarrasine.* But *this*, in our most intertextual of periods, inspired Roland Barthes to write that 'seminal' work of postmodern discourse *S/Z.* Here is Barthes on Italian music:

> Italian music, an object well defined historically, culturally, mythically . . . connotes a 'sensual' art, an art of the voice. An erotic substance, the Italian voice was produced *a contrario* (according to a strictly symbolic inversion) by singers without sex: this inversion is *logical* ('*That angelic voice, that delicate voice would be an anomaly coming from any body but yours,*' Sarrasine says to La Zambinella . . .), as though, by selective hypertrophy, sexual density were obliged to abandon the rest of the body and lodge in the throat, thereby draining the organism of all that *connects* it. Thus, emitted by a castrated body, a wildly erotic frenzy is returned to that body: the star castrati are cheered by hysterical audiences, women fall in love with them.[61]

Such excess of delight (Barthes goes on to describe this music as orgasm) seems far removed from the proprieties of London in the 1720s, but it is certainly true that the castrati were fêted as idols by some, and that their attraction was sexually asexual. There are some interesting matters of casting that reveal the riot of sexual uncertainty in the operas of the period, such as the problem of Nireno in Giulio Cesare. Here was a rare opportunity to have a castrato actually play a castrato, as Nireno is a eunuch. So, in the first production of February 1724, Giuseppe Bigonzi fulfilled that most logical of castings as 'alto castrato'. But the castrati were generally the expensive stars, and Nireno is a minor part. A revision in January 1725 saw Nireno 'cut' to a 'mute'. But for the last few nights of the 1725 run, Handel revived Nireno as a singing part, renaming the erstwhile eunuch Nirena and making 'her' a lady-in-waiting to Cleopatra, sung by a female soprano. (One can imagine what Barthes might have made of this, especially as the woman playing the new role was called Benedetta *Sorosina*!) By the next revival, in 1730, Nireno had been 'cut' again, but in Germany s/he had been playing an equally complicated role. A production there in 1725 saw Nireno played by a bass (!), Johann Koulhaas (while his wife, Christina Koulhaas played Sesto, a manly boy!).

Suffice it to say the castrato added spice to an already perplexing travesty of 'normality'. But for those with less salacious, nobler, interests, there was of course the, to us, unknowable pleasure of the castrato *voice*. Our falsettists and counter-tenors are increasingly impressive in this period of baroque revival, but they cannot, presumably, match the purity of sound heard by London opera-goers in the period of this study. Heriot quotes the opinion, in terms not far removed from the ecstasy of Barthes, of Enrico Panzacchi, the nineteenth-century music historian:

> Imagine a voice that combines the sweetness of the flute, and the animated suavity of the human larynx – a voice which leaps and leaps, lightly and spontaneously, like a lark that flies through the air and is intoxicated with its own flight; and when it seems that the voice has reached the loftiest peaks of altitude, it starts off again, leaping and leaping still with equal lightness and equal spontanteity, without the

> slightest sign of forcing or the faintest indication of artifice or effort; in a word, a voice that gives the immediate idea of sentiment transmuted into sound . . . a calm, sweet, solemn and sonorous musical language that left me dumbstruck, and captivated me with the power of a most gracious sensation never before experienced.[62]

It is with an odd feeling of regret (odd because of the barbarity involved) that we cannot share this pleasure with Handel's contemporaries.

This is a fitting invitation, finally, to return to the pleasures of music. It is difficult, adequately, to summarise the achievements of Handel's operas in the period 1720–1728. His music shows a mastery of human emotion and dramatic incident unsurpassed in his age and, in many cases, unequalled since. But he also developed a profound ability to portray character in depth. As the highest expression of this art his portrayal of Cleopatra, in *Giulio Cesare* (1724) has often, aptly, been seen as the equal of Shakespeare's, and that accolade is sufficient to justify this chapter's final example.

Cleopatra has nine arias and in them Handel explores every side of her notoriously Protean personality: dismissive, rude, playfulness ('Non disperar', Act I, Scene v); a coquettish enjoyment of the female arts of love ('Tutto può donna', I, vii); her optimism, gaiety, and radiance ('Tu la mia stella', I, viii); her beguiling graces ('Venere bella', II, vii); her capacity for profound tragic feeling ('Che sento?', II, viii); her sublime sense of noble pathos ('Piangerò', III, iii); her joyous energy ('Da tempeste' III, vii); and, finally, her unaffected love ('Caro/Bella', III, x).

The list omits one aria, because that aria best reveals that all these human capacities are expressed musically with a power that language cannot imitate. 'V'adoro pupille' is perhaps the greatest seduction aria in musical history. It has the equivalent force of Enobarbus's famous speech in *Antony and Cleopatra*:

> The barge she sat in, like a burnish'd throne
> Burn'd on the water: the poop was beaten gold;
> Purple the sails, and so perfumed that
> The winds were love-sick with them; the oars were silver,
> Which to the tune of flutes kept stroke, and made

> The water which they beat to follow faster,
> As amorous of their strokes. For her own person,
> It beggar'd all description . . .[63]

Shakespeare, here, follows his source, North's *Plutarch* very closely. But *Plutarch* gives an additional detail: 'her voyce and words were marvelous pleasant: for her tongue was an instrument of musicke to divers sports and pastimes'.[64] Shakespeare also economises on the music that attends her. His 'tune of flutes' is based on *Plutarch*'s 'sounde of the musicke of flutes, howboyes, citherns, violls, and such other instruments as they played upon in the barge'.[65] Cleopatra's legendary power is one naturally expressed by the metonym and metaphor of music. In Handel's score it is her *song* that seduces Caesar. And Handel overtrumps Plutarch with his instruments, as Winton Dean notes:

> Handel deploys a double orchestra: a group of nine instruments played by the nine Muses on stage or behind the scenes, including harp, theorbo and viola da gamba, is contrasted and combined with the main body in the pit, the violins of both orchestras being muted. The senses of the audience must have been as ravished as Caesar's.[66] [See Example 4.][67]

Dean's comment is well judged. We do not need contemporary testimony (though we do *have* it) to assume that the first audiences were as 'ravished' by this music as we are hearing it two hundred and seventy years later. It is true that for many London opera-goers Bononcini was a more popular composer in the Academy than Handel. It is true that Handel's London opera venture began with the polite mockery of Addison, and reached a climax with the polite mockery of Gay. But it is equally true that from 1711 onwards Handel and his Italian operas contributed inestimable pleasures to an elite public who could afford to take their pleasure where they chose, and chose to take it at the King's Theatre, Haymarket.

Example 4

Largo.
Oboe.
unis.
Sordini.
Viol.
Oboe, e Violino I.
Violino II.
Viola.
Viola da Gamba.
Teorba, Harpe, Bassons e Violoncelli.
Cleopatra.
Va - do - ro, pu - pil - le, sa - et - te — d'A - mo - re, le vo - stre fa - vil - le son
Violino I.
Sordini.
Violino II.
Orchestra.
Viola.
Bassi.
tr
gra - te nel sen: va - do - ro, pu - pil - le, le vo - stre fa - vil - le son gra - te, son
gra - te nel sen, va -

APPENDIX : A GUIDE TO RECORDINGS OF HANDEL'S OPERAS 1711–28

There has never been more opportunity for the student of Handel's operas to hear excellent recordings, and the period 1711–28 is particularly well represented in the catalogues. In the 1990s there have been a series of important releases, and in the last couple of years there have been two superb original instrument premières of *Radamisto* (1720) and *Scipione* (1726).

In *Radamisto* (Harmonia Mundi HMU907111/3; 1993) Nicholas McGegan directs the Freiburg Baroque Orchestra and a fine group of soloists in a thrilling production of Handel's heroic score. The recorded version incorporates the revisions Handel made for the second run in December 1720 (Senesino singing the title role). The counter-tenor Ralf Popken gives a noble and lucid reading of the part here. His rendering of 'Ombra cara' (the opera's most famous aria) is powerful and moving. He is ably supported by the other high voices: Tigrane and Fraarte (both played here by women who manage the right timbre for their male roles); Juliana Gondek's Zenobia (which gives an impressive range of emotion, particularly expressive in its passages of defiant resignation, as in 'Son contento di morire'); and, in the role of Polissena, Lisa Saffer, who makes the rather unaccountable fidelity to her tyrannical husband Tiridante musically and dramatically credible. The lower roles, also, are sung with great verve and conviction. The orchestral playing is compelling, and the recording is first rate.

In terms of material *Scipione* (FNAC Music 592245; 1994) cannot compete with this masterpiece, but it is given a convincing and enthusiastic performance by 'Les Talens Lyriques', directed by the accomplished baroque harpsichordist Christophe Rousset. Derek Lee Ragin, here in the title role, is one of the best counter-tenors now singing and gives a joyous lightness to the love songs ('Pensa, Oh Bella'; 'Gioia si, speri si'). The rest of the cast is equally effective. Lucejo, orginally played by Senesino, is beautifully sung by Doris Lamprecht. She has the best numbers in the opera, conveying the range of emotions from plaintive regret ('Lamentandomi corro a vuolo') to confident optimism ('Come al nazio boschetto'). The accompaniment throughout is elegant and supportive and the recording balance between voices and instruments is just right.

Perhaps one of the best 1990's recordings of any of Handel's operas is René Jacobs' *Giulio Cesare* (1724) a justly award-winning set of discs (Harmonia Mundi HMC 901385.87; 1991). This is the most recorded of all of Handel's operas, and there are other successful versions (notably the English National Opera's (EMI CMS7 69760–2), with fine singing from Janet Baker (Caesar), James Bowman (Ptolemy) and Valerie Masterson's sublime Cleopatra). But Jacobs' original period-instrument Italian version is ultimately the most satisfying, capturing the full dramatic impact of the masterful score over a never-tedious four hours. There is no obvious weakness but the main roles are beautifully sung by Jennifer Larmore (Cesare), Barbara Schlick (Cleopatra, full of vivacity, though not quite as eloquent as Masterson), and Ragin (who finds the right tone of petulant, impotent villainy as Tolomeo). Anyone who needs to be convinced of the virtues of the best opera seria need do no more than listen to this set of discs.

There are two versions of *Ottone* (1723) (McGegan: Hungaroton HCD31304/6; 1992 and King: Hyperìon CDA66751/3; 1993), and both have been underestimated, as has the opera itself. Robert King's version, for Hyperìon, particularly, explains Burney's claim that 'there is scarce a song in the opera that did not become a general favourite'. The singing of James Bowman, Claron McFadden and Jennifer Smith gives full expression to an astonishing sequence of winning melodies. If you want good tunes look no further than this.

In the 1990s, also, Marc Minkowski and 'Les Musiciens du Louvre' have been making a convincing case for the 'magic' operas. Their *Amadigi di Gaula* (1715) (Erato 2292–45490–2; 1991) is very dramatic, the orchestra responding with brilliance to Handel's energetic score. Eiddwen Harrhy's sorceress Melissa steals the show, even managing to answer some of the criticism of the inconsistency of Handel's characterisation ('Io godo, scherzo e rido', for instance *does* convey her 'gloating', though Dean and Knapp suggest Handel's score fails in this sense). Nathalie Stutzman's *Amadigi* is an equally expressive reading (her 'Sussurate' is certainly sussurant).

Minkowski's *Teseo* (1713) (Erato 2292–45806–2; 1992) doesn't quite reach these heights but is still a welcome piece. There are some great moments including a furious, sizzling 'Sibillando' curse from the sorceress Medea (played by Della Jones) and a range of infernal sound effects for her devious conjurings. This opera has particularly fine parts for the orchestra, and the 'Musiciens du Louvre' do them full justice.

Nicholas McGegan (again) directs a full performance of *Floridante* (1721) (Hungaroton HCD31304/6; 1993), though this is less compelling than a one disc selection from the 'Tefelmusik Baroque Orchestra' directed by Alan Curtis (SM5000 SMCD5110; 1991). This collection avoids the simple approach of giving only arias, and the included recitative passages do give a sense of the drama. The highlight (of the recording as well as the opera itself) is the highly dramatic sequence 'Notte cara'.

René Jacobs succeeds with another Handel opera (recorded before the accolades of his *Giulio Cesare*) in his *Flavio* (1723). The wit of this opera was rather lost on its first audiences, but is not lost on Jacobs, his orchestra ('Ensemble 415'). or his singers (Harmonia Mundi HMC 901312.13; 1990). The 'charm and the smiles' are perfectly captured in the aria that explicitly evokes them, 'Con un vezzo, con un riso', as indeed throughout the three acts. Derek Lee Ragin's singing, as Guido, is again irresistible, and he throws off the showpieces with aplomb (the simile aria 'L'armellin vita non cura', where he implausibly compares his sense of honour with the ermine's protection of its fur, is dazzling).

John Eliot Gardiner's *Tamerlano* (1724) (Erato 2292–45408–2; 1985) lacks dramatic tautness, but again has some fine singing (Regin is less impressive here, as Tamerlano, but Robson is excellent in the more important role of Bajazet and Nancy Argenta is fully supportive of her 'father', as Asteria). Bajazet's death scene is the best part of the set (thankfully, as it is also the best part of the score).

Other operas of the period do exist in currently available recordings. Indeed, only *Silla* (1713); *Admeto* (1727); *Riccardo Primo* (1727); and *Tolomeo* (1728) are not in any of the catalogues. But the above recordings offer the best insights into the power and beauty of Handel's opera output in the period.

8. The Pleasure of Terror: Paradox in Edmund Burke's Theory of the Sublime

E. J. CLERY

luxury is always creeping on

Lord Kames

I

In 1694 it was possible for the critic Charles Gildon to question the value of terror as a literary effect. He explained that while love dilates the soul, grief and fear contract it.[1] Terror is a shrinking condition, foreign to the heroic purposes of tragedy. Judged by a secular ethic of honour and valour, terror is an emotion natural enough when exhibited by women, children or the lower orders, but a weakness in a gentleman. In religious terms, the terrors of superstition reveal weakness and ignorance, a failure to grasp the assurances of rational religion and rely upon the wisdom of providence.

Four decades later, Garrick was electrifying the audiences at Drury Lane with his performance in the ghost scenes from *Hamlet*. Spectators of the time recorded the impact, 'His whole demeanor is so expressive of terror that it made my flesh creep even before he began to speak. . . . What an amazing triumph it is'.[2] It is not the actor's virtuosity alone that is celebrated here, but equally the triumph of terror as a source of aesthetic pleasure. No matter that ghosts have little credit in an age of enlightenment. Garrick's perfect simulation of fear transmits itself to the audience by a sympathetic contagion, and they learn, by his example, to value fear for its own sake. William

Collins' 'Ode to Fear', written in 1746, is the manifesto of a new sensibility:

> O thou whose spirit most possessed
> The sacred seat of Shakespeare's breast!
> By all that from thy prophet broke,
> In thy divine emotions spoke,
> Hither again thy fury deal,
> Teach me but once like him to feel:
> His cypress wreath my meed decree,
> And I, O Fear, will dwell with thee!

In the 1790s, the production of artificial terror becomes an industry, with Horace Walpole's experimental modernising of 'Gothic' romance in *The Castle of Otranto* (1764) as main prototype. Such titles as *Horrid Mysteries, The Necromancer, The Spectre Chief, The Midnight Groan, More Ghosts!* and *Astonishment!!!* fill the shelves of the circulating libraries. In *Northanger Abbey* (1818), Jane Austen's mildly satirical tribute to the delights of the 'horrid' school of fiction, even sensible Henry Tilney admits to having read *The Mysteries of Udolpho* (1794) by the celebrated Mrs Radcliffe, 'my hair standing on end the whole time'. A contemporary correspondant to one journal is less sanguine about the fact that terror is now 'the *order of the day*': the success of the 'Terrorist' novel means that any modern author now 'blushes to bring about a marriage by ordinary means, but conducts the happy pair through long and dangerous galleries, where the light burns blue, the thunder rattles, and the great window at the end presents the hideous visage of a *murdered* man, *uttering* piercing groans, and developing shocking mysteries'.[3] Whereas once Garrick and Collins had looked to Shakespeare as the originator of a finite number of grand effects of terror, now an army of hack writers have sprung up to supply an apparently inexhaustible demand.

What brought about this mass indulgence in the pleasures of terror? Faced with the phenomenon, some contemporaries, like the letter-writer just quoted, expressed their bewilderment in condemnation and satire. But a few were engaged in evolving new theories of terror and, more specifically, in finding ways of explaining how it is that pleasure and pain can be combined.

The main concern of my essay will be with this revaluation of terror in aesthetic theory, rather than with the production and consumption of the terrible. For while an investigation of this theoretical material won't necessarily tell us why people longed to be frightened, it can tell us something about the cultural value attached to fear, the status of effects of terror, and the ideological rewards to be reaped from an educated response to them, and thus contribute to a genuinely historical understanding of the products of the late eighteenth-century terror boom. In the context of aesthetic experience, fear will never be purely physiological, nor a timeless effusion of the unconscious. As anyone who has read *The Castle of Otranto* or *The Mysteries of Udolpho* unmoved can witness, their fear is not our fear.

In this period, the career of terror as a source of pleasure is inextricably linked with that of the sublime. They arrived together, bolstered by classical authority, in *Peri Hupsous*, attributed to a philosopher of the 3rd century AD, Longinus, and translated as *Le Traité du Sublime* by Boileau in 1674. The term 'sublime' was quickly taken up in England, where it was used interchangeably with the 'high' or 'elevated'. But as these synonyms indicate, terror at this stage was not crucial to the definition of sublimity. It is just one of a number of effects of rhetoric conducive to the extension of the mental faculties, and then only if accompanied by some idea of grandeur.

John Dennis and Joseph Addison are notable among early critics for the emphasis they place on terror, and their interest in contradictory states of mind associated with the sublime. Dennis includes terror among the 'Enthusiastick Passions': ''tis this sort of Terror, or Admiration, or Horror . . . which expres'd in Poetry make that Spirit, that Passion, and that Fire, which so wonderfully please'.[4] Addison, in his essays on 'The Pleasures of the Imagination', expresses the paradox more concisely in such formulations as 'agreeable Horrour' or 'a pleasing kind of Horrour'.[5] Milton's verse, the Coliseum and the Alps all inspire mingled terror and pleasure. But the only explanation Addison offers for this paradox effectively neutralises the terrible, by making pleasure depend on reflective distance from it. Written representations are the ideal source of this experience:

> If we consider . . . the Nature of this Pleasure, we shall find that it does not arise so properly from the Description of what is Terrible, as from the Reflection we make on our selves at the time of reading it. When we look on such hideous Objects, we are not a little pleased to think we are in no Danger of them. We consider them at the same time, as Dreadful and Harmless; so that the more frightful Appearance they make, the greater is the Pleasure we receive from the Sense of our own Safety.[6]

Edmund Burke's *Philosophical Enquiry into the Origin of our Ideas of the Sublime and Beautiful* (1757) represents a new phase in the progress of terror. Here it is made central to the definition of the sublime:

> Whatever is fitted in any sort to excite the ideas of pain, and danger, that is to say, whatever is in any sort terrible, or is conversant about terrible objects, or operates in a manner analogous to terror, is a source of the *sublime*; that is, it is productive of the strongest emotion which the mind is capable of feeling.[7]

In this scheme there can no longer be any drift of the sublime towards the beautiful, or emotions of joy, or complacent admiration. Terror must always have a part in the experience, for 'terror is in all cases whatsoever, either more openly or latently the ruling principle of the sublime' (p. 58), it is 'the common stock of every thing that is sublime' (p. 64).[8]

As well as making terror the key to the sublime, Burke crucially revises its relation to pleasure. He describes pain and pleasure as positive emotions: they cannot be combined and nor are they interdependent, in the sense that the absence of one automatically implies the presence of the other. Terror inspires pain, and therefore cannot be associated with pleasure. Instead a third term is introduced, 'delight', which *can* accompany pain, for it is a 'species of relative pleasure' (p. 36). Burke apologises for the neologism, but claims the philosopher's prerogative to adapt existing words to speculative usage, and redefines delight as 'the sensation which accompanies the removal of pain or danger' (p. 37). As Tom Furniss has observed, it is not obvious precisely how delight combines with terror; whether it is produced simultaneously with terror on the basis of conscious distance from danger, or as a result of an act removing danger, subsequent to a state of terror.[10] This vagueness about the sequence or synchronicity of 'delightful Terror' suggests that Burke's interest lies elswhere: whichever version is chosen, they both rule out the association of pleasure and terror, since the two can neither coexist nor replace each other.

Strangely enough, neither the insistence on terror, nor the sharp differentiation of 'pleasure' and 'delight' has received much attention in twentieth-century commentary on the *Enquiry*. The place of terror is either taken for granted, or obscured due to a post-Kantian conception of the sublime in which terror scarcely figures.[11] And because Burke claims that 'pleasure' and 'delight' are different without offering much explanation, the distinction is generally ignored.[12] What I will want to show is that it is these two features that tied Burke's aesthetic theory most closely to contemporary debate about social change, a debate conducted in terms quite alien to twentieth-century assumptions. Terror, it will emerge, is at once a political and an aesthetic affect, and pleasure has a powerful ideological resonance. But before moving on to examine the implications of Burkean terror, it is worth looking more closely at the way it operates within his general scheme.

Terror combined with delight is a law unto itself; in Burke it resists sublimation into pleasure. Delight does not supersede terror, it is generated by it and held in suspension with it. 'Terror is a passion which always produces delight when it does not press too close' (p. 46): this may sound like an echo of Addison, but here the distinction between positive pleasure and relative delight comes into effect. In Addison, the pleasure of terror involves the negation of terror; terror is assimilated by rational reflection on the absence of danger, to become a form of elevation or exaltation, a positive pleasure. Burke, by contrast, is concerned to maintain the separateness of terror, accompanied by its own variety of enjoyment. Whereas pleasure would imply transcendence, delight preserves the alterity of terror and pain.

The immediate reason why the delight of terror must differ from, say, the pleasure of beauty, is that they are directed towards entirely different ends, or 'final causes' as Burke calls them.[13]

Society is the final cause of the pleasure of beauty: the experience of beauty arouses desire, teaches sympathy, unites individuals in such a way as to promote the smooth-running and reproduction of the social totality. Self-preservation is the final cause of the sublime, but here the definition is more obscure:

> As the performance of our duties of every kind depends upon life, and the performing them with vigour and efficacy depends upon health, we are very strongly affected with whatever threatens the destruction of either; but as we were not made to acquiesce in life and health, the simple enjoyment of them is not attended with any real pleasure, lest satisfied with that, we should give ourselves over to indolence and inaction. (p. 41)

On the face of it, this seems inadequate as an explanation for the delight in sublime terror. Surely the instinct to preserve one's own life is natural enough? Why should it be desirable to rehearse moments of pain and danger with regard to objects of terror that pose no real threat? What kind of self-preservation is being spoken of here?

The clue lies in the final clause of this passage: life and health are not invested with 'real pleasure' since this might lead to 'indolence and inaction'. This vocabulary points the reader back to the first section of the *Enquiry* which concerns directly neither the sublime nor the beautiful, but novelty: 'The first and the simplest emotion which we discover in the human mind, is Curiosity' (p. 31). For children, in the first stage of life, everything is new and arouses curiosity. But with time novelty is inevitably diminished and curiosity slackens:

> In short, the occurrences of life, by the time we come to know it a little, would be incapable of affecting the mind with any other sensations than those of loathing and weariness, if many things were not adapted to affect the mind by means of other powers besides novelty in them, and of other passions besides curiosity in ourselves. (p. 31)

The natural tendency of the mind is towards entropy. Remedial stimulation of the passions is called for, in order to lift the mind above 'stale unaffecting familiarity'. The artificial production of pain and pleasure prevents the mind from settling into a fatal state of indifference. What is at stake is the 'life' of the individual will to survive.

It is in this context that sublime terror shows its worth, for 'it is productive of the strongest emotion which the mind is capable of feeling' (p. 39). How the sublime actually operates to preserve the 'life' of the mind is not revealed until Part Four, in sections V–VII: 'How the Sublime is produced', 'How pain can be a cause of delight', and 'Exercise necessary for the finer organs'. Here terror is shown operating on the nervous system with a rigour that Robert Miles has aptly termed 'hygienic'.[14] The description of this process should be quoted at length:

> Providence has so ordered it, that a state of rest and inaction, however it may flatter our indolence, should be productive of many inconveniencies; that it should generate such disorders, as may force us to have recourse to some labour, as a thing absolutely requisite to make us pass our lives with tolerable satisfaction; for the nature of rest is to suffer all the parts of our bodies to fall into a relaxation, that not only disables the members from performing their functions, but takes away the vigorous tone of fibre which is requisite for carrying on the natural and necessary secretions. At the same time, that in this languid inactive state, the nerves are more liable to the most horrid convulsions, than when they are sufficiently braced and strengthened. Melancholy, dejection, despair, and often self-murder, is the consequence of the gloomy view we take of things in this relaxed state of body. The best remedy for all these evils is exercise or *labour*; and labour is a surmounting of *difficulties*, an exertion of the contracting power of the muscles; and as such resembles pain, which consists in tension and contraction, in every thing but degree. Labour is not only requisite to preserve the coarser organs in a state fit for their functions, but it is equally necessary to these finer and more delicate organs, on which, and by which, the imagination, and perhaps the other mental powers act. (pp. 134–5)

Just as exercise is necessary to the 'coarse muscular parts of the constitution' so the 'finer parts' must be 'shaken and worked to the proper degree' (p. 134); the pain inspired by terror (a terror 'not conversant about the present destruction of the person'), can 'clear the parts . . . of a dangerous and troublesome incumbrance' leaving 'a sort of delightful horror, a sort of tranquillity tinged with terror' (p. 136).

This version of the operations of the sublime is so arresting that, as Frances Ferguson notes, few critics have spared much thought for Burke's other principle object, the idea of the beautiful.[15] The imbalance has its origin in the *Enquiry* itself. The 'final cause' of the sublime is given greater weight than that of the beautiful; the drama of self-preservation overshadows the imperative of the social passions promoted by beauty. But the hierarchy does not end here; for rather than being simply the answer to a lesser need, beauty comes to be framed as part of the problem that the sublime must remedy. This takes us back to the original statement on self-preservation and the assertion that the normal enjoyment of life and health is 'not attended with any real pleasure' lest it deteriorate into 'indolence and inaction' (p. 41). For beauty, unlike the sublime, *is* of course, attended by 'real pleasure'; and while it is designed, like the sublime, to lift the mind out of familiarity and indifference, the passions it inspires are weaker and pose the yet worse danger of deteriorating into 'indolence and inaction'. Beauty does not stimulate, but relaxes and softens. Although not openly stated, the sublime, it seems, must counter not only the mind's native indifference, but the consequences of pleasure itself. The paradox of the pleasure of terror leads us to another: the terror of pleasure.

II

Indifference, we have seen, is a threat to the health of the mind and, by extension, to life itself. Beauty, as the primary source of positive pleasure, seduces the mind out of indifference but only at the risk of leaving it in a state of langour and self-neglect which merely accelerates the effects of indifference. But in what schema could the beautiful logically figure as more dangerous than the terrible? How can pleasure be construed as life-threatening?

The suspicion of pleasure found in the *Enquiry* is less puritan than patrician. Burke's image of the body under siege from *ennui*, prey to the consequences of self-indulgence, is the *locus classicus* of a political discourse which posited 'the absolute opposition of pleasure to virtue'.[16] 'Civic humanism' is the name attached to the discourse (both conceptual system and system of value), which sought to define personal identity strictly in terms of citizenship. First connected by modern scholarship with the Renaissance revival of the republican ideal, civic discourse has more recently been described as the dominant mode in eighteenth-century debate in Britain on political morality and social transformation.[17] By identifying virtue with the ability to comprehend the public interest and act on it, civic discourse served to legitimate a ruling class of aristocratic landowners. For only those in possession of the leisure and wealth which came with landed property could be expected to set aside personal interest and devote themselves wholly to public service, whether by bearing arms or by governing, and had the time and opportunity to acquaint themselves with the needs of all sections of society. The majority, without the necessary qualifications, must take their lead from above. Women of whatever rank need not apply.[18]

Significantly, then, the perks of inherited wealth – leisure and display – could be seen in these terms not as pleasures but rather as a guarantee of disinterested views. Pleasure was associated instead with the expansion of trade and manufactures, under the opprobrious title of 'luxury'. This is not to say that commerce as such was condemned; rather, some of its symptoms gave cause for alarm. Without careful management, the existence of a unified, public body would be fatally undermined by the fragmentation of interests that accompanied commercial expansion. Even more insidious was the new potential for self-gratification on a wide scale opened up by economic prosperity. A sense of crisis was attached to every outgrowth of luxury or improvement, from cities to novel-reading; all served in varying degrees to corrupt individuals by encouraging them to neglect their public duty in favour of private dissipation, which would result cumulatively in the decline of the nation.

The relation of the sublime to the civic humanist critique of luxury could be traced back to Longinus's founding text. In the final section of *On the Sublime* the author attributes the 'Corruption of Genius' in the present age to peace, avarice and voluptuousness: 'Love of Money is the Disease which renders us most abject, and Love of Pleasure is that which renders us most corrupt.'[19] William Smith's 1739 translation employs the standard vocabulary of condemnation: when the 'corruption' spreads, the 'Faculties of the Soul . . . grow stupid' and men cease to 'cultivate Virtue'; 'Life in general . . . is thrown away in Indolence and Sloth [and] deadly Lethargy.'[20] This process, once properly underway, is unstoppable, the loss of sublime genius is irredeemable, and examples of the sublime can be admired only retrospectively: this is the message Smith underlines in the preface to his edition. It would be taken up by Hugh Blair as he accounts for the sublimity of the primitive Highland poet 'Ossian' – 'The two dispiriting vices, to which Longinus imputes the decline of poetry, covetousness and effeminacy, were as yet unknown;'[21] and by William Duff in his *Essay on Original Genius* (1767), where the loss of poetry in modern life is attributed to luxury, which 'enfeebles the mind, as it corrupts the heart, and gradually suppresses that strenuous exertion of the mental faculties, by which consummate excellence is to be attained'.[22] The civic discourse recognises no separation of political economy and the aesthetic. The arts are ideally the training ground for virtuous citizens, and taste is properly a medium for translating the private consumption of art into public purpose. It was this conviction that led critics to regard the literature of the sublime or of elevation as the trace of all that had been lost, or was in the process of being lost, as a result of the refinements of modernity.

Burke's figuring of an enervated body in relation to the sublime demonstrates a subscription to republican concerns, as does his censure of pleasure. Yet these tropes are not made the occasion for lamenting anew the decline of virtue and genius. The text swerves from committing itself to the 'already said'. The *Enquiry* is marked out as a work of transition by its refusal to go through the motions of the Polybian cycle, the irreversible movement from ancient virtue to modern decay.[23] Counter to the logic of civic discourse, Burke offers a cure for the ills of luxury, without acknowledging the need to abolish luxury (pleasure, the beautiful) itself. Luxury is a fixture in his system, though it continues to be seen as a threat. The sublime is posited as a way of maintaining the vitality of a body which can never be free of the risk of pleasure. The body, in other words, must learn to live with the new conditions of commercial society. By making this concession to economic and social change, Burke locates himself within contemporary, late eighteenth-century developments in political discourse aiming to reconcile commerce with a modified language of virtue.

Foremost among the innovators were the philosophers of the Scottish Enlightenment, notably David Hume, Adam Smith and Adam Ferguson. In their writings, discursive techniques of empirical science are brought to bear, disjunctively, on the conventional objects of civic discourse: property, history, morality, politics. And through this disjunction, the progress of commerce is reconceived within a space of neutral fact. Commerce, of course, had had its supporters prior to Hume and Smith; but Daniel Defoe and especially Bernard de Mandeville, author of *The Fable of the Bees; or Private Vices, Public Benefits* (1714), simply invert the moral schema of civic discourse rather than revising it, and can consequently be dismissed as part and parcel of the 'corruption' they defend. The beauty of the new science of political economy is its objectivity. It is on the strength of this objectivity that an alternative morality of trade can be articulated, and bourgeois interests mobilised. Burke's *Enquiry*, with its promise of a 'sober and attentive investigation of the laws of nature' (p. 1), and its catalogue of observed objects and effects, enacts a comparable strategy, neutralising an aesthetic category, the sublime, that, as we have seen, was frequently taken as an occasion for rehearsing alarmist prescriptions about social change. It was perhaps Hume's recognition of a fellow traveller that led him to recommend the *Enquiry* to Adam Smith, as 'a very pretty treatise on the sublime' in a letter of April 1759.[24]

What kind of solution does Burke's aesthetic theory offer to the problems defined by civic humanism? One recent suggestion has been that the operations of Burke's sublime 'follow the dictates of the work ethic'.[25] Frances Ferguson's hint has been elaborated at length by Tom Furniss in *Edmund Burke's Aesthetic Ideology*, where he proposes that the *Enquiry* 'develops a revolutionary aesthetic ideology which contributes to the hegemonic struggle of the middle class' in the period. According to this thesis, Burke, in spite of his conservative equating of luxury (read consumer capitalism) with corruption, revolutionises the notion by implicitly associating it not with the trading classes, but primarily with the idle and pleasure-loving aristocracy. His concept of the sublime, on the other hand, attempts to identify 'commercial endeavour with the supposed bracing effects of physical labour and with the independent virtue traditionally attributed to more "barbarous" societies', anticipating 'nineteenth-century images of virtuous labour'.[26]

There is not room here to review all the evidence for this argument, but it is certainly true that in the sections on the mechanisms of sublime terror, Burke uses the analogy of 'common labour' (p. 136), and even places the word 'labour' in italics (p. 135). But more important than references to labour, is the claim that Burke sees labour as an act of mastery, an overcoming of difficulty that gives rise to a heroic sense of self. The taste for the sublime would, in this sense offer a moral foundation for economic individualism. Two passages in particular have been cited with reference to this notion of the sublime as in essence the ethic of the 'self-made man'. One is from the section on 'Power' which presents God the creator as the ultimate manifestation of this idea: 'When the prophet David contemplated the wonders of wisdom and power, which are displayed in the œconomy of man, he seems to be struck with a sort of divine horror, and cries out, *fearfully and wonderfully am I made!*' (pp. 68–9; original emphasis). Frances Ferguson refers to this as an example of exaltation arising from identification with power – man recognises himself as made in God's image.

Identification with a sublime object also seems to play a part in the second passage, from the section on 'Ambition':

> Now whatever either on good or upon bad grounds tends to raise a man in his own opinion, produces a sort of swelling and triumph that is extremely grateful to the human mind;

> and this swelling is never more perceived, nor operates with more force, than when without danger we are conversant with terrible objects, the mind always claiming to itself some part of the dignity and importance of the things which it contemplates. Hence proceeds what Longinus has observed of that glorying and sense of inward greatness, that always fills the reader of such passages in poets and orators as are sublime; it is what every man must have felt in himself upon such occasions. (pp. 50–1)

This passage, with its phallic imagery, can also be taken to introduce into aesthetics by metaphor the gendered division of spheres within bourgeois ideology which makes work the preserve of men. It has often been quoted by recent commentators to convey the essence of Burke's idea of the sublime – masculine, strenuous, self-empowering;[27] yet it is in fact one of the most perplexing sections of the work. Burke actually locates ambition as one of the three principal passions directed towards maintaining 'the great chain of society' – the others being sympathy and imitation (p. 44). It should therefore, properly speaking, be aligned with the taste for the beautiful. Certainly, the rhetoric of virility accords with the function of sexual and social reproduction: the 'final cause' of ambition, which, like beauty, stimulates desire. However, the image of the mind 'swelling' to encompass its object has recalled to Burke a passage from Longinus, resulting in a confusing hybrid definition. He has strayed across the central division of his system, and the laconic appeal to personal feeling which ends the section seems a case of special pleading.[28]

There are also difficulties raised by the other examples. David's cry '*fearfully and wonderfully am I made*!' may appear an exalted affirmation of man's resemblance to God, but read in context the relation to divinity appears otherwise: 'whilst we contemplate so vast an object . . . we shrink into the minuteness of our own nature, and are, in a manner, annihilated before him.' What is fearful and wonderful is not the end-product – man – but the act of making itself, the idea of which keeps the reflecting subject suspended in a permanent state of fear and wonder. There is no climactic overcoming, or transcendant identification with the maker.[29] Similarly, when Burke describes the exercise of the finer organs by the sublime as labour, this does not amount to a labour theory of value. It is a work of consumption, internalising the envigorating effects of terror, not a productive labour.[30] Finally, an identification of the sublime with a 'work ethic' cannot incorporate convincingly the terms which we have found to be crucial in the *Enquiry*: 'terror', 'self-preservation' and 'delight' (as opposed to pleasure). None of them formed a part of discourse on trade and industry as it existed at the time.[31]

There can be no clean break with the order of civic discourse. The fact that Burke is brought to subscribe to the perceived crisis of luxury, or rather, to inscribe his aesthetic theory within the field of civic debate, rules out the possibility of elaborating a new, bourgeois system of value in answer to the problem. The solution must be sought in the republican ideal of citizenship. The primacy of terror and its 'final cause' of stimulating instincts of self-preservation indicate that it can be found in a return to the most fundamental public virtue: willingness to bear arms and risk life and limb in the nation's defence, in order to keep the spirit of patriotism alive.

The *Enquiry* was written and published at a time of heightened interest in Britain's military forces. Since the 1690s, as a result of frequent wars on the Continent, the size and importance of the standing army had been increasing. This was in spite of vocal opposition. Added to practical arguments against the expense of a permanent force were other, moral and political, objections: professional soldiers were mercenaries, motivated by personal gain rather than public spirit; it was in their interest to prolong war, and in peacetime they became parasites on civil society, prone to idleness and dissipation, or else potentially a tool in the hands of an autocratic government.[32] The histories of imperial Rome and of the English Commonwealth showed the capacity of a standing army to become the 'great instrument of tyranny and oppression'.[33] The alternative was the militia, a citizen's army: men trained to act in the nation's defence in time of need. In the 1740s, the threat of invasion by France and actual invasion by a Jacobite army, drew attention to England's feeble powers of resistance. Particularly humiliating was the spectacle of warlike Highlanders progressing virtually unchallenged through the docile northern counties, and there arose as a consequence 'an agitation for the reform of the militia, beginning in 1745, reaching a climax in 1756 and finally victorious in 1757'.[34] The Militia Act, passed in the same year that Burke's *Enquiry* was published, made provision for a more streamlined and effective force, though it was never in fact to be involved in any decisive action against an invader. However, just as important was its symbolic role in defence of the spirit of liberty and patriotism. Training in the use of firearms and practice of manoeuvres were vital to this symbolic purpose: at least the illusion that life-threatening action might arise must be maintained.

Debate over the decline of martial spirit occupies a distinctive place in the writings of the Scottish Enlightenment. It is on the topic of the relative effects of peace and war that impassive, mildly approving surveys of the progress of civil society tend to collapse abruptly into pessimism:

> Industry, manufactures, and wealth, are the fruits of peace; but advert to what follows. Luxury, a never-failing concomitant of wealth, is a slow poison, that debilitates men, and renders them incapable of any great effort: courage, magnanimity, heroism, come to be ranked among the miracles that are supposed never to have existed but in fable; and the fashionable properties of sensuality, avarice, cunning, and dissimulation, engross the mind. . . . Such are the fruits of perpetual peace with respect to individuals.[35]

For civilians, the professionalising of military service meant a narrowing of vision. In a primitive warrior society, private interest was always subordinated to public ends, encouraging a spirit of liberty. But in a modern commercial society, the thoughts of the majority are never lifted beyond their daily round of business and pleasure, and they become slaves to necessity or to vice.

Even those of the Scottish school most convinced of the benefits of modernity were inclined to favour the militia as a moral supplement. Hume was singular in opposing the axiom that men in a commercial society 'will lose their martial spirit' for '[t]he arts have no such effect in enervating either the mind or body'.[36] Yet his vision of a 'Perfect Commonwealth' involves a militia on the celebrated Swiss model, not a standing army which would allow the majority of men to remain permanently in peaceful occupations.[37] In *The Wealth of Nations* (1776) Adam Smith demonstrates at length the practical inferiority of militias compared to a well-regulated standing army, but when he comes to consider the role of education in an improved society, the militia reappears as a means of repairing the deformation of men caused by living in a peaceful, commercial state. For,

> a coward, a man incapable either of defending or of revenging himself, evidently wants one of the most essential parts of the character of a man. He is as much mutilated and deformed in his mind, as another is in his body, who is either deprived of some if its most essential members, or has lost the use of them. . . . Even though the martial spirit of the people were of no use towards the defence of the society, yet to prevent that sort of mental mutilation, deformity and wretchedness, which cowardice necessarily involves in it, from spreading themselves through the great body of the people, would still deserve the most serious attention of government.[38]

The militia mediates the contradiction created between material transformation and civic values. Like Burke in the *Enquiry*, Smith visualises mental or spiritual ailments by analogy with bodily disfunction or deformation, the image serving to restate an ideal identity of the private body of the individual with the public body of the nation.[39] And the militia, like the sublime, is to be a remedial simulation of the horrors of war.[40]

The martial spirit debate offers a way of understanding Burke's claim that the taste for terror is providentially ordained and, equally, why delight in terror takes the passive form that it does. The sublime subject of the *Enquiry* is not self-affirming but, on the contrary, eager for annihilation; he finds delight in being penetrated and dissolved. This delight is opposed to that positive pleasure which involves an indulgence of private desires and leads to another kind of dissolution. The sublime describes in aesthetic terms an ideal of virtue founded in self-sacrifice; it is a militia of the imagination. And yet the stimulation it provides can find no practical outlet. Because for the vast majority in a modern, commercial society there can be no progression from imaginary warfare to public action, the sublime must remain, as I have called it elsewhere, a 'private war without consequences'.[41]

III

Burke's *Enquiry* constitutes a point of negotiation and contradiction in the gradual shift from aristocratic to bourgeois hegemony. His aesthetic theory derives moral significance from an established opposition within contemporary political discourse, of private luxury versus public virtue. The sublime operates in opposition to pleasure, as an antidote for the corrupting effects of a commercial society. Virtue is so absolutely opposed to pleasure that a new name must be found for the enjoyment that attaches to the sublime: 'delight'. But this strategem cannot entirely erase the irony that sublime terror offers, after all, a variety of pleasurable consumption, and is therefore a symptom of the very corruption it is designed to correct.

The irony is heightened by the fact that the novel was to become the principle medium of aesthetic effects of terror. Popular fiction was frequently denounced as one of the very worst products of modern commercial culture. What's more, a conventional association with overheated female sensibilities, and the actual prominence of female writers and readers, made the novel mode the antithesis, or perhaps, rather, a gross parody, of the civic ideal of political formation through rational appreciation of the fine arts.

Most writers of fiction were, indeed, more interested in plundering the *Enquiry* as a handbook of sublime tropes, than in its social or political bearing. But there were exceptions. The prose poems *Fingal* (1762) and *Temora* (1763), attributed to the ancient Gaelic bard Ossian (but in fact fabricated by the 'editor' James Macpherson), are a perfect realisation of the principles of the civic sublime. Hugely popular well into the nineteenth century – 'Ossian' was the favourite reading matter of Napoleon – the numerous battle scenes improved with spine-chilling supernaturalism were designed to teach readers of the present the value of primitive warrior virtues through the experience of terror. There are also signs that a few of the more sophisticated novelists writing in the terror genre perceived what was at stake in Burke's theory and felt some residual sense of civic responsibility in producing images of the sublime. M. G. Lewis's *The Monk* (1796) was denounced on publication as degrading and sensationalist. Yet the characterisation of the eponymous anti-hero owes something to the notion that the stimulus of terror is necessary to virtue. Lewis's reflection, 'He had a Warrior's heart, and He might have shone with splendour at the head of an Army' (p. 236) could be set beside Lord Kames's claim that 'Monks are commonly pusillanimous: their way of life, which removes them from danger, enervates the mind, and renders them spiritless and cowardly.'[42] Sublimity comes too late to save Ambrosio from self-destruction, but it is implied that the scenes of danger and terror depicted in the novel will fortify the reader. Ann Radcliffe's first novel, *The Castles of Athlin and Dunbayne* (1789) differs from her best known works in taking two male characters as the main protagonists, and the earlier chapters perfectly illustrate the complementary relation of sublime landscape and warrior virtues. Her move to heroine-centred narratives, and the impact of her example on the fiction writing of the 1790s, appear all the more significant in the context of a civic humanist conception of the sublime. With the accompanying turn towards domestic nightmare, the public function of terror is abandoned, and the popular literature of terror becomes unequivocally the site of consoling, though still paradoxical, pleasures.[43]

9. Burns and Wordsworth: Art and 'The Pleasure which there is in life itself'

SUSAN MANNING

'Tomes of aesthetic criticism,' writes the philosopher George Santayana, 'hang on a few moments of real delight and intuition.'[1] Aesthetics, the 'science of art', has always existed not only to describe (and in some cases quantify) the pleasure human beings take in art, but also to *control* it: to legislate an acceptable balance between pleasure and moral instruction. Pleasure is the wicked fairy of aesthetics, competing for status with its sister-imperatives Beauty, Truth, the Good, Instruction, Mimesis. Conflicts arise not because of the weakness of pleasure as an ingredient of art, but because of its strength. Plato (reluctantly) went so far as to banish poets – even his beloved Homer – from the ideal republic, not because they failed to please, but, on the contrary, because the pleasure they gave was so strong that it was liable to overturn the principles of good order which underpinned the moral education of his rulers.[2] Aesthetics has traditionally attempted to neutralise pleasure's subversive potential by co-opting it for art's beneficial power over its audience: right representations please, art teaches by pleasing, the beautiful gives pleasure. It becomes 'safe' as the sugar coating on the bitter moral pill.

The eighteenth century was not, then, unique in the moral defences it erected against the purely pleasureable in art. One of the things which makes its literature so compelling is the openness with which, in a newly secular age, the problematics of pleasure can be discussed and incorporated in the pleasure of the text: R. B. Sheridan's play *The Rivals* (1775) provides a graphic and itself pleasurably comic illustration of morality's tendency to act as a cover (in the sense both of a *lid*, and a *disguise*) for pleasure, in a scene where its heroine, Lydia Languish, maintains her public image and moral advantage by hurriedly concealing the novel she is reading – *The Innocent Adultery* – within the covers of William Law's *The Whole Duty of Man*, that most impeccable ethical volume.

The relation of pleasure and art became a particular concern of eighteenth-century writing with the rise of literary criticism as a newly specialised branch of aesthetics. During the course of the century, critical attention shifted away from defining the intrinsic qualities of a work of art towards understanding its effect on the reader. Richard Hurd's 'Dissertation on the Idea of Universal Poetry' (1766) typifies a certain orthodoxy:

> When we speak of poetry, as an *art*, we mean *such a way or method of treating a subject as is found most pleasing and delightful to us.* In all other kinds of literary composition, pleasure is subordinate to USE: in poetry only, PLEASURE is the end, to which use itself . . . must submit.[3]

Hurd, like other mid-century theoreticians, evaded the problematics of the aesthetic equation by asserting – quite against the evidence – that what pleases is representations of virtue, and only representations of virtue please. It is doubtful whether any art ever *actually* worked like this; but such a straightforward accommodation of morality and pleasure became increasingly hard to sustain, even in theory, against developing and closer interest in the nature of the pleasure-experience, and in its relationship, if any, to virtuous behaviour. This shift in critical thinking away from *a priori* principles and towards the effect on an audience accompanies a new confidence in the authority of sense-based evidence, and the concomitant advance of empiricism in epistemology and ethics.[4] Once one grants the primacy of response over intention, to say that 'the Good' pleases, in no way guarantees that what pleases will be 'the Good.'

It is precisely this uncertain area between two aesthetic imperatives, which increasingly appeared openly antagonistic rather than harmoniously aligned, which became the poetic territory of Robert Burns (1759–96) and William Wordsworth (1771–1850). The association demonstrates both their profound poetic affinity, and the deep rift created by the course of eighteenth-century aesthetics between the poetry of pleasure and writing about poetic pleasure:

> Some rhyme a neebor's name to lash;
> Some rhyme (vain thought!) for needfu' cash;
> Some rhyme to court the countra clash,
>   An' raise a din;
> For me, an aim I never fash;
>   I rhyme for fun.[5]

> The Poet writes under one restriction only, namely, the necessity of giving immediate pleasure. . . . it is a homage paid to the native and naked dignity of man, to the grand elementary principle of pleasure, by which he knows and feels, and lives, and moves. We have no sympathy but what is propagated by pleasure: . . . We have no knowledge, that is, no general principles drawn from the contemplation of particular facts, but what has been built up by pleasure, and exists in us by pleasure alone.[6]

Burns and Wordsworth are both poets of Pleasure: daily pleasures and special moments are their subjects, and both agree that the poet's work is vitally connected with receiving and imparting pleasure. Wordsworth revered Burns as a poetic example, cited and admired his poetry throughout life, and made a pilgrimage through Ayrshire in 1803 using the works of the Scottish poet as his guidebook. His Burns is an ideal figure who came near to representing in person the 'Poet' characterised by the 'Preface' to *The Lyrical Ballads*, in daily touch with that 'low and rustic life' where the passions of men might be most readily 'incorporated with the beautiful and permanent forms of nature' ('Preface', p. 245). In the epitaph 'At the Grave of Burns,' Wordsworth laments his particular loss:

> I mourned with thousands, but as one
> More deeply grieved, for He was gone
> Whose light I hailed when first it shone
>   And showed my youth
> How verse may build a princely throne
>   On humble truth.[7]

The poet-ploughman – that inspired marketing compound of the Edinburgh critic Henry Mackenzie – readily became a Romantic icon, he 'who walked in glory and in joy/Behind his plough, upon the mountain-side', self-deified by the natural greatness of his spirit.[8] This essay will argue that the poetic legacy of Burns was actually much more problematic for Wordsworth's theory of 'Poetic Pleasure' than Wordsworth's idealisation of the Scottish poet could acknowledge; that mistaking Burns for a rustic bard of simple pleasures and 'Sensibility', he was bound to overlook or deny the disruptive, revolutionary nature of *his* poetry of Pleasure; and that the solemnity of Wordsworth's elevation of 'Pleasure' into 'an elementary principle' of the universe leads his own writing in directions far from the rooted immediacy of Burns's art.

In his philosophical work *A Treatise of Human Nature* (1739–40), David Hume took delight in demonstrating that good and evil, virtue and vice, were not axiomatic or objectively demonstrable, but only available to us as sensations of pleasure and displeasure. Around the philosophy of empiricism, which located all knowledge in the impressions made on the senses, there grew up during the eighteenth century a system of ethical thought based, broadly, on notions of pleasure and pain or – in relation to other people – of sympathy and aversion. The economy of Pleasure, in other words, became the only foundation for ethics. Hume's *Enquiry Concerning the Principles of Morals* of 1751 and Adam Smith's *The Theory of Moral Sentiments* of 1759 maintained that morality is determined by sentiment, not by reason, and defined virtue as whatever action or quality would give a spectator a pleasing feeling of approbation. Adam Smith, discussing 'The Pleasure of Mutual Sympathy,' declares

> whatever may be the cause of sympathy, or however it may be excited, nothing pleases us more than to observe in other men a fellow feeling with all the emotions of our own breast; nor are we ever so much shocked as by the appearance of the contrary. . . . Sympathy enlivens joy and alleviates grief. It enlivens joy by presenting another source of satisfaction; and it alleviates grief by insinuating into the heart almost the only agreeable sensation which it is at that time capable of receiving.[9]

The cult of Sensibility defined virtue not in terms of action or reason but by the acuteness with which the individual sympathised with the feelings of another, and the *pleasureableness* of this identification. The freedom and informality of Burns's epistle 'To James Smith' finds a basis for social intercourse by looking inward to personal response. It appears, in its easy directness, to overcome at a stroke the difficulties of communication between self and world which empiricism bequeathed to eighteenth-century and subsequently to romantic and modern literature. But Burns was neither oblivious of nor immune to these difficulties; the very personal authority of his poetic voice conceals a whole weight of philosophical ethics within its carelessness. Burns's lifetime almost exactly coincided with the lifespan of Sensibility. He was born in the year not only of *The Theory of Moral Sentiments,* but of the first two volumes of *Tristram Shandy,* and died on the eve of the publication of Schiller's essay *Naive and Sentimental Poetry.* All Burns's work shows the influence of 'feeling' and the centrality of sentiment and Sympathy to the poetics of pleasure; he professed to venerate Henry Mackenzie's *The Man of Feeling* (1771) 'next to the Bible,' and carried a copy always around with him. His letters reach repeatedly for the whimsical 'feeling' tones of Sterne.

Squeezed almost from expression by real and unromantic poverty in Ayrshire in the 1780s, Burns's writing at first found pleasure in mere sympathetic fellowship through unrelenting circumstances.[10] In his 'Epistle to John Lapraik', a distinctive and potentially disruptive personal voice suddenly crumples before the forces of wealth and power, to take refuge in the safe poses of sentiment:

But ye whom social pleasure charms,
Whose hearts the *tide of kindness* warms,
Who hold your *being* on the terms,
  'Each aids the others',
Come to my bowl, come to my arms,
  My friends, my brothers!

Real poetic pleasure comes to the *reader,* however, in the second epistle to Lapraik, as greater confidence in the relationship with his fellow Ayrshire poet (who had in the interim replied to the earlier verses) liberates Burns's voice from cautious virtue to gleeful defiance, and 'sociability' takes on a sharper edge:

> Ne'er mind how Fortune *waft* an' *warp*;
> She's but a b-tch.

The pleasures of personal freedom to curse the world and its constraints are the necessary prelude in Burns's poetry to finding community of a less attenuated kind than the aesthetics of Sensibility could offer. Confidence that a reader is there, listening and sympathetic (something the earlier epistle could not quite trust), returns individual insecurity to a public voice of challenging immediacy. It also, in more than one sense, returns Pleasure to Art, as the desire to write is confronted by the disenabling conditions of life:

> Forjesket sair, with weary legs,
> Rattlin the corn out-owre the rigs,
> Or dealing thro' amang the naigs
> Their ten-tours bite,
> My awkwart Muse sair pleads and begs,
> I would na write.
>
> The tapetless ramfeezl'd hizzie
> She's saft at best an' something lazy,
> Quo' she, 'Ye ken we've been sae busy
> This month an' mair,
> That trouth, my head is grown right dizzie,
> An' something sair.'
>
> Her dowf excuses pat me mad;
> 'Conscience', says I, 'ye thowless jad!
> I'll write, and that a hearty blaud,
> This vera night;
> So dinna ye affront your trade,
> But rhyme it right.
>
> 'Shall bauld L*****K, the *king o'hearts*,
> Tho' mankind were a *pack o' cartes*,

Roose ye sae weel for your deserts,
  In terms sae friendly,
Yet ye'll neglect to shaw your pairts
  An' thank him kindly?'

The poet's reluctance to honour the obligation is immediate, direct and specific in the freedoms it takes with eighteenth-century poetic decorum. Confident in its own literariness, the poem liberates strongly personal poetic energies in the manner of Pope's 'Epistle to Arbuthnot':

Shut, shut the door, good *John*! fatigu'd I said,
Tie up the knocker, say I'm sick, I'm dead,
The Dog-star rages! nay 'tis past a doubt,
All Bedlam, or *Parnassus* is let out.[11]

But the colloquial virtuosity of Pope is only part of Burns's poetic cast: here is a voice at once claiming the authority of labour, and anticipating the rhythmic flexibility of Byron's cosmopolitan narrator in *Don Juan* in defiantly local terms:

Sae I gat paper in a blink,
An' down gaed *stumpie* in the ink:
Quoth I, 'Before I sleep a wink,
  I vow I'll close it;
An' if ye winna make it clink,
  By Jove I'll prose it!'

Sae I've begun to scrawl, but whether
In rhyme, or prose, or baith thegither,
Or some hotch-potch that's rightly neither,
  Let time mak proof;
But I shall scribble down some blether
  Just clean aff-loof.

The quality of pleasure centres on the debate between poetic form and conversational directness: the antagonists are held in a collusion of self-knowledge which brushes aside questions of poetic decorum even as it exploits them. Affectionate sympathy and acknowledgment not scrutiny and censure structure the exchange between the poet and his personified Muse, a layabout 'jade' well versed in all the too-recognisable forms of prevarication. Like a reluctant mule, she has to be cuffed gently into action and warned to behave properly: 'So dinna ye affront your trade,/ But rhyme it right.' Colloquial almost to dialect, these lines also trade fully on the eighteenth-century public manner of the mock-heroic.

From the personification of the 'Muse' (recalcitrant and ramshackle though she may be) to the elaborately self-conscious metaphor of the suit of cards which recurs from *The Rape of the Lock* to (ironically) *The Prelude,* it was precisely this poetic inheritance which Wordsworth programmatically cast off in the name of a 'pure' poetic pleasure in the critical essay appended to his *Poems* of 1815, where rejection of the Popean social voice and comic innuendo becomes the prerequisite for a newly purified Romantic Art of Pleasure based on innocence of the corrupt accretions of neo-Classical diction. In the 'Preface' to the *Lyrical Ballads,* he declares categorically,

> The Reader will find that personifications of abstract ideas rarely occur in these volumes; and, I hope, are utterly rejected as an ordinary device to elevate the style, and raise it above prose. I have proposed to myself to imitate, and, as far as possible, to adopt the very language of men; and assuredly such personifications do not make any natural or regular part of that language. (1802, p. 250)

In these terms, Wordsworth could only see the complexity of Burns's poetic diction as the unfortunate consequence of imitating bad models, an insufficiently complete sloughing-off of the past. However, as I shall suggest, something is lost to the Pleasure equation, as well as gained, by Wordsworth's paradigmatic association of poetic pleasure with tonal and experiential innocence of the ambivalent inheritance of verbal play.

Burns's poetry brought an intensely personal idiom of pleasure and pain into the public realm, speaking always *from* rather than *at* rural life. It is this close connection which Wordsworth so admired, and which his poetic experiments of the 1790s aimed to imitate. The 1798 'Advertisement' to *The Lyrical Ballads* declares the poems to have been 'written chiefly with a view to ascertain how far the language of conversation in the middle and lower classes of society is adapted to the purposes of poetic pleasure'. Wordsworth's faith that the battle against the depraved taste created by eighteenth-century poetic artifice had to be won by appealing to the responses and the pleasures of the 'common reader' or 'real men' was belied by the baffled and hostile initial response to his pared down diction and simplified poetic register: what pleased most people, apparently, was exactly the language he most opposed. 'The pleasure which I have proposed to myself to impart', he declared in the Preface to the second edition of 1800, 'is of a kind very different from that which is supposed by many persons to be the proper object of poetry.' Different, and 'higher': in the 'Preface' to *The Lyrical Ballads*, Wordsworth attempted to reclaim Pleasure from the realms of mere entertainment – rope-dancing, sherry and Frontiniac, as he disparagingly enumerates them.[12] It is a distinction which Burns's poetry (remaining, as the epistle 'To James Smith' shows, unashamedly and aggressively populist) consistently refuses to make. Despite its claim on the common touch, Wordsworth's poetic pleasure was inherently more exalted and un-popular than that which it claimed to supplant.

To whom does the poet address himself, Wordsworth asked in his Preface, 'and what language is to be expected from him?' The answer, like the form of the question, makes it clear that the sociability which characterises Burns's epistles has become an abstracted ideal of poetic utterance:

> He is a man speaking to men: a man, it is true, endued with more lively sensibility, more enthusiasm and tenderness, who has a greater knowledge of human nature, and a more comprehensive soul, than are supposed to be common among mankind; a man pleased with his own passions and volitions, and who rejoices more than other men in the spirit of life that is in him. ('Preface', pp. 255–6)

Both Wordsworth's debt to the eighteenth-century aesthetics of Pleasure-through-Sympathy and his crucial departures from it are clear here. The poet produces pleasure in his reader by his ability to provoke their natural, sympathetic responses to shared experience. But this passage stresses not so much common humanity, as the quantitative *difference* – which becomes in effect a qualitative one – of the poet's sensibilities from those of his audience. His special ability to receive and then to give pleasure comes from his peculiar affinity with the fundamental elements of the universe, and is not a 'common' but a quite exceptional degree of human sensibility. And, when he does not 'find' the necessary sympathetic emotions in the world beyond, he is 'habitually impelled to *create*' them within the magic circle of his own self (p. 256).

It is a turning-point for the eighteenth-century aesthetics of pleasure: sympathetic response has, in the balance of a single sentence, re-focussed itself in the direction of Romantic solipsism. When sympathy turns to find its responses within, aesthetics can become a one-man show able to dispense entirely with the 'other', moving easily from community to transcendence. Wordsworth's own 'sympathy' with his poetic subjects was of an altogether different kind from Burns's. Coleridge wrote, 'dear Wordsworth appears to me to have hurtfully segregated and isolated his being. Doubtless his delights are more deep and sublime; but he has likewise more hours that prey upon the blood.' Like Goethe, he said, Wordsworth had 'this peculiarity of utter non-sympathy with the subjects of . . . poetry. They are always, both of them, spectators *ab extra* – feeling *for*, but never *with*, their characters.'[13]

Where Wordsworth's human sympathy with his subjects in the *Lyrical Ballads* comes from a consciousness which comprehends their joys and pains in the largeness of its own humanity, and through a self-denying ordinance of stylistic puritanism, Burns's more elaborate diction is intimately involved in the clash of imperatives within the poetic frame, a sympathy derived not from an ethical benevolence but from common experience. Even the starkest of the *Lyrical Ballads* ('Love', p. 122) contains nothing like the directness of Burns's mixed diction:

Her Bosom heav'd – she stepp'd aside;
As conscious of my Look, she stepp'd –
Then suddenly with timorous eye
  She fled to me and wept.

The simplicity of the language here courts bathos without making the riskiness of the experiment part of the texture of the poem, and a major source of its enjoyment, as it is in Burns (*Love and Liberty: A Cantata*):

> The caird prevail'd: th'unblushing fair
> In his embraces sunk,
> Partly wi' love o'ercome sae sair,
> An' partly she was drunk.

Out of the comical clash of incongruous idioms, the Scots and the English, the formal and the bawdy, emerges a voice which has no need to turn aside from any aspect of experience. This is a 'sanctioned Babel', a mixing of tongues whose indecorous gaiety joins chaos and constraint into play.[14] A-social (if not positively anti-social) impulse is elevated in this cycle of poems to heroic proportions within a brutally comic context which acknowledges the controlling framework of existing Scots tunes even as it defies all the norms of history and community:

> Sir Wisdom's a fool when he's fou;
> Sir Knave is a fool in a Session,
> He's there but a prentice, I trow,
> But I am a fool by profession.

Wordsworth's poetry, standing as it does upon the 'native and naked dignity of man,' is never foolish. But Burns's verbal echo of Swift is considered and active. Madness, '*a perpetual Possession of being well deceived*', is described in *A Tale of a Tub* as 'the Serene Peaceful State of being a Fool among Knaves'.[15] Folly is the last refuge of the pleasure principle against the punitive sanctimonious alliance of wisdom and knavery. As Burns wrote in July 1787, to his friend Robert Ainslie, 'I never was a rogue, but have been a fool all my life; and, in spite of all my endeavours, I see now plainly that I never shall be wise' (*Letters*, I, pp. 129–30). His art of pleasure always has to do with acknowledging and accepting the self's claims, sometimes in relation to, sometimes in defiance of, everything beyond: time, circumstances, other people, life itself and death itself – all those things which threaten the continuance and the pleasure of the naked ego. This kind of pleasure is not a promise of futurity; it does not lay claim to virtue or to ultimate truth (Sir Wisdom) or to expediency (Sir Knave) – but it does confer value on the here and now, a value which cannot be denied by time, deprivation or death.

In *Love and Liberty*, sensibility and sympathy leave the domain of polite society and align themselves, like the desolates on the heath in *King Lear*, with the community of need. The personal voices in this sequence of songs speak a polemic against conventional identity straight from the sources of selfhood; they celebrate natural instinct and anarchic impulses, but their random coming-together provides a focus for all in human nature that is extreme, attractive and impossible to realise in a normal social context:[16]

Life is all a VARIORUM,
  We regard not how it goes;
Let them cant about DECORUM,
  Who have character to lose.
A fig for those by law protected!
  LIBERTY'S a glorious feast!
Courts for cowards were erected,
  Churches built to please the PRIEST!

Such cynical gaiety would be desperate, were it not that convivial feelings come to override other imperatives through the rollicking dynamics of the verse. Here is 'sympathy' of a very different – and politically dangerous – kind. It offers poetic freedoms not available to a writer who like Wordsworth is always himself, and whose sympathy begins in and returns to the strong base of eidetic ego. 'Radical pleasures' *are* available to Wordsworth's writing, but their source and expression stem from a different understanding of community. In the 1790s, Wordsworth's political impulses were galvanised into celebratory expression of a more *self*-containing kind at the outset of the French Revolution, as the 'Poet' of *The Prelude* revels in the fantasy of coming universal freedom:

  O pleasant exercise of hope and joy!
For great were the auxiliars which then stood

Upon our side, we who were strong in love!
Bliss was it in that dawn to be alive,
But to be young was very Heaven!
(*The Prelude*, X, 690–4)

Far from 'yield[ing] up moral questions in despair' as Wordsworth described himself in Book X of *The Prelude* when the French Revolution reneged on his blissful expectations, *Love and Liberty* rolls over them. It passes beyond conventional political process to expose the revolutionary possibilities of small private acts and moments of pleasure, moments whose value is held in a form the State cannot control, tax or appropriate to larger ends. In this poem, personal happiness is unashamedly equated with the gratification of impulses.

Burns's poetry of pleasure repeatedly courts moral disaster by its refusal to keep concealed the interface between pleasure-as-taste – reasonable enjoyment – and appetite, the delights of the senses unashamedly enjoyed without sublimation or what David Hartley had called 'coalescence' into higher pleasures.[17] In sympathetic identification with Elizabeth Paton, the mother of his first illegitimate child, the poet celebrates at once the pleasures of defying decorum, and the larger consciousness implied by accepting the consequences of vaulting the moral pale for the sake of pleasure:

O wha my babie-clouts will buy,
O wha will tent me when I cry;
Wha will kiss me where I lie,
The rantin dog the daddie o't. . . .

When I mount the Creepie-chair,
Wha will sit beside me there,
Gie me Rob, I'll seek nae mair,
The rantin dog, the Daddie o't.

Wha will crack to me my lane;
Wha will mak me fidgin fain;
Wha will kiss me o'er again
The rantin dog the Daddie o't.

This is a poem which moves precisely in the interface of rational pleasure and sensual hunger, desire and loss; it openly acknowledges, too, the place of appetite as an ingredient in poetic pleasure. All the decisions have already been made by the speaker; her commitment to pleasure *seems* inevitable and unconsidered, but its consequences are those of choice. The 'Creepie chair' (the stool of repentence in the kirk where fornicators did humiliating public penance), the responsibilities brought by the child itself, the times of crying the girl knows to await her: all these suggest reflection and desolation beyond the sensual pleasures of the moment, an awareness of the cost of gratification which brings poignancy and gaiety tautly together. The poem is full of conflict: the self which asserts the right to pleasure against the world's censure is still arguing the point inside. The debate within the speaker raises all the possibilities of desolation ('wha will tent me when I cry'), all the moments beyond the here and now of pleasure. The repeated answer to these questions, arrived at with relief in the anchoring refrain at the end of every stanza, is only just, riskily, adequate. It stills the anxious movement of the verse, but hardly quiets the fears. Having a 'Daddie' who is a 'rantin dog' is a fine and exciting thing indeed, but it guarantees nothing for the future. But still, the poem opts for pleasure, turns aside doubts. Security looks dull, and the rantin dog carries the day.[18]

It seems to have been this quality in Burns's poems which troubled Francis Jeffrey, when he reviewed Cromek's *Reliques of Robert Burns* for *The Edinburgh Review* in 1809. Jeffrey's article attempted to move beyond the sentimentalists' appropriation of Burns; taking issue with Henry Mackenzie's idea of the ploughman poet who celebrated the simple pleasures of rural life and love, he pointed out that many of Burns's poems are in fact quite heartless in terms of the ethics of sympathy: the pleasure they announce is implicitly, if not overtly, achieved *at the expense* of another:

> That profligacy is almost always selfishness, and that the excuse of impetuous feeling can hardly ever be justly pleaded for those who neglect the ordinary duties of life, must be apparent, we think, even to the least reflecting of those sons of fancy and song. It requires . . . [only] the information of an honest

> heart, to perceive that it is cruel and base to spend, in vain superfluities, that money which belongs of right to the pale industrious tradesman and his famishing infants; or that it is a vile prostitution of language, to talk of that man's generosity or goodness of heart, who sits raving about friendship and philanthropy in a tavern, while his wife's heart is breaking at her cheerless fireside, and his children pining in solitary poverty.[19]

Jeffrey's harsh words point out the problematic relationship of 'pleasure' to social imperatives; even 'sociability,' it seems, may be only disguised gratification of selfish impulse. The charge cannot be lightly dismissed, for here is Jeffrey challenging the very source of Burns's poetic pleasure: 'He is perpetually making a parade of his thoughtlessness, inflammability and imprudence, and talking with much complacency and exultation of the offence he has occasioned to the sober and correct part of mankind' (p. 183). Burns's best poetry, putting itself definitively outside the comfortable ethical equation of pleasure and instruction, makes it perfectly clear (against all Pope's hopeful precepts in *The Essay on Man,* or the imperatives of sympathy) that 'self-love and social' were *not* in fact, or need not be, the same.[20] The moral *bono publico* cannot weigh against the pleasures of the moment; when it comes to the naked operation of the pleasure principle, sociability of sentiment cannot be relied upon to harness instinct. It is a crucial argument against an ethics of sympathy. Jeffrey was surely right to be troubled, and to point to the dangerousness of this art of Pleasure.

Wordsworth, like Jeffrey refusing to be turned aside from the problem, tried to make a different kind of accommodation between pleasure and morality in Burns's poetry:

> it is the privilege of poetic genius to catch . . . a spirit of pleasure wherever it can be found, – in the walks of nature, and in the business of men. – The poet, trusting to primary instincts, luxuriates among the felicities of love and wine, . . . nor does he shrink from the company of the passion of love though intemperate. . . . Frequently and admirably has Burns given way to these impulses of nature; both with reference to himself, and in describing the condition of others. . . . I

> pity him who cannot perceive that, in all this, though there was no moral purpose, there is a moral effect.[21]

Wordsworth's defence of Burns creates a sanitised and sentimentalised Poet of Pleasure and keeps concealed the contested boundary between sociable pleasure and personal appetite, the very region in which Burns's poetry plays, and which the rhetoric of sympathy seeks always to deny. Abstracting morality from intention, Wordsworth is able to assimilate it to pleasure (also elevated to a 'spirit') with less appearance of inconsistency. He recognised, however, that the heightened sense of pleasure in Burns's writing is not contradicted by, but rather depends upon the fact that he 'was a man who preached from the text of his own errors'.[22] The disparity between moral desires and their accomplishment became part of the 'Burns myth' that the poet died victim to his failure to find a measuring relationship to pleasure, flying between bouts of extreme gloom and dizzy intemperance.

And yet Burns seemed undeniably and supremely a *poet* of pleasure, celebrating and turning to delight the appetites which, in their excess, destroyed him. Knowing strongly 'the pleasure which there is in life itself', *his* acute ear for human foolishness might well have mocked the absence of self-irony in Wordsworth's tone; *his* self-characterisations have nothing of the stature of Wordsworth's 'Poet': 'I have yet fixed on nothing with respect to the serious business of life. I am just, as usual, a rhyming, mason-making, rattling, aimless, idle fellow' (*Letters*, I, p. 126). The native and naked dignity of man was only one side of the story; equally strong and constantly present in his writing is an awareness of weakness, incapacity and pitiful smallness. 'Good God!' he wrote melodramatically to Deborah Duff Davies in 1793, 'why this disparity between our wishes & our powers!' (*Letters*, II, p. 202). This doubleness of perception *required* a poetic diction whose voices could entertain antipodes. Put differently, there is nothing naive about either Burns's directness or his adoption of the poetic voices of others.

Criticising Currie's 'Life of Burns' in 1816, Wordsworth's defence of the poet's memory is equivocal and uneasy: Currie's account, he writes, 'is incomplete, – in essentials it is deficient; so that the most attentive and sagacious reader cannot explain how a mind, so well established by knowledge, fell – and continued to fall, without power to prevent or retard its own ruin' ('Letter to a Friend . . .,' p. 206). Wordsworth's regretful observation that 'the order of [Burns's] life but faintly corresponded with the clearness of his views' (p. 215) actually provides an important handle into the particular quality of pleasure in Burns's poetry. Wordsworth's views and his life are almost uncannily of a piece; his biography gives a sense of a man unusually self-contained, with a settled sense of purpose and secure sense of poetic mission, a man whose needs were nicely attuned to his ability to fulfil them and whose life was scarcely blighted by a discrepancy between reach and grasp. His defence of Burns is coloured by his mystification about the relationship between the poetry he admired and the life he could not understand.[23] Looking for a consistency which the poetry itself declares would not – could not – be there, he elevates the principle of poetic pleasure into a transcending, unifying condition of Being.

Such alignment with life was never possible for Burns, who dramatised (with a powerful leaven of enjoyment) his self-destructive vacillations in a letter to Margaret Chalmers in 1787:

> My worst enemy is *Moimême.* I lie so miserably open to the inroads & incursions of a mischievous, light-armed well-mounted banditti, under the banners of imagination, whim, caprice, & passion; and the heavy armed veteran regulars of wisdom, prudence & fore-thought, move so very, very slow, that I am almost in a state of perpetual warfare, & alas! frequent defeat. There are just two creatures that I would envy, a horse in his wild state traversing the forests of Asia, or an oyster on some of the desart [*sic*] shores of Europe. The one has not a wish without enjoyment, the other has neither wish nor fear. (*Letters*, I, p. 185)

Byron, having been granted a glimpse of some of Burns's letters, regarded as quite unpublishable, exclaimed in his journal, 'What an antithetical mind! – tenderness, roughness – delicacy, coarseness – sentiment, sensuality – soaring and grovelling, dirt and deity – all mixed up in that one compound of inspired clay!'[24] There must be a large amount of self-recognition in such an observation; but with respect to Burns, it highlights precisely that antithetical co-existence of extremes from which oblivion is the only refuge. It is also, though, out of the very instability of passion that the self learns to value the pleasure of the moment. The emotional equation does not *easily* resolve itself in favour of what Wordsworth calls an overbalance of pleasure. Burns's language contains always a consciousness of the compound of opposites which does not deny (though it may regret) the connection of pleasure and appetite. To feel the utmost pleasure of life is also to open oneself most fully to its pains.

> Had we never lov'd sae kindly,
> Had we never lov'd sae blindly!
> Never met – or never parted,
> We had ne'er been broken-hearted.

In Burns's poetry, pleasure is scarcely ever separable from a double consciousness of power *and* weakness, delight *and* desertion, satisfaction *and* yearning, belonging *and* alienation.

As Wordsworth and Jeffrey both recognised, the moral crux of pleasure comes in *Tam O'Shanter*. The poem begins, easily enough, with a scene of sociable pleasure of a perfectly sanctioned, seemingly harmless kind:

> Ae market-night,
> *Tam* had got planted unco right;
> Fast by an ingle, bleezing finely,
> Wi' reeming swats, that drank divinely;
> And at his elbow, Souter *Johnny*,
> His ancient, trusty, drouthy crony;
> Tam lo'ed him like a vera brither;
> They had been fou for weeks thegither.
> The night drave on wi' sangs and clatter;
> And aye the ale was growing better:
> The landlady and *Tam* grew gracious,
> Wi' favours, secret, sweet, and precious:
> The Souter tauld his queerest stories;
> The landlord's laugh was ready chorus:
> The storm without might rair and rustle,
> Tam did na mind the storm a whistle.

These pleasures Wordsworth readily defended in the *Letter to a Friend of Robert Burns*:

> Who, but some impenetrable dunce or narrow-minded puritan in works of art, ever read without delight the picture which he has drawn of the convivial exaltation of the rustic adventurer Tam O'Shanter? . . . This reprobate sits down to his cups, while the storm is roaring, and heaven and earth are in confusion; – the night is driven on by song and tumultuous noise – laughter and jest thicken as the beverage improves upon the palate – conjugal fidelity archly bends to the service of general benevolence – selfishness is not absent, but wearing the mask of social cordiality – and, while these various elements of humanity are blended into one proud and happy composition of elated spirits, the anger of the tempest without doors only heightens and sets off the enjoyment within. . . . The poet, penetrating the unsightly and disgusting surfaces of things, has unveiled with exquisite skill the finer ties of imagination and feeling. (pp. 213–14)

The 'finer ties of imagination and feeling' belong perfectly to the aesthetics of Sensibility, but hardly to Tam O'Shanter. The poem's pleasures are not all as innocently convivial as Wordsworth would have them. It celebrates life not in the face of death but in the face of damnation. The obverse side of the tipsy amorousness of the tavern emerges in the wildly abandoned witches' dance in the wood where the decorous fiction of seduction is cast aside and frankly revealed as desire:

> As *Tammie* glowr'd, amaz'd, and curious,
> The mirth and fun grew fast and furious:
> The piper loud and louder blew;
> The dancers quick and quicker flew;
> They reel'd, they set, they cross'd, they cleekit,
> Till ilka carlin swat and reekit,
> And coost her duddies to the wark,
> And linket at it in her sark!

As Carol McGuirk has finely put it, the 'witches give up a hope for a feeling, a concept of redemption for a sensation of present pleasure'.[25] The temptations of the Devil are so irresistibly laid on for Tam that 'Even Satan glowr'd, and fidg'd fu' fain,/ And hotch'd and blew wi' might and main' at the effects of his own work. The danger of Tam's instant and eternal damnation is present and real, and not to be obscured by any of the euphemisms with which Wordsworth (and most of the poem's other readers) attempted to recuperate it for innocent social pleasures. Scott was nearer the mark when he wrote that 'In the inimitable tale of 'Tam O'Shanter', [Burns] has left us sufficient evidence of his ability to combine the ludicrous with the awful and even the horrible. No poet, with the exception of Shakespeare, ever possessed the power of exciting the most varied and discordant emotions with such rapid transitions.'[26] Real terror and real damnation lurk in the comic extravaganza:

> Coffins stood round, like open presses,
> That shaw'd the dead in their last dresses;
> And by some devilish cantraip slight
> Each in its cauld hand held a light. –
> By which heroic *Tam* was able
> To note upon the haly table,
> A murderer's banes in gibbet airns;
> Twa span-lang, wee, unchristened bairns . . .

The tone tells us that it is not to be taken *too* seriously: this is a complex mock-epic which can accommodate many voices, many forms of pleasure, amongst which is enjoyment of its own power to evoke the terror of wildly exploited Gothic sensations. But neither is it nugatory. The pleasure of the poem is intense because the terror that informs it is real. The delight of its mastery of tone and its hero's victory over circumstances are in fact a kind of revenge: against life, against death, against the powerful logic of Calvinist determinism. *Tam O'Shanter* promises no ultimate victory, but, like few other poems, it commits itself fully to the present pleasures of living, without counting their cost; its moments of wistfulness and its visions of the ideal have to take their chance between the wild whirl of existence here and now, and the formless threats of the future:

But pleasures are like poppies spread,
You seize the flower, its bloom is shed;
Or like the snow falls in the river,
A moment white – then melts for ever;
Or like the borealis race,
That flit ere you can point their place;
Or like the rainbow's lovely form
Evanishing amid the storm. –

Burns's narrative of *Tam O'Shanter* brings the full rhetorical range of sophisticated diction and poetic allusion to bear on Tam's abandonment to the powerful impulses of the moment. The doubleness does not cancel the delight, but complicates it into an 'Art' (rather than a rendition, or a discovery) of Pleasure. The timeless moment of the pleasure-principle and its costs in time are equally part of the poem's currency. The language keeps alive the physical component of sensations of the most contradictory kinds against the tendency of the aesthetics of sensibility to sublimate them to 'tender feelings' or moral imperatives. It seems a huge narrowing of emotional and poetic possibility to arrive at Wordsworth's address to the question of poetry's tempering relationship to 'raw', unruly pleasure of the type dramatised in *Tam O'Shanter*:

> The end of Poetry is to produce excitement in coexistence with an overbalance of pleasure. Now, . . . excitement is an unusual and irregular state of the mind; ideas and feelings do not in that state succeed each other in accustomed order. But if the words by which this excitement is produced are in themselves powerful, or the images and feelings have an undue proportion of pain connected with them, there is some danger that the excitement may be carried beyond its proper bounds. Now the co-presence of something regular, something to which the mind has been accustomed when in an unexcited or a less excited state, cannot but have great efficacy in tempering and restraining the passion by an intertexture of ordinary feeling. ('Preface', p. 264)

Poetic expression tames the transmission of pleasure; it imposes stability and form on 'unusual and irregular states of mind'.

In Wordsworth's poetry, 'pleasure' is almost always either an emotion recollected and recorded in this way by the poetic voice in tranquillity, or regarded in the behaviour and mien of observed subjects: the dancers in 'By Their Floating Mill,' or the audience of the street-musicians in 'The Power of Music,' for example (*Poems,* 1807). It becomes part of the poet's mission to seek out hidden and humble instances, to find 'Joy' in the life of the small celandine or the daisy:

> Thus pleasure is spread through the earth
> In stray gifts to be claim'd by whoever shall find.
> ('By Their Floating Mill')

Despite Hazlitt's percipient sarcasm,[27] Wordsworth (perhaps under the influence of his admiration for Burns's power to evoke the pleasures of life) seeks also to recover the 'natural' pleasures of physical sensation from the attenuating grasp of sensibility, but without awakening the concomitant dangers of appetite:

> O there is blessing in this gentle breeze
> That blows from the green fields and from the clouds
> And from the sky: it beats against my cheek,
> And seems half-conscious of the joy it gives.
> (*The Prelude* (1805), I, 1–5)

The Prelude opens in this way with a vision of the pleasure of poetic being; 'the mind's affirmation of itself', as Ross Woodman puts it, 'the blessing that it confers upon itself in the presence of its own activity'.[28] The pleasures of the poetry written under this impulse are a large and grand testimony to human dignity:

> these fields, these hills,
> Which were his living being even more
> Than his own blood (what could they less?), had laid
> Strong hold on his affections, were to him
> A pleasurable feeling of blind love,
> The pleasure which there is in life itself.
> ('Michael: A Pastoral Poem')

This 'pleasure which there is in life itself' is fundamental. It has, in both Wordsworth's and Burns's poetry, a solidity which does not render it liable to coalescence towards the transcendent. In this sense, their poetry shares a sense of satisfaction in the moment, rather than that restless, sublimating pain or dissatisfaction which drives the poetry of other Romantic writers (Shelley being perhaps the prime example) quickly towards the 'higher' pleasures of abstraction or philosophy.

Wordsworth shares their poetic impulse to transcendence too, however. Drink, love, lust and good company are distinctly secondary pleasures in the epic of the growth of the Poet's mind. Pleasure in Wordsworth's poetry always tends towards *joy* removed from sensual impulse, a pure and irreducible absolute in human experience and memory. 'Joy' is associated in both his poetry and critical writings not with weakness or impermanence but with the consciousness of power, of mastery and control not only over himself, but in relation to everything which lies beyond him, be it language, other people or the natural universe: 'the Poet binds together by passion and knowledge the vast empire of human society, as it is spread over the whole earth and over all time'. It is the Poet's duty to add 'the gleam, the light that never was, on sea, or land, / The consecration and the poet's dream.'[29]

It is a vision to which Burns's art of pleasure, rooted as it is in the senses, cannot aspire. His diction is at its most insecure when (as in 'The Vision') he attempts the transcendent. He cannot rise to Wordsworth's sublime simplicity. Barred from the mystical and the elevated, his best lyrics commit themselves and their reader recklessly to experiences which know the pain of impossible desire at the heart of the intensest delight:

As fair art thou, my bonie lass,
  So deep in luve am I,
And I will luve thee still, my dear,
  Till a' the seas gang dry.

Till a' the seas gang dry, my dear,
  And the rocks melt wi' the sun!
And I will luve thee still, my dear,
  While the sands o' life shall run.

And fare thee weel, my only love,
  And fair thee weel a while!
And I will come again, my luve,
  Tho' it were ten thousand mile!
    ('My luve is like a red, red rose')

The verse incorporates the ideal into the real without denying it or giving up everything else to it. Human yearning for impossible perfection remains; the lines hold out the possibility of making a relationship, perhaps only that of disparity, between desire and the loss which inheres in the actual. And having taken a hard look at everything which is beyond the pleasure principle, Burns's poetry returns to affirm the pleasures of the senses as the only thing which can hold against the progressive privations of life:

I ha'e been blithe wi' comrades dear;
  I ha'e been merry drinking;
I ha'e been joyfu' gathering gear;
  I ha'e been happy thinking;
But a' the pleasures e'er I saw,
  Though three times doubled fairly,
That happy night was worth them a',
  Amang the rigs o' barley.

'The Rigs o' Barley' canvasses a whole range of possible pleasures in its memory of the moment of supreme pleasure: it is here that both the extent and the limits of his poetic sympathies and capacity for pleasure become evident.[30] Sociability, the convivial and physical satisfactions of drinking, the pursuit of wealth and profit, solitary meditation: all are sanctioned sources of rational hedonism by the end of the eighteenth century, the acceptable faces of gratification – and all, here, simply overwhelmed by the power of experience. The verse, of course, controls the reader's pleasure in the redacted moment which is the transcription of the pleasure-moment: the hyperbole of 'tho' three times doubled fairly' heightens before dropping simply to the conclusive assertion 'That happy night was worth them a'.' This is where the *art* of pleasure has the power Plato identified in *The Republic* to intensify its audience's involvement beyond the scope of reason's control. Here, finally, past rhetorical effect, past aesthetic purpose or even rational explanation, is experience known, 'something' (to borrow a phrase from George Herbert) 'understood'.[31] Such art brings the moment of pleasure irresistibly from poetic memory into the present of the reader. Elbowing aside Beauty, Truth and the Good, it expands the intensity of the immanent, but promises nothing beyond. To read Burns's poetry is to feel that this is enough; to move to that of Wordsworth is to acknowledge again, perhaps inevitably, the impulse to yoke pleasure to the cause of a larger morality. Uniquely, Burns's poetry takes the Art of Pleasure outside the co-ordinates of eighteenth-century aesthetic debate; reintroducing poetics to the poetry of pleasure, Wordsworth sets out a Romantic aesthetic in which the newly-recognised problems of the pleasure equation resolve in a transcendent ethical dimension.

Notes and References

PREFACE *Marie Mulvey Roberts*

1. This line is spoken by Lord Illingworth in *A Woman of No Importance*; see Oscar Wilde, *Works*, ed. G. F. Maine (London: Collins, 1948), p. 428.
2. Michel Foucault, *The History of Sexuality*, vol. 1: *An Introduction*, trans. Robert Hurley (London: Penguin, 1990), p. 71.
3. Roland Barthes, *The Pleasure of the Text*, trans. Richard Miller (Oxford: Blackwell, 1990), p. 58.
4. Ibid., p. 57.
5. Ibid.
6. See Peter Quennell, *The Pursuit of Happiness* (London: Constable, 1988).
7. See Wilde, *Works*, p. 1113.

1. ENLIGHTENMENT AND PLEASURE *Roy Porter*

1. For the Greeks, see A. W. H. Adkins, *From the Many to the One: A Study of Personality and Views of Human Nature in the Context of Ancient Greek Society, Values and Beliefs* (London: Constable, 1970); C. M. Bowra, *The Greek Experience* (London: Weidenfeld and Nicolson, 1957); H. North, *Sophrosyne: Self-knowledge and Self-restraint in Greek Literature* (Ithaca, NY: Cornell University Press, 1966).

   On these and other issues, there is a wealth of learning in John Passmore, *The Perfectibility of Man* (London: Duckworth, 1972); see also Peter Quennell, *The Pursuit of Happiness* (London: Constable, 1988).
2. For Renaissance ideas of human nature and destiny, see Marsilio Ficino, *Three Books on Life*, trans. Carol V. Kaske and John R. Clark (Binghamton, NY: The Renaissance Society of America, 1989); Paul Kristeller, *Renaissance Thought and its Sources* (New York: Columbia University Press, 1979); Herschel Baker, *The Dignity of Man* (Cambridge, MA: Harvard University Press, 1947); J. B. Bamborough, *The Little World of Man* (London: Longman, Green, 1952).
3. R. Williams, *The Country and the City* (London: Chatto & Windus, 1973); Ronald Hutton, *The Rise and Fall of Merry England* (Oxford: Oxford University Press, 1994).
4. For Christian attitudes, see Peter Brown, *The Body and Society: Men, Women and Sexual Renunciation in Early Christianity* (New York: Columbia University Press, 1988).

5. W. Kaiser, *Praisers of Folly* (Cambridge, MA: Harvard University Press, 1963); M. M. Bakhtin, *Rabelais and his World*, trans. H. Iswolsky (Cambridge, MA: MIT Press, 1968); for the ambiguities of the traditonal body, see Gail Kern Paster, *The Body Embarrassed: Drama and the Disciplines of Shame in Early Modern England* (Ithaca, NY: Cornell University Press, 1993).

6. Eric Dodds, *The Greeks and the Irrational* (Berkeley, CA: University of California Press, 1951).

7. See the excellent section in Alisdair Macintyre, *A Short History of Ethics* (London: Routledge & Kegan Paul, 1966), and Peter Brown, *The World of Late Antiquity: From Marcus Aurelius to Muhammad* (London: Thames & Hudson, 1971).

8. For Christianity see E. Pagels, *Adam, Eve and the Serpent* (London: Weidenfeld & Nicolson, 1988); T. S. R. Boase, *Death in the Middle Ages: Mortality, Judgement and Remembrance* (New York: McGraw-Hill, 1972); M. W. Bloomfield, *The Seven Deadly Sins* (East Lansing, MI: Michigan State University Press, 1952); John Bowker, *Problems of Suffering in Religions of the World* (Cambridge: Cambridge University Press, 1970); Jean Delumeau, *Sin and Fear: The Emergence of a Western Guilt Culture, 13th–18th Centuries* (New York: St Martin's Press, 1990). Theological rigorism and ecclesiastical repression are explored in R. I. Moore, *The Formation of a Persecuting Society: Power and Deviance in Western Europe A.D. 950–1250* (Oxford: Basil Blackwell, 1987); Jeffrey Richards, *Sex, Dissidence and Damnation. Minority Groups in the Middle Ages* (London: Routledge, 1990); Piero Camporesi, *The Fear of Hell: Images of Damnation and Salvation in Early Modern Europe*, trans. Lucinda Byatt (Oxford: Basil Blackwell, 1990).

9. For death, see L. P. Kurtz, *The Dance of Death and the Macabre Spirit in European Literature* (New York: Institute of French Studies, 1934); J. M. Clark, *The Dance of Death in the Middle Ages and the Renaissance* (Glasgow: Jackson, 1950); Nigel Llewellyn, *The Art of Death* (London: Reaktion Books, 1991); Philippe Ariès, *Western Attitudes Towards Death: From the Middle Ages to the Present* (London: Marion Boyars, 1976). For later, less macabre attitudes, see John McManners, *Death and the Enlightenment* (Oxford: Clarendon Press, 1981).

10. John Sekora, *Luxury: The Concept in Western Thought – Eden to Smollett* (Baltimore, MD: The Johns Hopkins University Press, 1977); K. Sharpe, *Criticism and Compliment: The Politics of Literature in the England of Charles I* (Cambridge: Cambridge Univeresity Press, 1987). Not least, moralists denounced such traditions as sexually corrupt: Jonathan Goldberg, *Sodometries: Renaissance Texts, Modern Sexualities* (Stanford, CA: Stanford University Press, 1992).

11. The new rational theologies will be examined below, but for general viewpoints see G. R. Cragg, *From Puritanism to the Age of Reason: A Study of Changes in Religious Thought within the Church of England, 1660–1700* (Cambridge: Cambridge University Press, 1950); G. R. Cragg, *The Church and the Age of Reason* (Harmondsworth: Penguin, 1960); G. R. Cragg, *Reason and Authority in the Eighteenth Century* (Cambridge:

Cambridge University Press, 1964); N. Sykes, *Church and State in England in the Eighteenth Century* (Cambridge: Cambridge University Press, 1934); J. V. Price, 'Religion and Ideas', in Pat Rogers (ed.), *The Context of English Literature: The Eighteenth Century* (London: Methuen, 1978), pp. 120–52; E. G. Rupp, *Religion in England, 1688–1791* (Oxford: Clarendon Press, 1986).

12. There is no room here to explore contested interpretations of the Enlightenment: see Roy Porter, *The Enlightenment* (London: Macmillan, 1990). The discussion in this chapter endorses the optimistic view advanced by Peter Gay, *The Enlightenment: An Interpretation*, 2 vols (New York: Knopf, 1967–9). A keynote of Gay's Enlightenment is the deployment of reason to bring about human happiness.

See also Ernst Cassirer, *The Philosophy of the Enlightenment* (Boston, MA: Beacon, 1964); Robert Anchor, *The Enlightenment Tradition* (Berkeley, CA: University of California Press, 1967) is clear; useful on England are J. Redwood, *Reason, Ridicule and Religion: The Age of Enlightenment in England, 1660–1750* (London: Thames and Hudson, 1976) and Roy Porter, 'The Enlightenment in England', in R. Porter and M. Teich (eds), *The Enlightenment in National Context* (Cambridge: Cambridge University Press, 1981), pp. 1–18. For anthologies, see L. M. Marsak (ed.), *The Enlightenment* (New York: Wiley, 1972); L. G. Crocker (ed.), *The Age of Enlightenment* (New York: Harper, 1969).

13. Thomas Hobbes, *Leviathan*, ed. A. D. Lindsay (New York: Everyman Library, 1953; 1st edn, London: Crooke, 1651); for the debate over Hobbes, see Samuel I. Mintz, *The Hunting of Leviathan* (Cambridge: Cambridge University Press, 1962). The conflict between the self-interested rational individual and the hierarchical society forms the premise of J. L. Clifford (ed.), *Man Versus Society in Eighteenth Century Britain: Six Points of View* (Cambridge: Cambridge University Press, 1968).

14. Rudolf Dekker, '"Private Vices, Public Virtues" Revisited: The Dutch Background of Bernard Mandeville', *History of European Ideas*, XIV (1992), pp. 481–98.

15. Bernard de Mandeville, *The Fable of the Bees: or, Private Vices, Publick Benefits*, ed. Philip Harth (Harmondsworth: Penguin, 1970; first edn, London: J. Roberts, 1714), p. 64. For interpretation, see E. G. Hundert, *The Enlightenment's Fable: Bernard Mandeville and the Discovery of Society* (Cambridge: Cambridge University Press, 1994); R. I. Cook, *Bernard Mandeville* (New York: Twayne Publishers, 1974); M. M. Goldsmith, *Private Vices, Public Benefits: Bernard Mandeville's Social and Political Thought* (Cambridge: Cambridge University Press, 1985); T. A. Horne, *The Social Thought of Bernard Mandeville: Virtue and Commerce in Early Eighteenth-Century England* (London: Macmillan, 1978); Louis Dumont, *From Mandeville to Marx: the Genesis and Triumph of Economic Ideology* (Chicago, IL: University of Chicago Press, 1977); Dario Castiglione, 'Excess, Frugality and the Spirit of Capitalism: Readings of Mandeville on Commercial Society', in Joseph Melling and Jonathan

Barry (eds), *Production, Consumption and Values in Historical Perspective* (Exeter: University of Exeter Press, 1992), pp. 155–79.

16. Mandeville, *The Fable of the Bees,* pp. 67–8.
17. Ibid., p. 69.
18. Ibid., p. 76.
19. Ibid., p. 76.
20. Leslie Stephen, *English Thought in the Eighteenth Century,* 2 vols (New York: Brace & World, 1962); John Hedley Brooke, *Science and Religion: Some Historical Perspectives* (Cambridge: Cambridge University Press, 1991); Charles E. Raven, *Natural Religion and Christian Theology,* vol. 1: *Science and Religion* (Cambridge: Cambridge University Press, 1953); vol. 2: *Experience and Interpretation* (Cambridge: Cambridge University Press, 1953); A. O. Lovejoy, *The Great Chain of Being* (Cambridge, MA: Harvard University Press, 1936); R. N. Stromberg, *Religious Liberalism in Eighteenth-Century England* (London: Oxford University Press, 1954). For the decline of Hell, see Philip C. Almond, *Heaven and Hell in Enlightenment England* (Cambridge: Cambridge University Press, 1994). For theistic religious thought, see Peter Gay, *Deism. An Anthology* (Princeton, NJ: Princeton University Press, 1968). For secularisation, see Frank E. Manuel, *The Eighteenth Century Confronts the Gods* (Cambridge, MA: Harvard University Press, 1959; Frank E. Manuel, *The Changing of the Gods* (Hanover and London: University Press of New England and Brown University Press, 1983); Pieter Spierenburg, *The Broken Spell: A Cultural and Anthropological History of Preindustrial Europe* (London: Macmillan, 1991); Keith Thomas, *Religion and the Decline of Magic: Studies in Popular Beliefs in Sixteenth and Seventeenth-Century England* (London: Weidenfeld & Nicolson, 1971); W. O. Chadwick, *The Secularization of the European Mind in the Nineteenth century* (Cambridge: Cambridge University Press, 1975). A classic expression of the natural theology of an ordered world is Alexander Pope's 'Essay on Man', in J. Butt (ed.), *The Poems of Alexander Pope* (London: Methuen, 1965).
21. Margaret Jacob argues that such views were congruent with the optimistic philosophy of moderate Whigs who achieved power under the Hanoverians. They contended that the benificence of the system was a reason for obedience: M. C. Jacob, *The Newtonians and the English Revolution, 1689–1720* (Ithaca: Cornell University Press, 1976).
22. On such environmental views, see C. Glacken, *Traces on the Rhodian Shore: Nature and Culture in Western Thought from Ancient Times to the End of the Eighteenth Century* (Berkeley, CA: University of California Press, 1967); C. H. Vereker, *Eighteenth-Century Optimism* (Liverpool: Liverpool University Press, 1967).
23. Pat Rogers, *Johnson* (Oxford: Oxford University Press, 1993); Gloria Sybil Gross, *This Invisible Riot of the Mind: Samuel Johnson's Psychological Theory* (Baltimore, MD: University of Pennsylvania Press, 1992); C. Pierce, *The Religious Life of Samuel Johnson* (London: Athlone, 1983); R. B. Schwarz, *Samuel Johnson and the Problem of Evil* (Madison, WI: University of Wisconsin Press, 1975). Johnson's *bête noire* was the un-

thinking optimism of Soame Jenyns's *Free Inquiry into the Nature and Origin of Evil. In Six Letters* (London: printed for R. & J. Dodsley, 1757).

See also Peter Gay, *Voltaire's Politics: The Poet as Realist* (New York: Vintage, 1956). Good and evil were perceived to be deeply interwoven: see Jean Starobinski, *The Remedy in the Disease: Critique and Legitimation of Artifice in the Age of Enlightenment* (Cambridge: Polity Press, 1992).

24. Ernest Lee Tuveson, *Millennium and Utopia: A Study in the Background of the Idea of Progress* (New York: Harper & Row, 1964).

25. For moral philosophy, see L. A. Selby-Bigge, *British Moralists*, 2 vols (Oxford: Clarendon Press, 1897); S. C. Brown (ed.), *Philosophers of the Enlightenment* (Brighton: Harvester Press, 1979); Peter Jones (ed.), *The 'Science' of Man in the Scottish Enlightenment: Hume, Reid, and their Contemporaries* (Edinburgh: Edinburgh University Press, 1989); Richard Olson, *The Emergence of the Social Sciences, 1642–1792* (New York: Twayne 1993).

26. Lawrence E. Klein, *Shaftesbury and the Culture of Politeness* (Cambridge and New York: Cambridge University Press, 1994); Anthony, 3rd Earl of Shaftesbury, *An Inquiry Concerning Virtue and Merit*, in *Characteristicks of Men, Manners, Opinions, Times etc*, 2 vols, ed. J. M. Robertson (London: G. Richards, 1900); B. Rand, *The Life, Unpublished Letters and Philosophical Regimen of Anthony, Earl of Shaftesbury* (London: S. Sonnenschein, 1900).

On aesthetic pleasure, see B. Sprague Allen, *Tides in English Taste (1619–1800): A Background for the Study of Literature*, 2 vols (Cambridge, MA: Harvard University Press, 1937; Walter Jackson Bate, *From Classic to Romantic: Premises of Taste in Eighteenth-Century England* (Cambridge, MA: Harvard University Press, 1946); Samuel H. Monk, *The Sublime: A Study of Critical Theories in Eighteenth Century England* (Ann Arbor, MI: University of Michigan Press, 1960); S. Hipple, *The Beautiful, the Sublime and the Picturesque in Eighteenth Century British Aesthetic Theory* (Carbondale, IL: Southern Illinois University Press, 1957); M. H. Abrams, *The Mirror and the Lamp: Romantic Theory and the Critical Tradition* (London: Oxford University Press, 1953).

27. On benevolist views of human nature, see David Spadafora, *The Idea of Progress in Eighteenth-Century Britain* (New Haven, CT and London: Yale University Press, 1990); F. J. Barker-Benfield, *The Culture of Sensibility: Sex and Society in Eighteenth Century Britain* (Chicago, IL: University of Chicago Press, 1992), deals with generosity of heart.

28. Roy Porter, 'Medicine in the Enlightenment', in C. Fox, R. Porter and R. Wokler (eds), *Inventing Human Science: Eighteenth Century Domains* (Berkeley, CA: University of California Press, 1995).

29. C. B. Macpherson, *The Political Theory of Possessive Individualism: Hobbes to Locke* (Oxford: Oxford University Press, 1962); H. P. Dickinson, *Liberty and Property: Political Ideologies in Eighteenth-century Britain* (London: Weidenfeld & Nicolson, 1977).

30. For the psychological individualism entailed in such views, see

J. O. Lyons, *The Invention of the Self* (Carbondale, IL: Southern Illinois University Press, 1978); P. M. Spacks, *Imagining a Self* (Cambridge, MA: Harvard University Press, 1976); Charles Taylor, *Sources of the Self: The Making of the Modern Identity* (Cambridge: Cambridge University Press, 1989); G. S. Rousseau, 'Psychology', in G. S. Rousseau and Roy Porter (eds), *The Ferment of Knowledge* (Cambridge: Cambridge University Press, 1980), pp. 143–210.

31. This led to the image of 'economic man' within classical political economy, the notion that an optimal economic system involves competition between free individuals in a free market. See W. L. Letwin, *The Origins of Scientific Economics* (London: Methuen, 1963); J. O. Appleby, *Economic thought and Ideology in Seventeenth-Century England* (Princeton, NJ: Princeton University Press, 1978).

32. J. A. Passmore, 'The Malleability of Man in Eighteenth-Century Thought' in E. R. Wasserman (ed.), *Aspects of the Eighteenth Century* (Baltimore, MD: Johns Hopkins University Press, 1965), pp. 21–46; G. A. J. Rogers, 'Locke, Anthropology and Models of the Mind', *History of the Human Sciences,* VI (1993), pp. 73–88.

For Locke, see *An Essay Concerning Humane Understanding,* ed. P. Nidditch (Oxford: Clarendon Press, 1975); J. L. Axtell, *The Educational Works of John Locke* (Cambridge: Cambridge University Press, 1968); see also Maurice Cranston, *John Locke: A Biography* (London: Longmans, 1957); Ernest Lee Tuveson, *The Imagination as a Means of Grace: Locke and the Aesthetics of Romanticism* (Berkeley, CA: University of California Press, 1960).

33. John Locke, *An Essay Concerning Humane Understanding,* ed. P. Nidditch (Oxford: Clarendon Press, 1975), Book I, Ch. II, para. 15, p. 55.

34. For Locke's theory of mind and its influence, see John Yolton, *John Locke and the Way of Ideas* (New York: Oxford University Press, 1956); John Yolton, *Thinking Matter: Materialism in Eighteenth Century Britain* (Minneapolis, MIN: University of Minnesota Press, 1983); K. Maclean, *John Locke and English Literature of the Eighteenth Century* (New Haven, CT: Yale University Press, 1936); Gerd Buchdahl, *The Image of Newton and Locke in the Age of Reason* (London: Sheed & Ward, 1961); H. E. Allison, 'Locke's Theory of Personal Identity: A Re-Examination', in I. C. Tipton (ed.), *Locke on Human Understanding: Selected Essays* (Oxford: Clarendon Press, 1977), pp. 105–22.

35. Cosmic progress, driven by the quest of all creatures for happiness, was the theme of Erasmus Darwin's evolutionary speculations. See Maureen McNeil, *Under the Banner of Science: Erasmus Darwin and His Age* (Manchester: Manchester University Press, 1987).

36. For Hartley see Elie Halévy, *The Growth of Philosophic Radicalism* (London: Faber & Faber, 1928); Barbara Bowen Ogberg, 'David Hartley and the Association of Ideas', *Journal of the History of Ideas,* XXXVII (1976), pp. 441–54; C. U. M. Smith, 'David Hartley's Newtonian Neuropsychology', *Journal of the History of the Behavioral Sciences,* XXIII (1987), pp. 123–36; M. E. Webb, 'A New History of Hartley's *Observa-*

tions on Man', *Journal of the History of the Behavioral Sciences*, XXIV (1988), pp. 202–11; Margaret Leslie, 'Mysticism Misunderstood: David Hartley and the Idea of Progress', *Journal of the History of Ideas*, XXXIII (1972), pp. 625–32.

37. J. A. Passmore, *Priestley's Writings on Philosophy, Science and Politics* (New York: Collier Books, 1965); Anthony Hadley Lincoln, *Some Political and Social Ideas of English Dissent, 1763–1800* (Cambridge: Cambridge University Press, 1938); John Money, 'Joseph Priestley in Cultural Context: Philosophic Spectacle, Popular Belief and Popular Politics in Eighteenth-Century Birmingham', *Enlightenment & Dissent*, VII (1988), pp. 57–81; Jack Fruchtman, Jr, *The Apocalyptic Politics of Richard Price and Joseph Priestley: A Study in Late Eighteenth-Century English Republican Millennialism* (Philadelphia, PA: American Philosophical Society, 1983).

38. Phillipa Foot, 'Locke, Hume, and Modern Moral Theory: A Legacy of Seventeenth- and Eighteenth-Century Philosophies of Mind', in G. S. Rousseau (ed.), *The Languages of Psyche: Mind and Body in Enlightenment Thought* (Berkeley/Los Angeles/Oxford: University of California Press, 1991), pp. 81–106. Eighteenth-century thinking emphasised the pleasures of moral acts, as in philanthropy: Donna T. Andrew, *Philanthropy and Police: London Charity in the Eighteenth Century* (Princeton, NJ: Princeton University Press, 1989); Betsy Rodgers, *Cloak of Charity: Studies in Eighteenth Century Philanthropy* (London: Methuen, 1949); D. Owen, *English Philanthropy, 1660–1960* (Cambridge, MA: Harvard University Press, 1965).

39. F. L. Lucas, *The Search for Good Sense* (London: Cassell, 1958) has a sensible essay on Chesterfield. See also his *The Art of Living* (London: Cassell, 1959); S. M. Brewer, *Design for a Gentleman: the Education of Philip Stanhope* (London: Chapman & Hall, 1963); Charles Strachey (ed.), *The Letters of the Earl of Chesterfield to his Son* (London: Methuen, 1932).

40. Soame Jenyns, *Free Inquiry into the Nature and Origin of Evil. In Six Letters* (London: printed for R. and J. Dodsley, 1757).

41. For Bentham's life and thought see M. Mack, *Jeremy Bentham: An Odyssey of Idea, 1748–1792* (London: Heinemann, 1962); J. Dinwiddy, *Bentham* (Oxford: Oxford University Press, 1989); Ross Harrison, *Bentham* (London: Routledge & Kegan Paul, 1983). For changing views about pain, see Roy Porter, 'Pain and Suffering', in W. F. Bynum and Roy Porter (eds), *Companion Encyclopedia of the History of Medicine* (London: Routledge, 1993), pp. 1574–91. For hostility to cruelty towards animals, see Dix Harwood, 'Love for animals and how it Developed in Great Britain', PhD Thesis, Columbia University, New York (1928).

42. For Bentham's penal views, see Janet Semple, *Bentham's Prison: A Study of the Panopticon Penitentiary* (Oxford: Clarendon Press, 1993); M. Ignatieff, *A Just Measure of Pain: Penitentiaries in the Industrial Revolution, 1750–1850* (London: Macmillan, 1978). Bentham adopted liberal and hedonistic views on many issues, e.g. sexual preferences: Jeremy Bentham, 'Offenses Against One's Self: Paederasty', *Journal of*

Homosexuality, III (1978), pp. 389–405; IV (1979), pp. 91–109; respecting homosexuality, see G. S. Rousseau, 'The Pursuit of Homosexuality in the Eighteenth Century: "Utterly Confused Category" and/or Rich Repository?', in R. P. Maccubbin (ed.), *'Tis Nature's Fault: Unauthorized Sexuality during the Enlightenment* (Cambridge: Cambridge University Press, 1987), pp. 132–68.

43. See Erich Roll, *A History of Economic Thought* (London: Faber, 1938); J. A. Schumpeter, *History of Economic Analysis* (London: Allen & Unwin, 1954); Albert O. Hirschman, *The Passions and the Interests: Political Arguments for Capitalism before its Triumph* (Princeton, NJ: Princeton University Press, 1977); J. Viner, *The Role of Providence in the Social Order* (Philadelphia, PA: American Philosophical Society, 1972); I. Hont and M. Ignatieff (eds), *Wealth and Virtue. The Shaping of Political Economy in the Scottish Enlightenment* (Cambridge: Cambridge University Press, 1983); P. Deane, *The State and the Economic System: An Introduction to the History of Political Economy* (Oxford: Oxford University Press, 1989). For Locke and economics see C. G. Caffentzis, *Clipped Coins, Abused Words, and Civil Government. John Locke's Philosophy of Money* (New York: Autonomedia, 1989); W. George Shelton, *Dean Tucker and Eighteenth-Century Economic and Political Thought* (New York: St Martin's, 1981).

44. Joyce Appleby, 'Consumption in the Early Modern Social Thought', in John Brewer and Roy Porter (eds), *Consumption and the World of Goods* (London and New York: Routledge, 1993), pp. 162–75.

45. J. G. A. Pocock, *Politics Language and Time: Essays in Political Thought and History* (London: Methuen, 1972); J. G. A. Pocock, *The Machiavellian Moment. Florentine Political Thought and the Atlantic Republican Tradition* (Princeton, NJ: Princeton University Press, 1975).

46. For the defence of capitalism within the Scottish theory of progress, see Frank E. Manuel and Fritzie P. Manuel, *Utopian Thought in a Western World* (Cambridge, MA: Belknap Press, 1979); Ronald L. Meek, *Social Science and the Ignoble Savage* (Cambridge: Cambridge University Press, 1975); G. Bryson, *Man and Society: The Scottish Inquiry of the Eighteenth Century* (Princeton, NJ: Princeton University Press, 1945); Charles Camic, *Experience and Enlightenment: Socialization for Cultural Change in Eighteenth-Century Scotland* (Chicago, IL: University of Chicago Press, 1983); Jane Rendell, *The Origins of the Scottish Enlightenment* (London: Macmillan, 1978); Anand Chitnis, *The Scottish Enlightenment and Early Victorian Society* (London: Croom Helm, 1986).

47. Janet Todd, *Sensibility: An Introduction* (London: Methuen, 1986); Ann Jessie Van Sant, *Eighteenth-Century Sensibility and the Novel: The Senses in Social Context* (Cambridge: Cambridge University Press, 1993); John Mullan, *Sentiment and Sociability: The Language of Feeling in the Eighteenth Century* (New York: Oxford University Press, 1990). Many of these outlooks were, of course, explored in fiction. See Michael McKeown, *The Origins of the English Novel 1660–1740* (Baltimore, MD and London: Johns Hopkins University Press, 1987).

48. D. Bond (ed.), *The Spectator*, 5 vols (Oxford: Clarendon Press,

1965); Edward A. Bloom, Lilian D. Bloom and Edmund Leites, *Educating the Audience: Addison, Steele, and Eighteenth-Century Culture* (Los Angeles, CA: William Andrews Clark Memorial Library, 1984). For background to the politeness movement, see Norbert Elias, *The Civilizing Process*, vol. 1: *The History of Manners* (New York: Pantheon, 1978); vol. 2: *Power and Civility* (New York: Pantheon, 1982); vol. 3: *The Court Society* (New York: Pantheon, 1983). For the rise of the author, who publicised this civilising mission, see I. Watt, *The Rise of the Novel* (London: Chatto & Windus, 1957); A. Beljame, *Men of Letters and the English Reading Public in the Eighteenth Century, 1660–1744* (London: Kegan Paul, Trench, Trubner, 1948); P. Rogers, *Grub Street* (London: Methuen, 1972); J. W. Saunders, *The Profession of English Letters* (London: Routledge & Kegan Paul, 1964).

49. There were also counter-currents in the last third of the eighteenth century including the reassertion of traditional, conservative, Christian thinking. See J. H. Plumb, 'Reason and Unreason in the Eighteenth Century: The English Experience', in his *In the Light of History* (London: Allen lane, 1972); Maurice J. Quinlan, *Victorian Prelude: A History of English Manners, 1700–1830* (London: Cass, 1941). At the close of the century, Enlightenment hedonism was also attacked by Romanticism in the name of higher values. See Marilyn Butler, *Romantics, Rebels and Reactionaries: English Literature and its Background 1760–1830* (Oxford and New York: Oxford University Press, 1981; 1982); Marilyn Butler, 'Romanticism in England', in Roy Porter and Mikuláš Teich (eds), *Romanticism in National Context* (Cambridge: Cambridge University Press, 1988), pp. 37–67; Marilyn Butler (ed.), *Burke, Paine, Godwin, and the Revolution Controversy* (Cambridge/New York: Cambridge University Press, 1984). Malthus was then arguing that population (that is, sexual drives) was dangerously outrunning resources: Patricia James, *Population Malthus: His Life and Times* (London: Routledge & Kegan Paul, 1979).

Finally, for international comparisons and contrasts, see Robert Mauzi, *L'Idée du Bonheur dans la Littérature et la Pensée Française au XVIII Siècle* (Paris: Colin, 1960), and largely for Italy, Piero Camporesi, *Exotic Brew: Hedonism and Exoticism in the Eighteenth Century* (Cambridge: Polity Press, 1992).

2. MATERIAL PLEASURES IN THE CONSUMER SOCIETY — Roy Porter

1. In the eighteenth century, Jeremy Bentham of course attempted to do just that – to create a calibration of pleasure as part of his utilitarian philosophy. For Bentham's 'felicific calculus', see the chapter on 'Pleasure and Enlightenment' in this volume.

2. For Britain as a commercial society generating consumerism and perhaps a 'consumer revolution', see Neil McKendrick, John Brewer and J. H. Plumb, *The Birth of a Consumer Society: The Commercialization*

of Eighteenth-Century England (London: Europa, 1982); John Brewer and Roy Porter (eds), *Consumption and the World of Goods* (London: Routledge, 1993); Joyce Appleby, 'Consumption in the Early Modern Social Thought', in John Brewer and Roy Porter (eds), *Consumption and the World of Goods* (London and New York: Routledge, 1993), pp. 162–75.

In many ways, the Dutch Republic created modern pleasures before Britain, and so the Dutch first had to come to terms with their moral dilemmas: Simon Schama, *The Embarrassment of Riches: An Interpretation of Dutch Culture in the Golden Age* (London: Fontana, 1988).

3. For 'material culture' and the historical and theoretical debates surrounding it, see D. Miller, *Material Culture and Mass Consumption* (Oxford: Basil Blackwell, 1987); A. Appadurai (ed.), *The Social Life of Things* (Cambridge: Cambridge University Press, 1986); Chandra Mukerji, *From Graven Images: Patterns of Modern Materialism* (New York: Columbia University Press, 1983); Alan Macfarlane, *The Culture of Capitalism* (Oxford: Basil Blackwell, 1987).

4. C. C. Gillispie, *The Montgolfier Brothers and the Invention of Aviation 1783–1784* (Princeton, NJ: Princeton University Press, 1983).

5. Morton W. Bloomfield, *The Seven Deadly Sins: an Introduction to the History of a Religious Concept with Special Reference to Medieval English Literature* (Michigan: State University Press, 1967).

6. On aristocratic lifestyles see David Cannadine, *The Decline and Fall of the British Aristocracy* (New Haven, CT: Yale University Press, 1990); J. V. Beckett, *The Aristocracy in England, 1660–1914* (Oxford: Basil Blackwell, 1986); G. E. Mingay, *English Landed Society in the Eighteenth Century* (London: Routledge & Kegan Paul, 1963); Lawrence Stone and Jeanne C. Fawtier Stone, *An Open Elite? England 1540–1880* (Oxford: Clarendon Press, 1984). For a magnificent collective biography of a pleasure-loving aristocratic family, see Stella Tillyard, *Aristocrats* (London: Chatto & Windus, 1994).

7. The classic discussion is Thorstein Veblen, *The Theory of the Leisure Class* (New York: Macmillan, 1912).

8. The pioneer work here came from J. H. Plumb, *The Commercialization of Leisure in Eighteenth Century England* (Reading: University of Reading, 1973); J. H. Plumb, *Georgian Delights* (London: Weidenfeld & Nicolson, 1980).

9. Ronald Hutton, *The Rise and Fall of Merry England* (Oxford: Oxford University Press, 1994).

10. Mark Girouard, *Life in the English Country House* (New Haven, CT and London: Yale University Press, 1978); Jeremy Black, *The British and the Grand Tour* (London: Croom Helm, 1985).

11. For the town as a site of enjoyment, see Peter Borsay, 'The English Urban Renaissance: The Development of Provincial Urban Culture, *c.* 1680–1760', *Social History*, v (1977), pp. 581–603; Peter Borsay, 'All the Town's a Stage', in P. Clark (ed.), *The Transformation of English Provincial Towns (1660–1800)* (London: Hutchinson, 1985), pp. 228–58; Peter Borsay, 'Urban Development in the Age of Defoe',

in Clyve Jones (ed.), *Britain in the First Age of Party, 1684–1750* (London: The Hambledon Press, 1987), pp. 195–219; Peter Borsay, *The English Urban Renaissance: Culture and Society in the Provincial Town, 1660–1770* (Oxford: Clarendon Press, 1989).

For London, see Lawrence Stone, 'The Residential Development of the West End of London in the Seventeenth Century', in Barbara C. Malament (ed.), *After the Reformation: Essays in Honor of J. H. Hexter* (Philadelphia, PA: University of Philadelphia Press, 1979), pp. 167–212; Roy Porter, *London: A Social History* (London: Hamish Hamilton, 1994), Ch. 7.

12. R. W. Malcolmson, *Popular Recreations in English Society 1700–1850* (Cambridge: Cambridge University Press, 1973); Peter Burke, *Popular Culture in Early Modern Europe* (London: Temple Smith, 1978); E. P. Thompson, 'Time, Work-discipline and Industrial Capitalism', in *Customs in Common* (London: Merlin Press, 1991), pp. 352–403.

13. On the poor and their pleasures see Gertrude Himmelfarb, *The Idea of Poverty: England in the Early Industrial Age* (London: Faber; New York: Knopf, 1984); A. Clayre, *Work and Play: Ideas and Experience of Work and Leisure* (London: Weidenfeld & Nicolson, 1974). For Hogarth, see Ronald Paulson, *Hogarth, The 'Modern Moral Subject'*, vol. 1: *High Art and Low, 1732–1750*; vol. 2: *Art and Politics, 1750–1764* (Cambridge: Lutterworth, 1993); Neil McKendrick, 'Josiah Wedgwood and Factory Discipline', *The Historical Journal*, IV (1961), pp. 30–55; K. Thomas, 'Work and Leisure in Pre-industrial Society', *Past and Present*, XXIX (1964), pp. 50–66.

Some regarded the pleasures offered by cities as civilising, others saw them as Sodom: see M. Byrd, *London Transformed: Images of the City in the Eighteenth Century* (New Haven, CT and London: Yale University Press, 1978); Arthur J. Weitzman, 'Eighteenth Century London: Urban Paradise or Fallen City?', *Journal of the History of Ideas*, XXXVI (1975), pp. 469–80; R. Williams, *The Country and the City* (London: Chatto & Windus, 1973).

14. For the new 'pleasure preference', see Paul Langford, *A Polite and Commercial People: England 1727–1783* (Oxford: Oxford University Press, 1989) – a magnificent account of the lifestyles of the English. For a lower social stratum, see J. M. Golby and A. W. Purdue, *The Civilization of the Crowd: Popular Culture in England, 1750–1900* (London: Batsford, 1984).

15. For cultural performers, entrepreneurs and the new entertainment industry and media, see Michael Foss, *The Age of Patronage: The Arts in England 1660–1750* (Ithaca: Cornell University Press, 1972); John W. Saunders, *The Profession of English Letters* (London: Routledge & Kegan Paul/ Toronto: Toronto University Press, 1964); Pat Rogers, *Grub Street: Studies in a Subculture* (London: Methuen, 1972); Emmett L. Avery (ed.), *The London Stage 1600–1800*, 2 vols (Carbondale, IL: Southern Illinois University Press, 1968); Paula R. Backscheider, *Spectacular Politics: Theatrical Power and Mass Culture in Early Modern England* (Baltimore, MD: Johns Hopkins University Press, 1994); on the

commercialisation of the visual arts, see Iain Pears, *The Discovery of Painting: The Growth of Interest in the Arts in England, 1680–1768* (New Haven, CT: Yale University Press, 1988); Louise Lippincott, *Selling Art in Georgian London: The Rise of Arthur Pond* (London and New Haven, CT: Yale University Press, 1983).

16. Theorists of progress approved the new material enjoyments: see David Spadafora, *The Idea of Progress in Eighteenth-Century Britain* (New Haven, CT and London: Yale University Press, 1990).

17. Maxine Berg, *The Age of Manufactures, 1700–1820* (London: Fontana, 1985); P. J. Cain and A. G. Hopkins, *British Imperialism*, vol. i: *Innovation and Expansion, 1688–1914* (London: Longman, 1993); Peter Mathias, *The First Industrial Nation: An Economic History of Britain 1700–1914*, 2nd edn (London: Routledge, 1983); D. E. C. Eversley, 'The Home Market and Economic Growth in England 1750–1800', in E. L. Jones and G. E. Mingay (eds), *Land, Labour and Population in the Industrial Revolution* (London: Edward Arnold, 1967), pp. 206–59; Roderick Floud and Donald McCloskey (eds), *The Economic History of Britain since 1700*, 2 vols (Cambridge: Cambridge University Press, 1981).

Essential to commercial quickening was an information revolution, spurred by the development of newspapers. See Jeremy Black, *The English Press in the Eighteenth Century* (London: Croom Helm, 1986); R. McK. Wiles, *Freshest Advices: Early Provincial Newspapers in England* (Columbus, OH: Ohio State University Press, 1965); Geoffrey Alan Cranfield, *The Development of the Provincial Newspaper, 1700–1760* (Oxford: Clarendon Press; Westport, CT: Greenwood Press, 1962).

18. For the growing availability of objects of pleasure, see Carole Shammas, *The Pre-Industrial Consumer in England and America* (Oxford: Clarendon Press, 1990); Lorna Weatherill, *Consumer Behaviour and Material Culture, 1660–1760* (London: Routledge, 1988); Lorna Weatherill, 'The Meaning of Consumer Behaviour in Late Seventeenth and Early Eighteenth-Century England', in John Brewer and Roy Porter (eds), *Consumption and the World of Goods* (London and New York: Routledge, 1993), pp. 206–27; T. H. Breen, '"Baubles of Britain": The American and Consumer Revolutions of the Eighteenth Century', *Past and Present*, CXIX (1988), pp. 73–104; T. H. Breen, 'The Meanings of Things: Interpreting the Consumer Economy in the Eighteenth Century', in John Brewer and Roy Porter (eds), *Consumption and the World of Goods* (London and New York: Routledge, 1993), pp. 249–60; B. Fine and E. Leopold, 'Consumerism and the Industrial Revolution', *Social History*, XV (1990), pp. 151–79.

19. Isabel Rivers (ed.), *Books and Their Readers in Eighteenth Century England* (Leicester: Leicester University Press, 1982); Ian Watt, *The Rise of the Novel: Studies in Defoe, Richardson and Fielding* (London: Chatto & Windus, 1957); John Feather, *The Provincial Book Trade in Eighteenth Century England* (Cambridge: Cambridge University Press, 1985). For popular reading, see Patricia Anderson, *The Printed Image and the Transformation of Popular Culture 1790–1860* (Oxford: Clarendon Press, 1991). For literacy, see David Cressy, 'Literacy in Context:

Meaning and Measurement in Early Modern England', in John Brewer and Roy Porter (eds), *Consumption and the World of Goods* (London and New York: Routledge, 1993), pp. 305–19; D. Vincent, *Literacy and Popular Culture. England 1750–1914* (Cambridge: Cambridge University Press, 1989); Paul Kaufman, *Borrowings from the Bristol Library, 1773–1784: A Unique Record of Reading Vogues* (Charlottesville, VA: Bibliographical Society of the University of Virginia, 1960).

20. Peter Borsay (ed.), *The Eighteenth Century Town: A Reader in English Urban History 1688–1820* (London/New York: Longman, 1990); Peter Borsay and Angus McInnes, 'The Emergence of a Leisure Town: Or an Urban Renaissance?', *Past and Present,* CXXVI (1990), pp. 189–202.

21. Alison Adburgham, *Shopping in Style: London from the Restoration to Edwardian Elegance* (London: Thames & Hudson, 1979); David Alexander, *Retailing in England During the Industrial Revolution* (London: Athlone Press, 1970); Hoh-cheung Mui and L. Mui, *Shops and Shopkeeping in Eighteenth-Century England* (London: Methuen, 1987; London: Unwin, 1988; London: Routledge, 1989). The development in London of the pavement – unknown in Paris – aided window-shoppers.

22. Clare Williams (ed. and trans.), *Sophie in London, 1786, Being the Diary of Sophie v. La Roche* (London: Jonathan Cape, 1933), p. 87.

23. *Ibid.*, p. 237.

24. Robert Southey noted the splendour of English shops, and noted that London had invented the fast-food take-away: *Letters from England,* ed. Jack Simmons (Gloucester: Allan Sutton, 1984), p. 361.

25. Edward Copeland, 'Jane Austen and the Consumer Revolution', in J. David Grey, A. Walton Litz and Brian Southam (eds), *The Jane Austen Handbook: With a Dictionary of Jane Austen's Life and Works* (London: Athlone Press, 1986), pp. 77–92.

26. C. W. Chalklin, *The Provincial Towns of Georgian England* (Montreal: McGill University Press, 1974); P. J. Corfield, *The Impact of English Towns 1700–1800* (Oxford: Oxford University Press, 1982); Trevor Fawcett, *The Rise of English Provincial Art: Artists, Patrons and Institutions Outside London, 1800–1830* (Oxford: Clarendon Press, 1974). For a lively contemporary account of provincial towns bursting into life, see Daniel Defoe, *A Tour Through the Whole Island of Great Britain* (London: Dent, 1974).

27. Phyliss Hembry, *The English Spa 1560–1815: A Social History* (London: Athlone, 1990); R. S. Neale, *Bath 1680–1850: A Social History, or, A Valley of Pleasure Yet a Sink of Iniquity* (London and Boston, MA: Routledge & Kegan Paul, 1981).

28. John Travis, *The Rise of the Devon Seaside Resorts, 1750–1900* (Exeter: University of Exeter Press, 1993); John K. Walton, *Wonderlands by the Waves* (Preston: Lancashire County Books, 1992); Alain Corbin, *The Lure of the Sea: The Discovery of the Seaside in the Western World, 1750–1840* (Cambridge: Polity Press, 1994); John Alfred Ralph Pimlott, *The Englishman's Holiday: A Social History* (London: Faber & Faber, 1947); Jane Austen, *Sanditon,* ed. M. Drabble (Harmondsworth: Penguin, 1974).

29. For pleasure resorts, see William Biggs Boulton, *The Amusements of Old London: Being a Survey of the Sports and Pastimes, Tea Gardens and Parks, Playhouses and Other Diversions of the People of London from the 17th to the Beginning of the 19th Century* (London: J. C. Nimmo, 1901); Mollie Sands, *Invitation to Ranelagh 1742–1803* (London: John Westhouse, 1946).

30. For the commercial theatre see Marc Baer, *The Theatre and Disorder in Late Georgian London* (Oxford: Clarendon Press, 1991); Paula R. Backscheider, *Spectacular Politics: Theatrical Power and Mass Culture in Early Modern England* (Baltimore, MD: Johns Hopkins University Press, 1994).

31. E. Howe, *The First English Actresses: Women and Drama 1600–1770* (Cambridge: Cambridge University Press, 1992) and Kristina Straub, *Sexual Suspects. Eighteenth-Century Players and Sexual Ideology* (Princeton, NJ: Princeton University Press, 1991) explore the cult of the actor and actress.

32. David Cressy, *Bonfires and Bells* (London: Weidenfeld & Nicolson, 1989); S. Rosenfeld, *The Theatres of the London Fairs in the Eighteenth Century* (Cambridge: Cambridge University Press, 1960).

33. On sport, see Hugh Cunningham, *Leisure in the Industrial Revolution, c.1780–c.1880* (London: Croom Helm, 1980); R. Longrigg, *The English Squire and his Sport* (London: Joseph, 1977); John K. Walton and James Walvin (eds), *Leisure in Britain 1780–1939* (Manchester: Manchester University Press, 1983); Dennis Brailsford, *Sport, Time and Society* (London: Routledge, 1990); Dennis Brailsford, *British Sport: A Social History* (London: Lutterworth Press, 1992); W. Vamplew, *The Turf: A Social and Economic History of Horse Racing* (London: Allen Lane, 1974).

34. D. Brailsford, *Bareknuckles: A Social History of Prize-Fighting* (Cambridge: Lutterworth, 1988); John Ford, *Prizefighting. The Age of Regency Boximania* (Newton Abbot: David and Charles, 1971). Boxing and other sports involved heavy gambling. See John Ashton, *The History of Gambling in England* (London: Duckworth, 1898). It should be remembered that Georgian England had a national lottery: Cecil Henry L'Estrange Ewen, *Lotteries and Sweepstakes: An Historical, Legal and Ethical Survey of Their Introduction, Suppression and Re-establishment in the British Isles* (London: Heath Cranton, 1932).

35. H. C. Robbins Landon, *Handel and His World* (London: Weidenfeld & Nicolson, 1984); Eric David Mackerness, *A Social History of English Music* (London: Routledge & Kegan Paul, 1964). Alongside the pleasure garden was the masquerade: Terry Castle, *Masquerade and Civilization: The Carnivalesque in Eighteenth Century English Culture and Fiction* (London: Methuen, 1986). For other metropolitan amusements, see E. J. Burford, *Wits, Wenchers and Wantons: London's Low Life: Covent Garden in the Eighteenth Century* (London: Robert Hale, 1992). For street life see James Boswell, *Boswell's London Journal, 1762–1763*, ed. Frederick A. Pottle (London: Heinemann, 1950); John Gay, *Trivia; or, The Art of Walking the Streets of London*, ed. W. H. Williams (London: Daniel O'Connor, 1922).

36. R. D. Altick, *The Shows of London: A Panoramic History of Exhibitions, 1600–1862* (Cambridge, MA: Belknap Press, 1978); Ricky Jay, *Learned Pigs and Fireproof Women* (New York: Warner Books, 1986), pp. 277–8.

37. Kenneth Hudson, *A Social History of Museums* (London: Macmillan, 1975); Edward Miller, *That Noble Cabinet: A History of the British Museum* (London: Andre Deutsch, 1973).

38. Admirably discussed by J. H. Plumb, *The Commercialization of Leisure in Eighteenth-Century England* (Reading: University of Reading, 1973) See also his *Georgian Delights* (London: Weidenfeld & Nicolson, 1980).

39. A new cultural entrepreneur was the itinerant scientific lecturer: John R. Millburn, *Benjamin Martin: Author, Instrument-Maker and Country-Showman* (Noordhoff: Leyden, 1976); A. E. Musson and Eric Robinson, *Science and Technology in the Industrial Revolution* (Manchester: Manchester University Press, 1969); Larry Stewart, *The Rise of Public Science: Rhetoric, Technology, and Natural Philosophy in Newtonian Britain, 1660–1750* (Cambridge: Cambridge University Press, 1992); Simon Schaffer, 'Natural Philosophy and Public Spectacle in the Eighteenth Century', *History of Science,* XXI (1983), pp. 1–43.

40. Roger Elbourne, *Music and Tradition in Early Industrial Lancashire 1780–1840* (Woodbridge, Suffolk: the Folklore Society, 1980).

41. R. Malcolmson, *Popular Recreations in English Society 1700–1850* (Cambridge: Cambridge University Press, 1973).

42. Richard Warner, *The History of Bath* (Bath: Cruttwell, 1801), p. 349, quoted in Roy Porter, 'Science, Provincial Culture and Public Opinion in Enlightenment England', *The British Journal for Eighteenth Century Studies,* III (1980), pp. 20–46.

43. Stephen Mennell, *All Manners of Food: Eating and Taste in England and France from the Middle Ages to the Present* (Oxford: Basil Blackwell, 1985).

44. Peter Clark, *The English Alehouse: A Social History, 1200–1830* (London: Longman, 1983); Roy Porter, 'The Drinking Man's Disease: The 'Pre-History' of Alcoholism in Georgian Britain', *British Journal of Addiction,* LXXX (1985), pp. 385–96. The 1730s and 1740s saw the gin craze: M. D. George, *London Life in the Eighteenth Century* (Harmondsworth: Penguin, 1966); Peter Clark, 'The "Mother Gin" Controversy in the Early Eighteenth Century', *Transactions of the Royal Historical Society,* XXXVIII (1988), pp. 63–84. See also Jordan Goodman, *Tobacco in History: The Cultures of Dependence* (London: Routledge, 1993).

45. Stella Margetson, *Regency London* (London: Cassell, 1971).

46. Peter Wagner, *Eros Revived: Erotica in the Age of Enlightenment* (London: Secker & Warburg, 1986); Lawrence Stone, *The Family, Sex and Marriage in England, 1500–1800* (London: Weidenfeld and Nicolson, 1977). Much may be discovered about sexual expectations and activities from Lawrence Stone, *The Road to Divorce, England 1530–1987* (Oxford: Oxford University Press, 1990); Lawrence Stone, *Uncertain Unions: Marriage in England 1660–1753* (Oxford: Oxford University Press, 1992);

Lawrence Stone, *Broken Lives: Separation and Divorce in England 1660–1857* (Oxford: Oxford University Press, 1993); Stanley Nash, 'Social Attitudes towards Prostitution in London, from 1752 to 1829', PhD thesis, New York University, 1980; P.-G. Boucé (ed.), *Sexuality in Eighteenth Century Britain* (Manchester: Manchester University Press, 1982).

47. John Cleland, *Memoirs of a Woman of Pleasure*, ed. by Peter Sabor (Oxford: Oxford University Press, 1985); for discussion, see Randolph Trumbach, 'Modern Prostitution and Gender in Fanny Hill: Libertine and Domesticated Fantasy', in G. S. Rousseau and Roy Porter (eds), *Sexual Underworlds of the Enlightenment* (Manchester: Manchester University Press, 1987), pp. 69–85.

48. A. D. Harvey, *Sex in Georgian England. Attitudes and Prejudices from the 1720s to the 1820s* (London: Duckworth, 1994); Desmond King-Hele, *Doctor of Revolution: The Life and Genius of Erasmus Darwin* (London: Faber & Faber, 1977); Roy Porter and Lesley Hall, *The Facts of Life: The History of Sexuality and Knowledge from the Seventeenth Century* (New Haven, CT: Yale University Press, 1994).

49. Derek Jarrett, *The Ingenious Mr Hogarth* (London: Joseph, 1976); Michael Duffy (ed.), *The English Satirical Print, 1600–1832*, 7 vols (Cambridge: Chadwyck-Healey, 1986). For the pleasures of the bourgeoisie, see Peter Earle, *The World of Defoe* (London: Weidenfeld & Nicolson, 1976); Peter Earle, *The Making of the English Middle Class: Business, Society and Family Life in London, 1660–1730* (London: Methuen, 1989); Peter Earle, *A City Full of People* (London: Methuen, 1994).

50. On the Victorian 'anti-sensual' reaction, see Michael Mason, *The Making of Victorian Sexual Attitudes* (Oxford: Oxford University Press, 1994); Muriel Jaeger, *Before Victoria: Changing Standards and Behaviour, 1787–1837* (London: Chatto & Windus, 1956).

3. THE PLEASURES OF THE TABLE *Simon Varey*

1. Charles Carter, *The Complete Practical Cook* (London, 1730), title page and unnumbered folding plate.

2. Lydia Fisher, *The Prudent Housewife; or, Complete English Cook, for Town and Country*, 12th edn (London, 1791), p. 35.

3. See Thomas Short, *Discourses on Tea, Sugar, Milk, Made-Wines, Spirits, Punch, Tobacco, &c* (London, 1750) for prices and quantities.

4. On *The London Art of Cookery* (London, 1783) and Farley's plagiarisms, see Fiona Lucraft, 'The London Art of Plagiarism', *Petits propos culinaires*, 42 (1992), pp. 7–24 and 43 (1993), pp. 34–46.

5. Farley speaks of mankind's 'rude, but natural state', in which for 2000 years 'the cook and physician were equally unknown' (John Farley, *The London Art of Cookery*, ed. Ann Haly, introduction by Stephen Medcalf (Lewes, 1988), p. 21).

6. Henry Fielding, *The Journal of a Voyage to Lisbon*, Everyman edn (London and New York, 1932; reprinted 1973), p. 262.

7. Ibid.

8. Daniel Defoe, *A Tour thro' the Whole Island of Great Britain*, ed. G. D. H. Cole, 2 vols (London 1927), vol. 1, p. 225.

9. Fielding, *Lisbon*, pp. 263–4.

10. Ibid., p. 264.

11. J. C. Drummond and Anne Wilbraham, *The Englishman's Food: A History of Five Centuries of English Diet*, ed. Dorothy Hollingsworth (1957; reprinted London, 1991), p. 192.

12. Isabella Beeton, *Mrs. Beeton's Book of Household Management*, rev. edn (1861; reprinted New York, 1986), item 607, p. 283.

13. Hans Sloane, *A Voyage to the Islands Madera, Barbados, Nieves, S. Christophers and Jamaica with the Natural History of the Herbs and Trees, Four-footed Beasts, Fishes, Birds, Insects, Reptiles, &c. of the last of those Islands*, 2 vols (London, 1707–25), vol. 1, p. xvi.

14. *The Expedition of Humphry Clinker*, ed. Thomas R. Preston (Athens, GA, 1990), p. 118.

15. Ibid., p. 120.

16. Ibid., pp. 118–19.

17. Drummond and Wilbraham, *The Englishman's Food*, pp. 193–4.

18. Petronius, trans. Michael Heseltine, Loeb Classical Library, rev. edn (London, 1930), pp. 34, 36, 40, 49. Discovered only in the mid-seventeenth century, the manuscript of Petronius quickly turned Trimalchio's Feast into a byword for extravagance.

19. *Hell upon Earth: or the Town in an Uproar* (London, 1729), p. 28.

20. Ibid.

21. *The London Art of Cookery*, ed. Haly, p. 167.

22. *Emma*, vol. 3, Ch. 2, *The Novels of Jane Austen*, ed. R. W. Chapman, 5 vols (Oxford, 1926), vol. 4, p. 329.

23. Fisher, *Prudent Housewife*, pp. 119–20.

24. Alice and Frank Prochaska (eds), *Margaretta Acworth's Georgian Cookery Book* (London, 1987), p. 19.

25. Prochaska and Prochaska, p. 19, citing Stephen Mennell, *All Manners of Food: Eating and Taste in England and France from the Middle Ages to the Present* (Oxford, 1985). They give no page reference. Mennell discusses Anglo-French culinary and cultural relations, pp. 102–33.

26. Swift, *Prose Works* 13 (Oxford, 1959), p. 30.

27. *Hell upon Earth*, 28. 'Cullis' is a coulis, 'pupton' (or 'poupeton' in French) is a stewed bird that is then breaded and baked.

28. *Hell upon Earth*, p. 27.

29. *Hell upon Earth*, p. 29.

30. Patrick Lamb, *Royal Cookery: or, the Compleat Court-Cook*, 3rd edn (London, 1726), pref., n.p.

31. Ibid.

32. John Arbuthnot, *An Essay concerning the Nature of Aliments*, vol. 2: *Practical Rules of Diet in the various Constitutions and Diseases of Human Bodies* (London, 1732), p. 296.

33. See, for example, Thomas Tryon, *Wisdom's Dictates: or, Aphorisms & Rules, Physical, Moral, and Divine* [with] *A Bill of Fare of Seventy Five*

Noble Dishes of Excellent Food (London, 1691), a passionate defence of vegetarianism on gustatory, dietary, and ecological grounds.

34. *The Art of Cookery, Made Plain and Easy* (London, 1778), frontispiece.

35. Henry Hobhouse, *Seeds of Change: Five Plants that Transformed Mankind* (1985; reprinted New York, 1987), p. 74.

36. Lawrence Durrell, *The Dark Labyrinth* (London, 1964), p. 30.

4. PLEASURES ENGENDERED BY GENDER *Marie Mulvey Roberts*

1. Donald McCormick, *The Hell Fire Club* (London: Jarrolds, 1958), p. 7.

2. The focus here will be on London, as it is here that the greatest variety of clubs appear. Most cities have records of active club activity, such as Dublin, the home of a Hell Fire Club, Glasgow, where the Banditti met and Edinburgh, which had spawned the Puissant Order of the Beggars' Benison.

3. See Walter Arnold, *The Life and Death of the Sublime Society of Beef Steaks* (London: Bradbury, Evans, 1871).

4. Roy Porter, *English Society in the Eighteenth Century* (Harmondsworth: Penguin, 1982), p. 25.

5. See Robert J. Allen, *The Clubs of Augustan London* (Cambridge, MA: Harvard University Press), p. 31.

6. See Dena Goodman, 'Enlightened Salons: The Convergence of Female and Philosophic Ambitions', *Eighteenth-Century Studies*, XXII (1988–9), pp. 329–50; 'Seriousness of Purpose: Salonnières, Philosophes, and the Shaping of the Eighteenth-Century Salon', *Proceedings of the Annual Meeting of the Western Society for French History*, XV (1988), pp. 111–18; Lawrence E. Klein, 'Gender, Conversation and the Public Sphere in Early Eighteenth-Century England', in Judith Still and Michael Warton (eds), *Textuality and Sexuality: Reading Theories and Practices* (Manchester: Manchester University Press, 1993), pp. 100–15.

7. See J. Habermas, *The Structural Transformation of the Public Sphere: An Inquiry into a Category of Bourgeois Society*, trans. Thomas Burger with the assistance of Frederick Lawrence (London: Polity Press, 1989).

8. See Janet M. Burke, 'Freemasonry, Friendship and Noblewomen: The Role of the Secret Society in Bringing Enlightenment Thought to Pre-Revolutionary Women Elites', *History of European Ideas*, 10, no. 3 (1989), pp. 283–94.

9. See Olwen H. Hufton, *Women and the Limits of Citizenship in the French Revolution* (Toronto: University of Toronto Press, 1988).

10. The different women's movements and clubs are described in Elizabeth Roudinesco, *Théroigne de Méricourt: A Melancholic Woman during the French Revolution* (London: Verso, 1991).

11. For an insight into Augustan society see Pat Rogers, *The Augustan Scene* (London: Methuen, 1974).

12. *The Spectator*, ed. Donald Bond (Oxford: Clarendon Press, 1965), 1, p. 34.
13. See George Saintsbury, *The Peace of the Augustans: A Survey of Eighteenth-Century Literature as a Place of Rest and Refreshment* (London: G. Bell & Sons, 1916).
14. *The Poems by Henry Carey*, ed. F. T. Wood (London: E. Partridge, 1730), p. 249. Alexander Hamilton apparently wrote his mock-epic *History of the Tuesday Club* (*c.* 1752–6) to burlesque the Freemasons. See Robert Micklus, 'The Secret Fall of Freemasonry in Dr Alexander Hamilton's *The History of the Tuesday Club*', in J. A. Leo Lemay (ed.), *Deism, Masonry, and the Enlightenment: Essays Honoring Alfred Owen Aldridge* (Newark, NJ: University of Delaware Press, 1987), pp. 127–36.
15. *The History of Whites*, p. 27.
16. The verse is from the anonymous poem, 'The Address', written earlier in 1704 that is reprinted in Allen, *The Clubs of Augustan London*, p. 34.
17. Jane Austen, *Emma*, ed. Ronald Blythe (Harmondsworth: Penguin, 1966), p. 106.
18. Dr Johnson, *A Dictionary of the English Language*, 3 vols (London: Longman, Rees, Orme, Brown & Green, 1827).
19. See Allen, *The Clubs of Augustan London*, pp. 136–45.
20. John Gay, *Poetry and Prose*, ed. Vinton A. Dearing (Oxford: Clarendon Press, 1974), p. 458.
21. Edward Ward, *The Secret History of Clubs* (printed and sold by the booksellers, London, 1709), The Epistle Dedicatory.
22. See Allen, *The Clubs of Augustan London*, p. 183.
23. Edward Ward, *The History of the London Clubs or the Citizen's Pastime, particularly the Lying Club, The Yorkshire Club, The Thieves' Club, The Beggars' Club, The Broken Shopkeepers' Club, The Basket Women's Club with a Sermon Preached to a Gang of Highway-Men* (London: J. Bagnall, 1711), p. 2.
24. See Allen, *The Clubs of Augustan London*, p. 158.
25. *The Spectator*, 1, p. 35.
26. Ward, *The Secret History of Clubs*, p. 9.
27. See John Timbs, *London Clubs of the Metropolis during the 17th, 18th and 19th Centuries*, 2 vols (London: privately printed, 1866), 2, p. 173.
28. Ward, *The Secret History of Clubs*, p. 62–6.
29. *The Spectator*, I, p. 36. In his poem *The Borough*, George Crabbe writes; 'A Club there is of *Smokers* – Dare you come/To that close, clouded, hot, narcotic Room?'. See George Crabbe, Letter X 'Clubs and Social Meetings', *The Complete Poetical Works*, ed. Norma Dalrymple-Champneys and Arthur Pollard (Oxford: Clarendon Press, 1988), 1, p. 456.
30. See Allen, *The Clubs of Augustan London*, p. 169.
31. Ward, *The Secret History of Clubs*, p. 30.
32. Ibid, p. 31.
33. Ibid., pp. 162–3.

34. Ibid., p. 16.
35. Ibid., p. 107.
36. Allen, *The Clubs of Augustan London*, p. 170.
37. Allen, *The Clubs of Augustan London*, pp. 89–91 describes Daniel Defoe's satiric *The Secret History of the October Club: From its Original to this Time* (1711).
38. See Pat Rogers, 'The Breeches Part', in Paul-Gabriel Boucé (ed.), *Sexuality in Eighteenth-Century Britain* (Manchester: Manchester University Press, 1982), pp. 244–58.
39. Mark Blackett-Ord, *Hell-Fire Duke; The Life of the Duke of Wharton* (Windsor Forest, Berks: The Kensal Press, 1982), p. 44.
40. H. T. F. Rhodes, *The Satanic Mass* (London: Arrow, 1973), p. 147.
41. Ward, *The Secret History of Clubs*, p. 42.
42. *The Spectator*, I, 111.
43. See *The Spectator*, I, p. 110.
44. See Immanuel Kant, 'Answer to the Question: What is "Enlightening"?', in Simon Eliot and Beverley Stern (eds), *The Age of Enlightenment: An Anthology of Eighteenth-Century Texts* (London: Ward Lock Educational in association with the Open University Press, 1979) 2, pp. 249–55.
45. See Margaret Jacob, 'Freemasonry, Women and the Paradox of the Enlightenment', *Women and History*, 9 (1984), pp. 69–93.
46. See Dorothy Ann Lipson, *Freemasonry in Federalist Connecticut* (Princeton, NJ: Princeton University Press, 1977), p. 190.
47. Anon, *The Masonic Minstrel: Being a Complete Collection of Odes, Anthems, Songs, Prologues, Epilogues* (London: Johnson, 1828), p. 133.
48. Ibid.
49. See also Marie Mulvey Roberts, 'Who wears the Apron? Masonic Misogyny and Female Freemasonry', *Transactions of the Eighth International Congress on the Enlightenment* (Oxford: The Voltaire Foundation), II, pp. 812–16; and 'Masonics, Metaphor and Misogyny: A Discourse of Marginality', in Peter Burke and Roy Porter (eds), *Languages and Jargons: Contributions to a Social History of Language* (Cambridge: Polity in association with Blackwells, 1995), pp. 133–54.
50. Martin Short, *Inside the Brotherhood: Further Secrets of the Freemasons* (London: Grafton Books, 1989), p. 102.
51. See B. B. Schnorrenberg, 'Is Childbirth any place for a Woman? The Decline of Midwifery in Eighteenth-century England', *Studies in Eighteenth Century Culture*, X (1981), pp. 393–408; Jean Donnison, *Midwives and Medical Men: A History of Inter-Professional Rivalry and Women's Rights* (London: Heinemann, 1977); and Roy Porter, 'A Touch of Danger: The Man-midwife as a Sexual Predator', in G. S. Rousseau and Roy Porter (eds), *Sexual Underworlds of the Enlightenment* (Manchester: Manchester University Press, 1987), pp. 206–33.
52. Ward, *The Secret History of Clubs*, XXV.
53. Alan Bray, *Homosexuality in Renaissance England* (London: Gay Man's Press, 1982), p. 86.
54. Ibid., p. 87. Bray claims that Ward's description of the Mollies'

effeminacy 'is remarkably close to first-hand descriptions of the molly houses', as in the passage cited above on p. 86. For accounts of the trials see Anthony E. Simpson, 'Masculinity and Control: The Prosecution of Sex Offences in Eighteenth-Century London', unpublished PhD dissertation, New York University (1984). To avoid confusion between Mollies and Sodomites, it is useful to consult the articles written by Randolph Trumbach. See 'London's Sodomites: Homosexual Behaviour and Western Culture in the Eighteenth Century', *Journal of Social History*, II (1977), pp. 9–11; and 'Sodomitical Subcultures, Sodomitical Roles, and the Gender Revolution of the Eighteenth Century: The Recent Historiography', in Robert Purks Maccubbin (ed.), *'Tis Nature's Fault: Unauthorized Sexuality during the Enlightenment* (Cambridge: Cambridge University Press, 1987), pp. 109–21.

55. See *Public Ledger* for 26 August 1776; and M. Coryn, *The Chevalier D'Eon* (London: Thornton Butterworth, 1932).

56. *An Epistle from Mademoiselle D'Eon to the right Honorable L—D M—D C—F J—E of the C—Y of the K—G's B—H On his Determination in Regard to her Sex* (London: M. Smith, 1778), p. 23. See also Lynne Friedli, '"Passing Women" – A Study of Gender Boundaries in the Eighteenth Century', in G. S. Rousseau and Roy Porter (eds), *Sexual Underworlds of the Enlightenment*, pp. 244–6.

57. *The Spectator*, 2, p. 183.

58. Allen, *The Clubs of Augustan London*, p. 102.

59. *The Spectator*, IV, pp. 60–5.

60. Allen, *The Clubs of Augustan London*, p. 167.

61. Jane Elizabeth Moore, *Miscellaneous Poems on Various Occasions* (Dublin: privately printed, 1797), p. 26. J. M. Roberts in *The Mythology of the Secret Societies* (St Albans: Granada, 1974), pp. 66, 389 n, says that women were admitted but takes account of the comment made by the author of *La Franc-Maçonne ou Révélation des Mystères des Franc-Maçons* (Brussels, 1744), pp. 11–15, that these may not have been genuine lodges but ploys to allay female curiosity and also, perhaps, strategies for seduction.

62. Douglas Knoop, G. P. Jones and Douglas Hamer, *Early Masonic Pamphlets* (Manchester: Manchester University Press, 1945), p. 307.

63. Janet M. Burke, 'Freemasonry, Friendship and Noblewomen', 291n.

64. Crabbe, *The Complete Poetical Works*, ed. Norma Dalrymple-Champneys and A. Pollard, 1, p. 459.

5. 'THE LUXURY OF DOING GOOD': BENEVOLENCE, SENSIBILITY, AND THE ROYAL HUMANE SOCIETY *Carolyn D. Williams*

1. Jonathan Swift, 'Thoughts on Various Subjects' (1711), in *Prose Works*, ed. Herbert Davis and Irvin Ehrenpreis, 14 vols (Oxford: Basil Blackwell, 1939–68), I, p. 241.

2. *The Works of the Most Reverend Dr John Tillotson, late Lord Archbishop of Canterbury*, 8th edn (London: T. Goodwin, 1720), p. 172.
3. Ibid., p. 173.
4. Ibid., p. 174.
5. Ibid., p. 175.
6. Anthony Ashley Cooper, Third Earl of Shaftesbury, 'Concerning Virtue or Merit', Book I, Part II, Section II, in *Characteristics of Men, Manners, Opinions, Times*, ed. John M. Robertson, intro. by Stanley Grean, 2 vols in one (Indianapolis and New York: Bobbs Merrill, 1964), I, p. 248.
7. Ibid., Book II, Part I, Section I; I, p. 280.
8. Ibid., Book II, Part II, Section I; I, p. 294.
9. Ibid., I, p. 295.
10. Ibid., Book I, Part III, Section III; I, p. 273.
11. Ibid., Part III, Section IV; I, pp. 84–5.
12. Ibid., Section IV; I, p. 27.
13. Ibid., I, pp. 27–8.
14. Bernard Mandeville, *The Fable of the Bees: Or, Private Vices, Publick Benefits*, ed. F. B. Kaye, 2 vols (Oxford: Clarendon, 1924), I, p. 253.
15. Ibid., I, p. 259.
16. Ibid., I, p. 57.
17. David Hume, *A Treatise of Human Nature*, ed. L. A. Selby-Bigge (Oxford: Clarendon, 1896), Book III, Part III, Section I, p. 574.
18. David Hume, 'An Enquiry Concerning the Principles of Morals', Section IX, Part II, in *Enquiries Concerning Human Understanding and Concerning the Principles of Morals*, ed. L. A. Selby-Bigge, 3rd edn, revised by P. H. Nidditch (Oxford: Clarendon, 1975), p. 279.
19. Ibid., p. 283.
20. John Brown, *Essays on the Characteristics*, ed. L. Davis and C. Reymers, 5th edn (London, 1764), pp. 220–1.
21. Ibid., p. 221.
22. William Paley, *The Principles of Moral and Political Philosophy* (London: R. Faulder, 1785), p. 56.
23. Ibid., p. 35.
24. Ibid., pp. 33–4.
25. Shaftesbury, 'Concerning Virtue and Merit', Book I, Part II, Section III, in *Characteristics*, I, p. 251.
26. Ibid., I, p. 252.
27. Francis Hutcheson, 'An Inquiry Concerning the Original of our Ideas of Virtue or Moral Good', Section II, VIII, in *An Inquiry into the Original of our Ideas of Beauty and Virtue* (1725), in *British Moralists: Being Selections from Writers Principally of the Eighteenth Century*, ed. L. A. Selby-Bigge, 2 vols (Oxford: Clarendon, 1897), I, p. 83.
28. Ibid., Section V, VIII; I, p. 140.
29. David Hume, *A Treatise of Human Nature*, Book III, Part III, Section I, pp. 574–5.
30. Ibid., Book III, Part III, Section I, p. 578.
31. Shaftesbury, 'Concerning Virtue or Merit', Book II, Part II, Sec-

tion I, *Characteristics*, I, p. 298.

32. Ibid., I, p. 310.
33. Hutcheson, 'Inquiry', Section V, VIII, *British Moralists*, I, p. 140.
34. Hume, *Treatise*, Book III, Part III, Section I, p. 579.
35. Shaftesbury, '*Sensus Communis*', Part IV, Section II, Characteristics, I, p. 90.
36. Hutcheson, 'Inquiry', Section V, VIII, *British Moralists*, I, p. 141.
37. Mandeville, 'Enquiry into the Origin of Moral Virtue', *The Fable of the Bees*, I, p. 56.
38. Adam Smith, *The Theory of Moral Sentiments*, ed. D. D. Raphael and A. L. Macfie (Oxford: Clarendon, 1976), Part IV, Chapter 2, Paragraph 10, pp. 190–1.
39. I am indebted for this quotation to Janet Todd, *Sensibility: An Introduction* (London and New York: Methuen, 1986), p. 141.
40. John Mullan, *Sentiment and Sociability: The Language of Feeling in the Eighteenth Century* (Oxford: Clarendon, 1988), p. 217; see also p. 239.
41. Todd, *Sensibility*, p. 47.
42. Ibid., p. 144.
43. I am indebted for this observation to a private communication from Catherine Crawford.
44. John Fothergill, 'Observations on a Case Published in the last Volume of the *Medical Essays*', *Philosophical Transactions*, no. 475 (1745), 280.
45. This identification can be found in J. M. Kuist, *The Nichols File of 'The Gentleman's Magazine': Attributions of Authorship and Other Documentation in Editorial Papers at the Folger Library* (Madison: University of Wisconsin Press, 1982).
46. William Dodd, *A Sermon, Preached March 10, 1776, at St Andrew's, Holborn* (London: for the Humane Society, 1776), p. 22.
47. Colin Milne, *A Sermon Preached at St Sepulchre's, London, on Sunday March 15th* (London: for the Humane Society, 1778), p. 23.
48. See John P. Griffin, 'A Tale of Two Paintings and the London Medical Scene of the Late 18th Century', *Journal of the Royal Society of Medicine*, 83 (1990), pp. 520–3.
49. Thomas Francklin, *A Sermon Preached at St George's, Bloomsbury* (London: for the Humane Society, 1779), p. 17.
50. A German text of *Der Opfer-Tod* can be found in August von Kotzebue, *Theater*, 40 vols (Vienna and Leipzig: Ignaz Klang and Eduard Kummer, 1840–2), vol. 8 (1840).
51. *Self Immolation; or, the Sacrifice of Love. A Play, in Three Acts: By Augustus von Kotzebue*, trans. Henry Neuman (Dublin: G. Folingsby, 1799), p. vi.

6. THE SEDUCTIONS OF CONDUCT *Vivien Jones*

1. Rev. Mr Wetenhall Wilkes, *A Letter of Genteel and Moral Advice to a Young Lady* (1740; 8th edn, 1766), in Vivien Jones (ed.), *Women in*

the Eighteenth Century: Constructions of Femininity (London and New York: Routledge, 1990), p. 30. Wilkes's definition of chastity is recycled from an earlier conduct book, Richard Allestree's *The Ladies Calling* (1673). The sentence about dreams is Wilkes's own.

2. Sarah Pennington, *An Unfortunate Mother's Advice to her Absent Daughters* (1761); reprinted in *The Young Lady's Pocket Library, or Parental Monitor* (1790); reprinted with a new introduction by Vivien Jones (Bristol: Thoemmes Press, 1995), pp. 85–7; Mary Wollstonecraft, *A Vindication of the Rights of Woman* (1792), ed. with an introduction by Miriam Brody Kramnick (Harmondsworth: Penguin, 1982), p. 173.

3. Margaret George, 'From "Goodwife" to "Mistress": The Transformation of the Female in Bourgeois Culture', *Science and Society*, 37 (1973), p. 155.

4. Mary Poovey, *The Proper Lady and the Woman Writer: Ideology as Style in the Works of Mary Wollstonecraft, Mary Shelley, and Jane Austen* (Chicago, IL and London: University of Chicago Press, 1984), pp. xvii, 23; Sandra M. Gilbert and Susan Gubar, *The Madwoman in the Attic: The Woman Writer and the Nineteenth-Century Literary Imagination* (New Haven, CT and London: Yale University Press, 1979).

5. Nancy Armstrong, *Desire and Domestic Fiction: A Political History of the Novel* (New York and Oxford: Oxford University Press, 1987), pp. 59, 66.

6. Nancy Armstrong and Leonard Tennenhouse (eds.), *The Ideology of Conduct: Essays on Literature and the History of Sexuality* (New York and London: Methuen, 1987), p. 11. On the domestic woman as a figure of power, see Armstrong, *Desire*, pp. 26–7.

7. See Bibliography.

8. I am grateful to Markman Ellis for suggesting this comparison. Armstrong is properly selfconscious about the need for strategic overstatement: see *Desire*, p. 26. For a much more complex account of the production of class identity, which is nevertheless comparatively uninterested in gender, see Michael McKeon, *The Origins of the English Novel 1600–1740* (Baltimore, MD: Johns Hopkins University Press, 1987; London: Radius, 1988). In a recent article, interestingly, McKeon focuses explicitly on gender; see Michael McKeon, 'Historicizing Patriarchy: The Emergence of Gender Difference in England, 1660–1760', *Eighteenth-Century Studies*, 28 (1995), pp. 295–322.

9. See, for example, Carol Houlihan Flynn, 'Defoe's Idea of Conduct: Ideological Fictions and Fictional Reality', in Armstrong and Tennenhouse, op. cit., pp. 73–95.

10. 'An Act for the better preventing of Clandestine Marriages', 26 Geo. 2. For an excellent summary of the debates and issues around the Marriage Act, see Erica Harth, 'The Virtue of Love: Lord Hardwicke's Marriage Act', *Cultural Critique*, 9 (1988), pp. 123–54.

11. James Fordyce, *Sermons to Young Women*, 2 vols (1766), in Jones, op. cit., pp. 177–78.

12. William Buchan MD, *Domestic Medicine: or, a Treatise on the Prevention and Cure of Diseases by Regimen and Simple Medicines*, 2nd

edn 'with considerable Additions' (London and Edinburgh, 1772), pp. 148–9n.

13. Judith Fetterley, *The Resisting Reader: A Feminist Approach to American Fiction* (Bloomington, IN, and London: Indiana University Press, 1978), pp. xxii–xxiii.

14. For an excellent summary of many of these arguments, see Ros Ballaster, Margaret Beetham, Elizabeth Fraser and Sandra Hebron, *Women's Worlds: Ideology, Femininity and the Woman's Magazine* (London: Macmillan, 1991), pp. 8–42. See also Bibliography.

15. Michel Foucault, *The History of Sexuality*, vol. I: *An Introduction*, trans. Robert Hurley (Harmondsworth: Penguin, 1978), p. 96.

16. Michel Foucault, *Power/Knowledge: Selected Interviews and Other Writings 1972–1977*, ed. Colin Gordon (Brighton: Harvester Press, 1980), p. 119.

17. See Margaret Whitford and Sadie Plant, 'Pleasure', in Elizabeth Wright (ed.), *Feminism and Psychoanalysis: A Critical Dictionary* (Oxford and Cambridge, MA: Blackwell, 1992), pp. 331–4.

18. Susan Staves, 'The Secrets of Genteel Identity in *The Man of Mode*: Comedy of Manners vs. the Courtesy Book', *Studies in Eighteenth-Century Culture*, 19 (1989), pp. 117–28 (119).

19. See, for example, Lynne Segal's excellent recent book on feminism and heterosexuality, *Straight Sex*, the subtitle of which is *The Politics of Pleasure* (London: Virago, 1994).

20. Wollstonecraft, op. cit., p. 192.

21. Pennington, op.cit., p. 97.

22. John Gregory, *A Father's Legacy to his Daughters* (1774); reprinted in *The Young Lady's Pocket Library, or Parental Monitor* (1790); reprinted with a new introduction by Vivien Jones (Bristol: Thoemmes Press, 1995), p. 15.

23. On the seduction narrative, see Susan Staves, 'British Seduced Maidens', *Eighteenth-Century Studies*, 14 (1980–1), pp. 109–34.

24. Michael McKeon, 'Historicizing', p. 321, n.72.

25. Foucault, *History*, p. 106.

26. George Savile, Marquis of Halifax, *The Lady's New-Year's Gift: or, Advice to a Daughter* (1688), in Jones, op. cit., pp. 17–18; Wilkes, in Jones, op. cit., p. 34.

27. Foucault, *History*, pp. 125–6.

28. Wilkes, in Jones, op. cit., p. 31.

29. See *Shamela* (1741), Henry Fielding's parody of *Pamela*, in which the heroine is a scheming hypocrite, trading on her 'Vartue': *Joseph Andrews & Shamela*, ed. by Douglas Brooks-Davies and Martin C. Battestin (Oxford: World's Classics, 1981).

30. On the classic romance paradigm, see Tania Modleski, *Loving with a Vengeance: Mass-Produced Fantasies for Women* (New York and London: Methuen, 1982), pp. 15–26, 35–58.

31. James Fordyce, *Sermons to Young Women*, 2 vols (1766; 3rd edn, London, 1766), I, p. 191; John Duncombe, *The Feminiad. A Poem* (1754), in Jones, op.cit., p. 173.

32. Eliza Haywood, 'Preface to *Lasselia: or, the Self-Abandon'd*' (1724), in Jones, op. cit., p. 153.

33. Eliza Haywood, *The British Recluse: or, the Secret History of Cleomira, Suppos'd Dead. A Novel*, 2nd edn (London, 1722), pp. 112–13.

34. Elizabeth Singer Rowe, *Letters Moral and Entertaining in Prose and Verse* (1728–32); reprinted in *Friendship in Death: in Twenty Letters from the Dead to the Living. To which are added, Letters Moral and Entertaining, in Prose and Verse. In Three Parts* (London, 1740), pp. 107–8.

35. Samuel Richardson, *Clarissa: or The History of a Young Lady* (1747–8), ed. with an introduction and notes by Angus Ross (Harmondsworth: Penguin, 1985), p. 890.

36. On the work of the Societies for the Reformation of Manners, see T. C. Curtis and W. A. Speck, 'The Societies for the Reformation of Manners: A Case Study in the Theory and Practice of Moral Reform', *Literature and History*, 3 (1976), pp. 45–64.

37. Cf. Pope, *Moral Essays*, 'Epistle II: To a Lady', l.216: 'Ev'ry Woman is at heart a Rake'.

38. Wollstonecraft, op. cit., pp. 192, 193, 194, 223.

39. Ibid., p. 206.

40. Gregory, op. cit., pp. 23–4; Wollstonecraft, op. cit., pp. 112, 192.

41. Pennington, op. cit., p. 98.

42. On the 'scandalous memoirists', such as Teresia Constantia Phillips, Laetitia Pilkington, and Frances Anne, Viscountess Vane, see Felicity Nussbaum, 'Heteroclites: The Gender of Character in the Scandalous Memoirs', in *The Autobiographical Subject: Gender and Ideology in Eighteenth-Century England* (Baltimore, MD and London: Johns Hopkins University Press, 1989).

43. Halifax, in Jones, op. cit., p. 17; Gregory, op. cit., p. 44. Gregory's promise of independence turned out to be somewhat ironic: the history of his elder daughter Dorothea, who became companion to the 'blue-stocking' Elizabeth Montagu, is told in Betty Rizzo, *Companions Without Vows: Relationships Among Eighteenth-Century British Women* (Athens, GA and London: University of Georgia Press, 1994), pp. 112–41.

44. Roger Lonsdale (ed.), *Eighteenth-Century Women Poets: An Oxford Anthology* (Oxford and New York: Oxford University Press, 1989), pp. 3, 207, 63.

45. *The Poems of Anne Countess of Winchilsea*, ed. by Myra Reynolds (Chicago, IL: University of Chicago Press, 1903), p. 74. Lonsdale's exerpt from this poem omits the section on female friendship.

46. [George Colman and Bonnell Thornton] *Poems by Eminent Ladies* (1755), and subsequent editions; republished in 1773 as *Poems by the most Eminent Ladies of Britain and Ireland*; a new edition 'with considerable Alterations, Additions, and Improvements' was published in 1785[?].

47. Haywood, op. cit., pp. 137, 138; Richardson, op. cit., p. 226; Sarah Scott, *A Description of Millennium Hall* (1762; London: Virago, 1986), p. 165.

48. Mary Astell, *A Serious Proposal to the Ladies, For the Advancement of their True and Greatest Interest* (1694), in Jones, op. cit., p. 205; Ruth Perry, *The Celebrated Mary Astell: An Early English Feminist* (Chicago, IL and London: University of Chicago Press, 1986), pp. 330–1.
49. Anne-Thérèse, Marchioness de Lambert, *Advice of a Mother to her Daughter* (first English trans. 1727); reprinted in *The Young Lady's Pocket Library, or Parental Monitor* (1790); reprinted with a new introduction by Vivien Jones (Bristol: Thoemmes Press, 1995), pp. 134, 162, 161.
50. Harth, op. cit., p. 147.
51. Rizzo, op. cit., pp. 4–5, 13–16. On a female culture maintained through letters, conversation, etc., see also Deborah Kaplan, *Jane Austen among Women* (Baltimore, MD: Johns Hopkins University Press, 1992).
52. Jane Austen, *Pride and Prejudice* (1813; Harmondsworth: Penguin, 1972), Ch. 14, p. 113.
53. Fordyce, in Jones, op. cit., p. 176.

7. 'STRAINS OF NEW BEAUTY' *Derek Alsop*

1. Quoted in Otto Erich Deutsch, *Handel: A Documentary Bibliography* (London: Adam & Charles Black, 1955), p. 218.
2. Deutsch, op. cit., p. 220.
3. Deutsch, op. cit., p. 223.
4. See Christopher Hogwood, *Handel* (London: Thames & Hudson, 1984), p. 50.
5. Winton Dean and John Merrill Knapp, *Handel's Operas 1704–1726* (Oxford: Clarendon Press, 1987), p. 141.
6. Dean and Knapp, op. cit., p. 142.
7. Jonathan Keates, *Handel: The Man and his Music* (London: Victor Gollancz, 1985), p. 54.
8. Dean and Knapp, op. cit., p. 144.
9. Deutsch, op. cit., pp. 206–7.
10. H. C. Robbins Landon, *Handel and His World* (London: Weidenfeld & Nicolson, 1984), p. 110.
11. John Gay, *The Beggar's Opera*, ed. Bryan Loughrey and T. O. Treadwell (Harmondsworth: Penguin Books, 1986), p. 41.
12. Gay, op. cit., p. 58.
13. Quoted by Roger Fiske, *English Theatre Music in the Eighteenth Century*, 2nd edn (Oxford: Oxford University Press, 1986), p. 33.
14. *The Librettos of Handel's Operas*, ed. Ellen T. Harris, 13 vols (New York and London: Garland, 1989), III, pp. 274–5. (This collected edition gives facsimiles of the original publication of the Italian librettos and their translations. Sometimes the translation is rather loose, and sometimes arias are not translated in full, but they offer a fascinating opportunity to read the material available to the contemporary audience.)

15. *The Librettos*, III, pp. 294–5.
16. Charles Burney, *A General History of Music from the Earliest Ages to the Present Period*, 4 vols (London: T. Becket *et al.*, 1776–89), IV, pp. 286–7.
17. Dean and Knapp, op. cit., p. 424.
18. Gay, op. cit., p. 121.
19. Deutsch, op. cit., p. 210.
20. Gay, op. cit., p. 93.
21. John Mainwaring, *Memoirs of the Life of the Late George Frederic Handel* (London: R. & J. Dodsley, 1760), pp. 110–11.
22. Deutsch, op. cit., p. 147.
23. Keates, op. cit., p. 101.
24. The musical examples are taken from the *Deutsche Händel–gesellschaft Edition*, edited by Friedrich Chrysander, here volume LXVI (Leipzig, 1881), p. 22.
25. Keates, op. cit., p. 101.
26. Burney, op. cit., IV, 637.
27. Gay, op. cit., p. 71.
28. John Dennis, *An Essay on the Operas After the Italian Manner, Which are about to be Establish'd on the English Stage, With some Reflections on the Damage which they may bring to the Publick* (London: John Nutt, 1706), Preface, p. 4.
29. Dennis, op. cit., Preface, p. 2.
30. Dennis, op. cit., Preface, p. 7.
31. Dennis, op. cit., Preface, p. 6.
32. Dennis, op. cit., main text, p. 13.
33. Dennis, op. cit., main text, p. 14.
34. Donald F. Bond (ed.), *The Spectator*, 5 vols (Clarendon Press, Oxford, 1965), I, p. 81.
35. Dean and Knapp, op. cit., p. 146.
36. *The Spectator*, I, p. 80.
37. *The Spectator*, I, p. 80.
38. *The Spectator*, I, p. 81.
39. Fiske, op. cit., p. 66.
40. Quoted by Robbins Landon, op. cit., p. 75.
41. *The Spectator*, I, pp. 23–4.
42. *The Spectator*, I, pp. 24–5.
43. Hogwood, op. cit., p. 65.
44. Deutsch, op. cit., p. 25.
45. *The Spectator*, I, p. 26.
46. Dean and Knapp, op. cit., p. 178.
47. Dean and Knapp, op. cit., p. 178.
48. Burney, op. cit., IV, 255.
49. Burney, op. cit., IV, 253.
50. *Deutsche Händelgesellschaft Edition*, vol. LXII (Leipzig, 1874), pp. 42–4.
51. Dean and Knapp, op. cit., p. 287.
52. Deutsch, op. cit., p. 52.

53. Mainwaring, op. cit., p. 93.
54. Mainwaring, op. cit., pp. 96–97.
55. Deutsch, op. cit., p. 86.
56. Mainwaring, op. cit., pp. 98–9.
57. Dean and Knapp, op. cit., p. 336.
58. Burney, IV, op. cit., 260.
59. *Deutsche Händelgesellschaft Edition*, vol. LXIII (Leipzig, 1875), pp. 11–12.
60. Angus Heriot, *The Castrati in Opera* (London: Secker & Warburg, 1956), p. 27.
61. Roland Barthes, *S/Z* transl. by Richard Miller (Oxford: Basil Blackwell, 1974), p. 109.
62. Heriot, op. cit., pp. 36–7.
63. William Shakespeare, *Antony and Cleopatra*, Act II, Scene ii, lines 191–98, ed. M. R. Ridley (London: Methuen, 1954), p. 62.
64. Shakespeare, op. cit., p. 263.
65. Shakespeare, op. cit., p. 262.
66. Winton Dean, notes for *Giulio Cesare* recording (Harmonia Mundi HMC 901385.87), booklet, p. 23.
67. *Deutsche Händelgesellschaft Edition*, vol. LXVIII (Leipzig, 1875), pp. 56–7.

8. THE PLEASURE OF TERROR *E. J. Clery*

1. Charles Gildon, *An Essay on the Vindication of Love in Tragedies*, 1694.
2. G. C. Lichtenberg, *Lichtenberg's Visits to England as Described in His Letters and Diaries*, trans. and ed. M. L. Mare and W. H. Quarrell (Oxford, 1938), pp. 10–11.
3. *The Spirit of the Public Journals for 1797* (London: R. Phillips, 1798), p. 223.
4. John Dennis, 'The Grounds of Criticism in Poetry' (1704), in E. N. Hooker (ed.), *The Critical Works of John Dennis*, 2 vols (Baltimore, MD: Johns Hopkins University Press, 1939), I, p. 339.
5. *Spectator*, no. 419 (1 July 1712), D. F. Bond (ed.), *The Spectator*, 5 vols (Oxford, 1965), p. 571.
6. *Spectator*, no. 418 (30 June 1712), op. cit., p. 568.
7. Edmund Burke, *A Philosophical Enquiry into the Origin of our Ideas of the Sublime and Beautiful*, ed. J. T. Boulton, revised edn (1958; Oxford: Basil Blackwell, 1987), p. 39. Subsequent page references will be shown in parentheses in the main body of the text.
8. While Dennis distinguised between terror, caused by a sudden disturbance, and fear, caused by a gradual disturbance, Burke uses terror, fear and horror interchangeably, and no distinctions will be observed here; see W. P. Albrecht, *The Sublime Pleasures of Tragedy: A Study of Critical Theory from Dennis to Keats* (Lawrence, Manhattan,

Wichita: University Press of Kansas, 1975), p. 18.

9. See Herbert A. Wicheln, 'Burke's Essay on the Sublime and its Reviewers', *Journal of English and Germanic Philology*, 21 (1922), pp. 645–61. Wicheln shows that when Burke was challenged by reviewers on controversial proposals like the positive nature of pleasure and pain, and the centrality of terror to the sublime, he responded by strengthening his position in revisions to the second edition, rather than by moderating it.

10. See Tom Furniss, *Edmund Burke's Aesthetic Ideology: Language, gender, and political economy in revolution* (Cambridge, 1993), p. 25. A third possibility, that delight is produced by an individual's active overcoming of the sense of danger, seems to be ruled out by Burke's description of an essentially passive experience.

11. Very often Burke's physiological explanation of the workings of terror has been dismissed as a reductive aberration in his argument. In *The Romantic Sublime* (Baltimore, MD and London, 1976), Thomas Weiskel finds the explanation of 'how terror becomes delight . . . cumbersome, not to say silly' (p. 88). He reinterprets terror as psychological 'anxiety' and reduces it to a step towards sublime transcendence (see especially pp. 96–8). Peter de Bolla has influentially connected eighteenth-century theories of the sublime with the creation of a modern, atomised subject, but dismisses terror as merely one of the 'origins or stimuli for sublime sensation' with 'very little bearing on our argument'; *The Discourse of the Sublime* (Oxford, 1989), p. 62.

12. For instance, Adam Phillips in his introduction to the World's Classics edition of the *Enquiry* sees it as a 'dubious distinction'; Edmund Burke, *A Philosophical Enquiry into the Origin of our Ideas of the Sublime and Beautiful*, ed. Adam Phillips (Oxford, 1990), p. xxi. Furniss notes the differentiation but, none the less, finds Addison's idea of the *pleasure* of terror 'strikingly Burkean'; Furniss op. cit., p. 23. Although Kant seems to adopt Burke's system by marking a difference between positive and negative pleasure he masks (by reusing the term 'pleasure') what I will be claiming is a vital qualitative distinction in Burke; I. Kant, *Critique of Judgment*, trans. Werner S. Pluhar (Indianapolis, IN, 1987), p. 129.

13. The term derives from the Aristotelian division of causality into four classes; the 'final' or 'efficient' cause is the aim of a change, which determines it retroactively.

14. Robert Miles, *Gothic Writing 1750–1820: A Genealogy* (London and New York, 1993), p. 71.

15. Frances Ferguson, 'The Sublime of Edmund Burke, or The Bathos of Experience', *Glyph*, 8 (1981), pp. 62–78, 69.

16. Shaftesbury quoted in John Barrell, *The Birth of Pandora and the Division of Knowledge* (London, 1992), p. 67; the present article owes a particular debt to an essay in this collection, '"The Dangerous Goddess": Masculinity, Prestige and the Aesthetic in Early Eighteenth-Century Britain' (pp. 63–87), for a fascinating discussion of the problems involved in representing Venus, both personification of and

stimulus to pleasure. Barrell also explores the discourse of civic humanism as 'the most authoritative fantasy of masculinity' in the period, raising issues highly relevant to the *Enquiry*.

17. See, for instance, J. G. A. Pocock, *The Machiavellian Moment: Florentine Political Thought and the Atlantic Republican Tradition* (Princeton, NJ and London, 1975); Stephen Copley (ed.), *Literature and the Social Order* (London, 1984), Introduction; Barrell, *Birth of Pandora*, Foreword.

18. The male monopoly on public virtue had a formative effect on the rhetoric of civic discourse: change in the social order is figured as a crisis of masculine identity; corruption is frequently described as 'effeminacy'. The vital role of this gendered rhetoric in discussion of the sublime can only be hinted at here.

19. Longinus, *On the Sublime: The 'Peri Hupsous' in Translations by Nicolas Boileau-Despreaux (1674) and William Smith (1739)* (Delmar, NY, 1975), p. 105.

20. Ibid., pp. 106–7.

21. Hugh Blair, 'A Critical Dissertation of the Poems of Ossian', in J. Macpherson (ed.), *The Works of Ossian*, 2 vols, 3rd edn (London, 1815), II, pp. 340–1.

22. William Duff, *An Essay on Original Genius and Its Various Modes of Exertion in Philosophy and the Fine Arts, Particularly in Poetry* (Gainesville, FL, 1964), p. 291.

23. On the influence of Polybius's model of cyclical history, see Pocock, *Machiavellian Moment*, pp. 77–80.

24. Wichelns, 'Burke's Essay', p. 646. Edmund Burke would, of course, go on to become one of the foremost politicians of the age. There have been a number of attempts to relate his aesthetic theory to his later, conservative response to the French Revolution, notably Neal Wood, 'The Aesthetic Dimension of Burke's Political Thought', *Journal of British Studies*, 4(1) (November 1964), pp. 41–64; Ronald Paulson, 'Burke, Paine and Wollstonecraft: The Sublime and the Beautiful', in *Representations of Revolution (1789–1820)* (New Haven, CT and London, 1983), pp. 57–87; and Furniss, *Edmund Burke's Aesthetic Ideology*, *passim*. In this essay I am interested in the political resonances of the sublime and the beautiful at the time of the *Enquiry*'s first publication.

25. Ferguson, 'The Sublime of Edmund Burke', p. 76.

26. Furniss, op. cit., p. 42.

27. See, for instance: Weiskel, *Romantic Sublime*, p. 98; Isaac Kramnick, *The Rage of Edmund Burke* (New York, 1977), p. 96; de Bolla, *Discourse*, p. 71 (though here the idea of empowerment is qualified); Terry Eagleton, *The Ideology of the Aesthetic* (Oxford, 1990), p. 54; Furniss, *Edmund Burke's Aesthetic Ideology*, pp. 31–2.

28. The image of the sublime subject in the section on 'Ambition' – egotistical and blatantly 'male' – is thus an anomaly in the *Enquiry*. It has been cited so frequently, I suspect, because it is the only description that seems to correspond to a post-Kantian notion of transcendental sublimity, on the one hand; and on the other, because

it supports the idea of a 'male' sublime and a 'female' beautiful as a straightforward dichotomy.

29. Cf. Frances Ferguson, 'The Sublime of Edmund Burke', pp. 72–5; her account of the identification of power and sublimity is complicated by the positing of a dialectic in which the subject alternates between self-abasement and self-empowerment to attain freedom from social relations.

30. While de Bolla's suggestion, that the *Enquiry* produces material for a '"romantic" egotistical reading' of the sublime without endorsing it, is useful (*Discourse,* p. 70), the evidence cannot support an absolute claim that Burke's treatise exhibits a 'third phase of the sublime' equivalent to that found in Longinus and Kant, 'a physical or psychological reaction which allows the subject to overcome or transcend its subjection, transforming potential annihilation into a sense of elevation', nor that it affirms 'the sense of self as a kind of heroic labourer, purging itself of weakness through individual effort'; as in Furniss, *Burke's Aesthetic Ideology,* pp. 27, 29. For an analogous theory of passive as opposed to active labour, see the discussion of how meaning is generated by words in Section Five of the *Enquiry.*

31. The use of the master/slave dialectic from Hegel's *Phenomenology of Spirit* (1807) to explain the self-empowering role of terror and self-preservation in relation to labour is anachronistic and, I find, unconvincing; Furniss, *Edmund Burke's Aesthetic Ideology,* pp. 49–51.

32. See Pocock, *Machiavellian Moment,* on the importance of the standing army controversy and the opposing 'myth of the English militia' (p. 414); pp. 410–17, 426–36.

33. John Millar, *The Origin of the Distinction of Ranks* [1771], revised edn 1779, reprinted in William C. Lehmann, *John Millar of Glasgow 1735–1801: His Life and Thought and his Contributions to Sociological Analysis* (Cambridge, 1960), p. 292. Cf. Adam Ferguson, *An Essay on the History of Civil Society* (London and Edinburgh, 1768): 'The boasted refinements, then, of the polished age, are not divested of danger . . . if they form disciplined armies, they reduce the military spirit of entire nations; and by placing the sword where they have given a distaste to civil establishments, they prepare for mankind the government of force', p. 385.

34. J. R. Western, *The English Militia in the Eighteenth Century: The Story of a Political Issue 1660–1802* (London and Toronto, 1965), p. 105.

35. Henry Home, Lord Kames, *Sketches of the History of Man* [1774], 2 vols, revised edn (London and Edinburgh, 1788); II, p. 301.

36. David Hume, 'Of Luxury', in *Essays Moral, Political, and Literary* [1741–2], ed. Eugene F. Millar (Indianapolis, IN, 1985)

37. Hume, 'Idea of a Perfect Commonwealth', op. cit.

38. Adam Smith, *An Inquiry into the Nature and Causes of the Wealth of Nations,* ed. R. H. Campbell, A. S. Skinner and W. B. Todd, 2 vols (Oxford, 1976), II, pp. 787–8.

39. For other remarks by Smith on the division of labour and the consequent decline of martial spirit, see Adam Smith, *Lectures on Justice,*

Police, Revenue and Arms, ed. E. Cannon, 1896 (New York, 1964), pp. 42–3, 259; and *Wealth of Nations*, II, p. 782.

40. Cf. Kant, *Critique of Judgment*, pp. 121–2; the correspondence of the sublime to the experience of war, as a remedy for 'a merely commercial spirit', is made explicit here but, typically, terror is dismissed as a factor.

41. E. J. Clery, *The Rise of Supernatural Fiction, 1762–1800* (Cambridge, 1995), p. 105.

42. Kames, *Sketches*, II, p. 300.

43. On the indoor terrors of the 'female gothic' see Ellen Moers, *Literary Women* (London, 1978); Mary Poovey, 'Ideology and the *Mysteries of Udolpho*', *Criticism*, 21 (Fall 1979), pp. 307–30; Kate Ferguson Ellis, *The Contested Castle: Gothic Novels and the Subversion of Domestic Ideology* (Urbana, 1989); E. J. Clery, *Rise of Supernatural Fiction*, pp. 95–130. On novel-reading as a harmless and consolatory pleasure, see 'The Female Castle-Builder. A Picture From Real Life', in *Flowers of Literature*, 2 (1802), pp. 215–17; and Walter Scott's discussion of Radcliffe in *The Lives of the Novelists* (London, 1910), p. 216.

9. BURNS AND WORDSWORTH *Susan Manning*

Full citations of works quoted will be found in the Bibliography for this chapter.

1. *The Life of Reason*, vol. 4: *Reason in Art* (London, 1905), p. 193.

2. *The Republic*, trans. Richard W. Sterling and William Scott (New York and London, 1985), pp. 296–7.

3. *The Works of Richard Hurd, D.D.*, 8 vols (1811; facsimile reprint, New York, 1967), II, p. 2.

4. The term 'aesthetics' (from the Greek) means, literally, 'things perceptible by the senses;' it is ironic that the eighteenth century should preside over the semantic shift in the term towards 'the study or appreciation of taste'.

5. Robert Burns, Epistle 'To James Smith'. Citations from Burns's poetry are all to be found in James Kinsley's edition of *The Poems and Songs of Robert Burns*, 3 vols (Oxford: Oxford University Press, 1968).

6. William Wordsworth, 'Preface' (1800 and 1802) to *The Lyrical Ballads*, pp. 257–8. Citations are subsequently identified in the text as 'Preface'.

7. Unless otherwise indicated, citations from Wordsworth's poetry may be found in *Poetical Works* (Oxford: Oxford University Press, 1936, 1974).

8. See Mackenzie's acclamation of Burns's Kilmarnock edition, in *The Lounger*, no. 97 (9 December 1786), *Collected Works of Henry Mackenzie*, 8 vols (Edinburgh, 1808), vol. VI, pp. 378–91. Wordsworth, 'Resolution and Independence,' *Poems of 1807*, p. 43.

9. *The Theory of Moral Sentiments* (1759), ed. D. D. Raphael and A. L. MacFie, *The Glasgow Edition of the Works and Correspondence of Adam Smith*, 6 vols (Oxford, 1976), I, pp. 13–14.

10. One of Burns's literary mentors, Sterne's Yorick, noted the 'sweet pliability of man's spirit, that can at once surrender itself to illusions, which cheat expectation and sorrow of their weary moments!' (*A Sentimental Journey Through France and Italy* (1767; London: J. M. Dent & Sons, 1927; 1976), p. 92).

11. *The Twickenham Edition of the Poems of Alexander Pope,* 1 vol., ed. John Butt (London: Methuen, 1963; 1973), pp. 597–8.

12. See Roy Porter's essay in the current volume on the 'material pleasures' increasingly available to a wider band of consumers.

13. Quoted by A. S. Byatt (1970), p. 42.

14. Roland Barthes, *The Pleasure of the Text,* trans. Richard Miller (New York: Hill & Wang, 1975), p. 4. Cf Friedrich Schiller, *On the Aesthetic Education of Man* (1795), ed. and trans. E. M. Wilkinson & L. A. Willoughby (Oxford: Clarendon Press, 1967), p. 97: 'The play-drive . . . since it annuls all contingency, [will] annul all constraint too, and set man free both physically and morally.'

15. Jonathan Swift, *A Tale of A Tub and Other Satires,* ed. Kathleen Williams (London: Dent, 1975), pp. 108, 110.

16. Sigmund Freud describes the self seeking to obey the 'pleasure-principle' and find happiness in the wretched conditions of existence, escaping into 'powerful diversions, which let us make light of our misery; substitute gratifications which diminish it; intoxicating substances, which make us insensitive to it.' *Civilisation and Its Discontents,* trans. Angela Richards, *The Pelican Freud Library,* vol. 12 (Harmondsworth: Penguin Books, 1985), p. 262.

17. Hartley identified a hierarchy of six classes of intellectual pleasures (and their obverse, the pains associated with their frustration): imagination,ambition, self-interest, sympathy, theopathy and the moral sense. Pleasures of sensation lead (by a process he calls 'coalescence') to intellectual pleasures that culminate in benevolence for men and animals, and, ultimately, love for God. He sees the fundamental motivation of human life to be the 'endless Grasping after Infinity' (*Observations on Man, His Frame, His Duty, and His Expectations,* 2 vols (London, 1749; reprinted Hildesham: George Olms Verlagsbuchhandlung, 1967), II, p. 247. See also Stephen Ford, '*Coalescence*: David Hartley's "*Great Apparatus*"', in Christopher Fox (ed.), *Psychology and Literature in the Eighteenth Century* (New York: AMS Press, 1987), pp. 199–223.)

18. Compare Wordsworth's conscience-stricken redaction of his love affair with Annette Vallon, under the allegory of Vaudracour and Julia, in Book IX of *The Prelude.* Guilt and pleasure cannot co-exist in Wordsworth's poetic register.

19. Reprinted in *Burns: The Critical Heritage,* p. 183.

20. *The Twickenham Edition of the Poems of Alexander Pope,* vol. iii (i): *An Essay on Man,* ed. Maynard Mack (London: Methuen, 1950, 1958), Epistle iii, l. 318.

21. Wordsworth, *Letter to a Friend of Robert Burns . . .,* 1816 (*Wordsworth's Literary Criticism*), p. 213. Wordsworth and Jeffrey were old enemies: Jeffrey had repeatedly savaged Wordsworth's work in *The Edinburgh*

Review, culminating in a notorious dismissal of *The Excursion* in 1814, two years before this letter was written.

22. 'Letter to a Friend of Burns', p. 216.

23. To contemporaries their work seemed diametrically opposed. As William Hazlitt put it in 1818, 'It is hardly reasonable to look for a hearty or genuine defence of Burns from the pen of Mr Wordsworth; for there is no common link of sympathy between them. Nothing can be more different or hostile than the spirit of their poetry. Mr Wordsworth's poetry is the poetry of mere sentiment and pensive contemplation: Burns's is a very highly sublimated essence of animal existence. With Burns, "self-love and social are the same" . . . Mr Wordsworth is "himself alone," a recluse philosopher, or a reluctant spectator of the scenes of many-coloured life: moralising on them, not describing, not entering into them' (*Lectures on the English Poets* (1818), ed. William Carew Hazlitt (London: George Bell & Sons, 1884), pp. 175–6).

24. *Byron's Letters and Journals*, ed. Leslie A. Marchand, 12 vols (London: John Murray, 1973–82), vol. III, p. 239 (entry for 13 December 1813). See also Burns's letter to Alexander Cunningham, written December 1789: 'What strange beings we are! Since we have a portion of conscious existence, equally capable of enjoying Pleasure, Happiness & Rapture, or of suffering Pain, Wretchedness & Misery, it is surely worthy of enquiry whether there be not such a thing as A SCIENCE OF LIFE; whether Method, Economy and Fertility of expedients, be not applicable to Enjoyment; and whether there be not a want of dexterity in Pleasure which renders our little scantling of happiness still less, and a profuseness, and intoxication in bliss, which leads to Satie[ty,] Disgust and Self-abhorrence (*Letters*, II, p. 15).

25. *Robert Burns and the Sentimental Era*, p. 159.

26. Review of *Cromek's Reliques of Robert Burns, Quarterly Review*, 1809. Reprinted in *Burns: The Critical Heritage*, p. 207.

27. 'In Mr Wordsworth there is a total disunion and divorce of the faculties of the mind from those of the body: the banns are forbid, or a separation is austerely pronounced from bed and board – *a mensa et thoro*. From the Lyrical Ballads, it does not appear that men eat or drink, marry or are given in marriage. If we lived by every sentiment that proceeded out of mouths, and not by bread and wine, or if the species were continued like trees . . . Mr Wordsworth's poetry would be just as good as ever. It is not so with Burns' (*Lectures on the English Poets*).

28. Ross Woodman, '*The Prelude* and the Fate of Madness', in Woodman (ed.), *New Casebooks: Wordsworth*, p. 24.

29. 'Elegaic Stanzas Suggested by a Picture of Peele Castle . . .'.

30. 'Whatsoever is not detrimental to Society, & is of positive Enjoyment, is of God the Giver of all good things, & ought be [*sic*] received & enjoyed by His creatures with thankful delight' (*Letters*, II, 73).

31. 'Prayer (1), *The English Poems of George Herbert*, ed. C. A. Patrides (London: Dent, 1974; 1986), p. 71.

Bibliography

1. ENLIGHTENMENT AND PLEASURE *Roy Porter*

Eighteenth-century attitudes to pleasure in Britain need to be seen in context of the wider history of morals and opinions about hedonism: see John Passmore, *The Perfectibility of Man* (London: Duckworth, 1972), and Peter Quennell, *The Pursuit of Happiness* (London: Constable, 1988).

They must also be contextualised against the broader ideologies of the Enlightenment, in particular its scientific views of human nature. The best introduction is still Peter Gay's *The Enlightenment: An Interpretation*, 2 vols (New York: Knopf, 1967–9); more specialised and up-to-date is Christopher Fox, Roy Porter and Robbey Wokler (eds), *Inventing Human Science: Eighteenth Century Domains* (Berkeley, CA: University of California Press, 1995).

Crucial in the legitimation of pleasure was the debate following Mandeville's work, which is superbly discussed in E. G. Hundert, *The Enlightenment's Fable: Bernard Mandeville and the Discovery of Society* (Cambridge: Cambridge University Press, 1994).

Also vital was the development of a theory of progress, especially associated with the Scottish Enlightenment. For this see G. Bryson, *Man and Society: The Scottish Inquiry of the Eighteenth Century* (Princeton, NJ: Princeton University Press, 1945); David Spadafora, *The Idea of Progress in Eighteenth-Century Britain* (New Haven, CT and London: Yale University Press, 1990).

The key English philosophical expression of pleasure theory was Benthamite Utilitarianism. Still the best discussion is Elie Halévy, *The Growth of Philosophic Radicalism* (London: Faber & Faber, 1928). The relations between utilitarianism, psychology and the rise of modern economic thinking are explored in Albert O. Hirschman, *The Passions and the Interests: Political Arguments for Capitalism before its Triumph* (Princeton, NJ: Princeton University Press, 1977); and J. Viner, *The Role of Providence in the Social Order* (Philadelphia, PA: American Philosophical Society, 1972).

Few intellectuals ever straightforwardly endorsed hedonism. For secular critiques of the dangers of the pursuit of material pleasure, see John Sekora, *Luxury: The Concept in Western Thought, Eden to Smollett* (Baltimore, MD: The Johns Hopkins University Press, 1977); for the religious debate as to whether Christianity should countenance a 'happy world', see Leslie Stephen, *English Thought in the Eighteenth Century*, 2 vols (New York: Brace & World, 1962).

2. MATERIAL PLEASURES IN THE CONSUMER SOCIETY *Roy Porter*

Eighteenth-century pleasures should be seen in several contexts. One is the wider history of leisure: see Hugh Cunningham, *Leisure in the Industrial Revolution, c.1780–c.1880* (London: Croom Helm, 1980), and for a theoretical perspective, Thorstein Veblen, *The Theory of the Leisure Class* (New York: Macmillan, 1912).

Another is the rise of commercial society in the Georgian era, oriented towards commodities and enjoyment: see Neil McKendrick, John Brewer and J. H. Plumb, *The Birth of a Consumer Society: The Commercialization of Eighteenth-Century England* (London: Europa, 1982); J. H. Plumb, *The Commercialization of Leisure in Eighteenth Century England* (Reading: University of Reading, 1973); J. H. Plumb, *Georgian Delights* (London: Weidenfeld & Nicolson, 1980); Carole Shammas, *The Pre-Industrial Consumer in England and America* (Oxford: Clarendon Press, 1990).

A further context is the great urban renewal occurring at the time. This is discussed by Peter Borsay in 'The English Urban Renaissance: The Development of Provincial Urban Culture, c. 1680–1760', *Social History*, V (1977), pp. 581–603; and Peter Borsay, 'All the Town's a Stage', in P. Clark (ed.), *The Transformation of English Provincial Towns, (1660–1800)* (London: Hutchinson, 1985), pp. 228–58

Amongst studies to particular forms of plesure-taking newly catered for – sports, entertainments and types of higher culture – the following are particularly insightful: Alison Adburgham, *Shopping in Style: London from the Restoration to Edwardian Elegance* (London: Thames and Hudson, 1979); Pat Rogers, *Grub Street: Studies in a Subculture* (London: Methuen, 1972); Emmett L. Avery (ed.), *The London Stage 1600–1800*, 2 vols (Carbondale, IL: Southern Illinois University Press, 1968); Paula R. Backscheider, *Spectacular Politics: Theatrical Power and Mass Culture in Early Modern England* (Baltimore, MD: Johns Hopkins University Press, 1994); W. Vamplew, *The Turf: A Social and Economic History of Horse Racing* (London: Allen Lane, 1974).

Popular and commercial enjoyments had many critics and sparked debate. For these see Ronald Hutton, *The Rise and Fall of Merry England* (Oxford: Oxford University Press, 1994); A. Clayre, *Work and Play: Ideas and Experience of Work and Leisure* (London: Weidenfeld & Nicolson, 1974); R. Malcolmson, *Popular Recreations in English Society 1700–1850* (Cambridge: Cambridge University Press, 1973).

3. THE PLEASURES OF THE TABLE *Simon Varey*

The enjoyment of food is a notoriously transient pleasure, so perhaps it is to be expected that there is relatively little scholarly work on food history, less still on the pleasure attached to food in eighteenth-century Europe. Probably the best single source for consistent exploration of the history of food and cooking all over the world is *Petits propos culinaires*, a journal that has just passed its first half-century of issues, whose high quality belies its modest appearance. The best scholarly treatment of food history in France is Barbara Wheaton's *Savoring the Past* (Philadelphia, PA: University of Pennsylvania Press, 1983), which takes the subject up to the French Revolution; the best overall account of food history in England is Sir Jack Drummond's classic, *The Englishman's Food*, revised edn (London: Pimlico, 1991). Stephen Mennell, *All Manners of Food* (Oxford: Basil Blackwell, 1985) is another useful survey, covering both sides of the English Channel. More general still, but always interesting, is Reay Tannahill, *Food in History* (Harmondsworth: Penguin, 1973, reprinted 1991). Several famous cookery books first published in the eighteenth century have been reprinted in facsimile, including a late edition of Hannah Glasse, *Art of Cookery* and John Farley's compendium of plagiarisms, *The London Art of Cookery*. Alice and Frank Prochaska have given Margaretta Acworth's cookery manuscript the kind of scholarly treatment it deserves, though it is typical of hundreds of such manuscripts, many of which survive as family heirlooms. Maggie Black's *Jane Austen Cookbook* (London: British Museum, 1995) is not quite what it seems, because it is a rehash of Martha Lloyd's manuscript (which Austen knew) with a few period additions; but it still adds up to a handy guide through the eating preferences of a fairly ordinary household at the end of the eighteenth century.

4. PLEASURES ENGENDERED BY GENDER *Marie Mulvey Roberts*

Relatively little work has been done on the clubs in recent years, which is why the best starting points are Robert J. Allen, *The Clubs of Augustan London* (Cambridge, MA: Harvard University Press, 1933) and Louis C. Jones, *The Clubs of the Georgian Rakes* (New York: Columbia University Press, 1942). These draw on the numerous accounts of fictional and factual clubs that appear in contemporary periodicals such as *The Gentleman's Magazine, The Spectator, The Tatler, and World.* Another major primary source which is not available in modern editions is the writing of Edward Ward, that includes *The Secret History of the London Club[s] or, the Citizens' pastime . . . With a sermon preached to a gang of Highway-men*, Part I (London, J. Dutton, 1709) and *A Complete and Humorous Account of all the Remarkable Clubs and Societies in the Cities of London and Westminster, from the R[oya]l S[ociet]y down to the Lumber Troop* (London: printed for the author, 1745). More accessible are various nineteenth-century accounts of clubs such as John Timbs, *London Clubs of the Metropolis during the 17th, 18th and 19th Centuries*, 2 vols (London: privately printed, 1866). This contains many curious details, as does his *History of Clubs and Club Life* (1872), along with C. Marsh, *Clubs of London, with Anecdotes of their Members, Sketches of Character and Conversation*, 2 vols (London: Henry Colburn, 1832). Most recent work is in the form of papers in scholarly journals or lectures, such as Peter Clark, *Sociability and Urbanity: Clubs and Societies in the Eighteenth-Century City*, published by the Victorian Studies Centre for the University of Leicester, 1986. Out of all the clubs, the Hell Fire Clubs have attracted more attention than most. However, much that has been written has been misleading and sensationalised. One of the most reliable accounts is Betty Kemp, *Sir Francis Dashwood; an Eighteenth-Century Independent* (London: Macmillan, 1967). Leading clubs like the Kit-Cat Club have come to the attention of modern scholars and portraits of members are included in Elizabeth Einberg, *Manners and Morals: Hogarth and British Painting 1700–1760* (London: Viking, 1987). For information about the coffee houses there is Bryant Lillywhite, *London Coffee Houses* (London: George Allen & Unwin, 1963) and W. B. Boulton, *A History of White's*, 2 vols (London: Hon. A. Bourke, 1892). Reproductions of coffee-house advertisements appear in A. S. Turberville, *English Men and Manners in the Eighteenth Century* 2nd edn, (Oxford: Clarendon Press, 1929). There is a concise account of clubs and coffee houses in G. Rudé, *Hanoverian London 1714–1808* (London: Secker & Warburg, 1971), pp. 71ff. General works on the social history of eighteenth-century London include Derek Jarrett, *England in the Age of Hogarth* (London: Hart-Davis, MacGibbon, 1974), M. D. George, *London Life in the Eighteenth Century* (Harmondsworth: Penguin 1985) and Roy Porter, *English Society in the Eighteenth Century* (Harmondsworth: Penguin, 1982), p. 25. More specific is E. J. Burford's *Wits, Wenchers and Wantons: London's Low Life: Covent Garden in the Eighteenth Century* (London: Hale, 1986) where it is alleged that the Mohocks used to roll innocent passers-by in barrels. In connection with homosocialism, for a scholarly approach to male bonding in the broadest sense consult Mary Ann Clawson, *Constructing Brotherhood. Class. Gender and Fraternalism* (Princeton, NJ: Princeton University Press, 1989). A more popularist and contemporary approach is made by Barbara Rogers, *Men Only: An Investigation in Men's Organisations* (Pandora: London, 1988) and Lionel Tiger, *Men in Groups* (London: Nelson, 1969). Many of these current observations hold true for men's clubs during the eighteenth century.

There has been much recent scholarly interest shown in the history of cross-dressing, mainly in connection with women. Two other burgeoning areas in Women's Studies focus on clubs of the French Revolution and female Freemasonry. Joan Landes, *Women and the Public Sphere in the Age of the French Revolution* (Ithaca, NY: Cornell University Press, 1988), provides a thoughtful discussion of the public/private spheres debate and draws on Jean Bethke Elshtain's *Public Man, Private Woman: Women in Social and Political Thought* (Princeton, NJ: Princeton University Press, 1981), while Margaret Jacob has pioneered studies of women and Freemasonry, particularly in Holland. Her *Living the Enlightenment: Freemasonry and Politics in Eighteenth-Century Europe* (Oxford: Oxford University Press, 1991) contains a useful chapter on 'Freemasonry, Women, and the Paradox of the Enlightenment'. Another important text is Janet Mackay Burke, "Sociability, Friendship and the Enlightenment among Women Freemasons in Eighteenth-Century France', unpublished PhD dissertation, Arizona State University (1986). For factual information see Dudley Wright, *Women and Freemasonry* (London: William Rider, 1922) and F. W. G. Gilby, *Women and Freemasonry in the Past and in the Present* (Birmingham: privately printed, 1925). The single most useful account of predominant male masonic societies during this period is J. M. Roberts, *The Mythology of the Secret Societies* (London: Secker & Warburg, London, 1972). For pointing me towards many of my sources I am indebted to Christoph Heyl, Mary Waldron and John Ashby who is the assistant librarian at Freemasons Hall. The kind permission of Grand lodge to reproduce the print of 'Mademoiselle de Beaumont, or the Chevalier D'Eon' is gratefully acknowledged as is that of the British Museum, for allowing me to reproduce William Hogarth's *The Mystery of the Freemasons Brought to Light by the Gormogons* (1724) and the anonymous painting of Mademoiselle de Beaumont, or the Chevalier D'Eon (n.d.). I am also grateful to Mark Watson-Gandy for extending my knowledge of clubs. Thanks go to Marion Glastonbury, Helen Boden, Roy Porter, John Charles Smith and Caroline Williams for making indispensable comments on my essay. Finally my appreciation goes to Robert Miles for simply deriving pleasure from it.

5. 'THE LUXURY OF DOING GOOD' *Carolyn D. Williams*:

Ayer, A. J., *Hume*, 'Past Masters' series (London and New York: Oxford University Press, 1980).

Raphael, D. D., *Adam Smith*, 'Past Masters' series (London and New York: Oxford University Press, 1985).

Monro, H., *The Ambivalence of Bernard Mandeville* (Oxford: Clarendon, 1975).

Todd, Janet, *Sensibility: An Introduction* (London and New York: Methuen, 1986).

Hagstrum, Jean, *Sex and Sensibility: Ideal and Erotic Love from Milton to Mozart* (Chicago, IL: Chicago University Press, 1980; paperback edn, 1982).

Owen, D., *English Philanthropy, 1660–1960* (Cambridge, MA: Belknap Press of Harvard University Press, 1964).

Bishop, P. J., *A Short History of the Royal Humane Society to Mark its 200th Anniversary* (London: Royal Humane Society, 1974).

Further Reading

No previously published work has ever brought together the full range of topics covered by this chapter. Consequently, this bibliography simply covers each topic in turn, in the order in which it is discussed in the chapter.

Many studies deal, wholly or in part, with eighteenth-century attempts to solve the problem of altruism. A helpful article is John Darling, 'The moral teaching of Francis Hutcheson', *British Journal for Eighteenth-Century Studies,* XII (1989), pp. 165–74. More lengthy and detailed treatments of eighteenth-century moral philosophy include: T. D. Campbell, *Adam Smith's Science of Morals* (London: George Allen & Unwin, 1971); Barry Stroud, *Hume* (London and New York: Routledge & Kegan Paul, 1977); paperback edn. (London and New York, 1981); and Richard Sher, *Church and University in the Scottish Enlightenment: The Moderate Literati of Edinburgh* (Princeton, NJ: Princeton University Press, 1985). Readers who wish to investigate the twentieth-century controversy over Hume's philosophy and its relationship with Hutcheson should compare Norman Kemp Smith, *The Philosophy of David Hume* (London, 1960) with David Fate Norton, *David Hume: Common-Sense Moralist , Sceptical Metaphysician* (Princeton, NJ: Princeton University Press, 1982).

Students who would like to investigate more advanced material on sensibility should consult *Sensibility in Transformation: Creative Resistance to Sentiment from the Augustans to the Romantics: Essays in Honor of Jean Hagstrum,* ed. Syndy McMillen Conger (London: Associated University Press, 1990) and John Mullan, *Sentiment and Sociability: The Language of Feeling in the Eighteenth Century* (Oxford: Clarendon 1988; paperback edn, 1990). Studies which trace important links between sensibility and science are R. F. Brissenden, *Virtue in Distress: Studies in the Novel of Sentiment from Richardson to Sade* (London and Basingstoke: Macmillan, 1974) – where reference is made to the Royal Humane Society in early nineteenth-century Gothic literature – and A. J. Van Sant, *Eighteenth-Century Sensibility and the Novel: The Senses in Social Context* (Cambridge: Cambridge University Press, 1993). Readers who wish to sample the literature of sensibility for themselves should try *The Life and Opinions of Tristram Shandy, Gentleman* (1759–67), a title often shortened to *Tristram Shandy,* and *A Sentimental Journey* (1768) by Laurence Sterne (1713–68). The issues raised in eighteenth-century controversy were still very much alive in the nineteenth century: see *Sense and Sensibility* (1811) by Jane Austen (1775–1817).

A sophisticated analysis of the politics of charity is Donna T. Andrew, *Philanthropy and Police: London Charity in the Eighteenth Century* (Princeton, NJ: Princenton University Press, 1989). An interesting article on the language associated with charity is Rita Goldberg, 'Charity Sermons and the Poor: A Rhetoric of Compassion', *The Age of Johnson,* IV (1991), pp. 171–216.

The most medically sound articles on the part played by the Royal Humane Society in the history of resuscitation techniques are Sir Arthur Keith, 'Three Hunterian Lectures on the Mechanism Underlying the Various Methods of Artificial Respiration Practised since the Foundation of the Royal Humane Society', *The Lancet,* I (1909), pp. 745–49, 825–8, 895–9; J. P. Payne, 'On the Resuscitation of the Apparently Dead. An Historical Account', *Annals of the Royal College of Surgeons of England*, 45 (1969), pp. 98–107; and Norah Schuster, 'The Emperor of Russia and the Royal Humane Society', *Journal of the Royal College of General Practitioners*, 21 (1971), pp. 634–44. Some interesting angles are opened up by John P. Griffin, 'A Tale of Two Paintings and the London Medical Scene of the Late 18th Century', *Journal of the Royal Society of Medicine*, 83 (1990), pp. 520–3. The best attempt so far to set eighteenth-century resuscitation lore into its social context is P. Linebaugh, 'The Tyburn Riot against the Surgeons', in D. Hay and P. Linebaugh (eds), *Albion's Fatal Tree: Crime and Society in Eighteenth-Century England* (London, 1976), pp. 65–117.

6. THE SEDUCTIONS OF CONDUCT *Vivien Jones*

Femininity and Writing

Armstrong, Nancy, *Desire and Domestic Fiction: A Political History of the Novel* (New York and Oxford: Oxford University Press, 1987).

Ballaster, Ros, *Seductive Forms: Women's Amatory Fiction from 1684 to 1740* (Oxford: Clarendon Press, 1992).

Gallagher, Catherine, *Nobody's Story: The Vanishing Acts of Women Writers in the Marketplace 1670–1820* (Oxford: Clarendon Press, 1994).

Jones, Vivien (ed.), *Women in the Eighteenth Century: Constructions of Femininity* (London and New York: Routledge, 1990).

McKeon, Michael, *The Origins of the English Novel 1600–1740* (Baltimore, MD: Johns Hopkins University Press, 1987; London: Radius, 1988).

Perry, Ruth, *The Celebrated Mary Astell: An Early English Feminist* (Chicago, IL and London: University of Chicago Press, 1986).

Poovey, Mary, *The Proper Lady and the Woman Writer: Ideology as Style in the Works of Mary Wollstonecraft, Mary Shelley, and Jane Austen* (Chicago, IL and London: University of Chicago Press, 1984).

Rizzo, Betty, *Companions without Vows: Relationships Among Eighteenth-Century British Women* (Athens, GA and London: University of Georgia Press, 1994).

Shevelow, Kathryn, *Women and Print Culture: The Construction of Femininity in the Early Periodical* (London and New York: Routledge, 1989).

Todd, Janet, *The Sign of Angellica: Women, Writing and Fiction, 1660–1800* (London: Virago, 1989).

Histories of Sexuality and the Family

Brown, Irene Q., 'Domesticity, Feminism and Friendship: Female Aristocratic Culture and Marriage in England, 1660–1760', *Journal of Family History*, 7 (1982), pp. 406–27.

Gillis, John R., *For Better, For Worse: British Marriages, 1600 to the Present*

(New York and Oxford: Oxford University Press, 1985).
Macfarlane, Alan, *Marriage and Love in England: Modes of Reproduction, 1300–1840* (Oxford: Basil Blackwell, 1986).
Okin, Susan Moller, 'Patriarchy and Married Women's Property in England: Questions on Some Current Views', *Eighteenth-Century Studies*, 17 (1983), pp. 121–38.
Staves, Susan, *Married Women's Separate Property in England 1660–1833* (Cambridge, MA: Harvard University Press, 1990).
Stone, Lawrence, *The Family, Sex and Marriage in England 1500–1800* (London: Weidenfeld & Nicolson, 1977); abridged edn (Harmondsworth: Penguin, 1982).
Trumbach, Randolph, *The Rise of the Egalitarian Family: Aristocratic Kinship and Domestic Relations in Eighteenth-Century England* (New York: Academic Press, 1978).

Women as Consumers of Popular Culture

Ballaster, Ros, Margaret Beetham, Elizabeth Fraser and Sandra Hebron, *Women's Worlds: Ideology, Femininity and The Women's Magazine* (London: Macmillan, 1991).
Gledhill, Christine, 'Pleasurable Negotiations', in E. Deirdre Pribram (ed.), *Female Spectators: Looking at Film and Television* (London and New York: Verso, 1988).
Kaplan, Cora, '*The Thorn Birds*: Fiction, Fantasy, Femininity', in *Sea Changes: Essays on Culture and Feminism* (London: Verso, 1986).
Kaplan, Cora, 'The Cultural Crossover', *New Socialist* (November, 1986), pp. 38–40 (response to Judith Williamson: see below).
Light, Alison, '"Returning to Manderley": Romance Fiction, Sexuality and Class', *Feminist Review*, 16 (1984), pp. 7–25.
Modleskir, Tania, *Loving with a Vengeance: Mass-Produced Fantasies for Women* (New York and London: Methuen, 1982).
Radway, Janice, *Reading the Romance: Women Patriarchy & Popular Literature* (London: Verso, 1987).
Williamson, Judith, 'The Problems of Being Popular', *New Socialist* (September, 1986), pp. 14–15.

7. 'STRAINS OF NEW BEAUTY' Derek Alsop

Further Reading

Dean Winton and Merrill Knapp, John, *Handel's Operas 1704–1726* (Oxford: Clarendon Press, 1987).
Deutsch, Otto Erich, *Handel: A Documentary Bibliography* (London: Adam & Charles Black, 1955).
Gay, John, *The Beggar's Opera*, ed. Bryan Loughrey and T. O. Treadwell (Harmondsworth: 1986 Penguin Books).

Keates, Jonathan, *Handel: The Man and his Music* (London: Victor Gollancz, 1985).

Robbins Landon, H. C., *Handel and His World* (London: Weidenfeld & Nicolson 1984).

8. THE PLEASURE OF TERROR *E. J. Clery*

For terror as an aspect of the sublime in the aesthetic theory of the period, the standard reference is still Samuel H. Monk, *The Sublime: A Study of Critical Theories in XVIII-Century England* (1935; reprinted Ann Arbor, MI, 1960); other useful surveys are W. P. Albrecht, *The Sublime Pleasures of Tragedy: A Study of Critical Theory from Dennis to Keats* (Lawrence, KS, 1975); Walter John Hipple, Jr, *The Beautiful, the Sublime, & the Picturesque in Eighteenth-Century Aesthetic Theory* (Carbondale, IL, 1957); Marjorie Hope Nicolson, *Mountain Gloom and Mountain Glory: The Development of the Aesthetics of the Infinite* (1959; reprinted New York, 1963).

Thomas Weiskel, *The Romantic Sublime: Studies in the Structure and Psychology of Transcendence* (Baltimore, MD, 1976) is a highly influential study informed by post-structuralist theory, which generated new interest in the sublime, mainly with reference to Romantic poetry. Recent works which have examined the relation of terror and the sublime to the philosophical and political debate and material history of the time are E. J. Clery, *The Rise of Supernatural Fiction* (Cambridge, 1995); Peter de Bolla, *The Discourse of the Sublime: History, Aesthetics and the Subject* (Oxford, 1989); Frances Ferguson, 'The Sublime of Edmund Burke, or the Bathos of Experience', *Glyph*, 8 (1981), pp. 62–78; Tom Furniss, *Edmund Burke's Aesthetic Ideology: Language, Gender, and Political Economy in Revolution* (Cambridge, 1993); Ronald Paulson, 'Burke, Paine and Wollstonecraft: The Sublime and the Beautiful', in *Representations of Revolution* (New Haven, CI, 1983), pp. 57–87; Neal Wood, 'The Aesthetic Dimension of Burke's Political Thought', *The Journal of British Studies*, 4 (1) (November 1964), pp. 41–64.

The role and significance of terror in art and literature are considered in Peter Bicknell, *Beauty, Horror and Immensity: Picturesque Landscape in Britain, 1750–1850* (Cambridge, 1981); Carrol Fry, 'The Concept of the Sublime in Eighteenth-Century Horror Fiction', *Mankato Studies in English*, 1 (1966), pp. 31–44; David B. Morris, 'Gothic Sublimity', *NLH*, 16(2) (Winter 1985), pp. 299–319; David Punter, *The Literature of Terror* (London, 1980); Marie [Mulvey] Roberts, *Gothic Immortals: The Fiction of the Brotherhood of the Rosy Gross* (London, 1990), Patricia Meyer Spacks, *The Insistence of Horror: Aspects of the Supernatural in Eighteenth-Century Poetry* (Cambridge, MA, 1962); James B. Twitchell, *Romantic Horizons: Aspects of the Sublime in English Poetry and Painting, 1770–1850* (Columbia, MO, 1983); Malcolm Ware, *Sublimity in the Novels of Ann Radcliffe: A Study of the Influence upon her Craft of*

Edmund Burke's 'Enquiry into the Origin of our Ideas of the Sublime and the Beautiful' (Uppsala, 1963).

For an insight into the contemporary medical use of terror as shock therapy, see Antonie Luyendijk-Elshout, 'Of Masks and Mills: The Enlightened Doctor and His Frightened Patient', in *The Languages of Psyche,* ed. G. S. Rousseau (Berkeley, CA, Los Angeles, CA, Oxford, 1990), pp. 186–230.

9. BURNS AND WORDSWORTH *Susan Manning*

Primary

Burns, Robert, *Poems, Chiefly in the Scottish Dialect,* ed. Donald A. Low (1786; London: Dent, 1985).

——*The Poems and Songs of Robert Burns,* ed. James Kinsley, 3 vols (Oxford: Oxford University Press, 1968).

——*The Letters of Robert Burns,* 2nd edn, ed. J. DeLancey Ferguson and G. Ross Roy, 2 vols (Oxford: Clarendon Press, 1985).

——*Commonplace Books,* ed. Raymond Lamont Brown (1872; reprinted Wakefield: S. R. Publishers, 1969).

Wordsworth, William, *Lyrical Ballads,* ed R. L. Brett and A. R. Jones (London: Methuen, 1963; reprinted 1971).

——*Poems of 1807 (Poems in Two Volumes*), ed. Alun R. Jones (London: Macmillan, 1987).

—— *The Ruined Cottage, The Brothers, Michael,* ed. Jonathan Wordsworth (Cambridge: Cambridge University Press, 1985).

——, *The Prelude: A Parallel Text,* ed. J. C. Maxwell (Harmondsworth: Penguin Books, 1971).

——, *Poetical Works,* 2nd edn, ed. E. de Selincourt (Oxford: Oxford University Press, 1936, 1974).

——, *Wordsworth's Literary Criticism,* ed. Nowell C. Smith and Howard Mills (Bristol: Bristol Classical Press, 1980).

——, *The Letters of William and Dorothy Wordsworth,* ed. E. De Selincourt; vol. I: *The Early Years,* vol. II: *The Later Years* (Oxford, 1935, 1937).

Secondary

Austin, Francis, *The Language of Wordsworth and Coleridge* (London: Macmillan, 1989).

Beer, John, *Wordsworth and the Human Heart* (1976; reprinted London: Macmillan, 1986).

Byatt, A. S., *Unruly Times: Wordsworth and Coleridge in their Time* (London: Hogarth Press, 1970; reprinted 1989).

Crawford, Thomas, *Burns: A Study of the Poems and Songs,* 2nd edn (Edinburgh, 1965).

Ford, Stephen, '*Coalescence*: David Hartley's "Great Apparatus"', in

Christopher Fox (ed.), *Psychology and Literature in the Eighteenth Century* (New York: AMS Press, 1987).
Gill, Stephen, *William Wordsworth: A Life* (Oxford: Oxford University Press, 1989).
Hartley, David, *Observations on Man, His Frame, His Duty, and His Expectations,* 2 vols (1749; reprinted Hildesheim: George Olms Verlagsbuchhandlung, 1967).
Hazlitt, William, *Lectures on the English Poets* (1818), ed. William Carew Hazlitt (London: George Bell and Sons, 1884).
Low, Donald (ed.), *Robert Burns: The Critical Heritage* (London: Routledge & Kegan Paul, 1974).
Mackay, James, *Burns: A Biography of Robert Burns* (Edinburgh: Mainstream, 1992).
McGuirk, Carol, *Robert Burns and the Sentimental Era* (Athens, GA: The University of Georgia Press, 1985).
Mullan, John, *Sentiment and Sociability: The Language of Feeling in the Eighteenth Century* (Oxford: Clarendon Press, 1988).
Noyes, Russell, 'Wordsworth and Burns', *Publications of the Modern Language Association of America,* LIX, no. 3 (September 1944), pp. 813–32.
Simpson, Kenneth (ed.), *Burns Now* (Edinburgh: Canongate Academic, 1994).
Tiger, Lionel, *The Pursuit of Pleasure* (Boston, MA: Little, Brown, 1992).
William, John, *New Casebooks: Wordsworth* (London: Macmillan, 1993).

Notes on Contributors

Derek Alsop is a senior lecturer in English at St Mary's University College, Twickenham. A specialist in seventeenth- and eighteenth-century literature, his publications include work on Rochester's poetry and Sterne's *Tristram Shandy*. His interest in music, combined with his literary background, has led to a wide range of broadcasts for BBC Radio 3. Present projects include a libretto for a choral work based on Rabelais, and a co-authored book on the novel and theories of response.

E. J. Clery is a lecturer in English at Keele University. She is the author of *The Rise of Supernatural Fiction, 1762–1800* and of a number of articles examining the relationship between literature and political economy in the eighteenth century. She is currently completing a revised edition of Horace Walpole's *The Castle of Otranto* and a sourcebook, *Gothic Documents, 1700–1820.*

Vivien Jones is a senior lecturer in the School of English at the University of Leeds. She is the editor of *Women in the Eighteenth Century: Constructions of Femininity* and has published books on Henry James and Jane Austen as well as articles on women and writing in the eighteenth century. She has edited *The Young Lady's Pocket Library, or Parental Monitor* and *Pride and Prejudice.*

Susan Manning is a lecturer in the English Faculty of the University of Cambridge. She is the author of *The Puritan–Provincial Vision* and has written extensively on Scottish and American literature. She has edited Walter Scott's *Quentin Durward* and Washington Irving's *The Sketch-Book of Geoffrey Crayon, Gent.* She is working on books on the art of pleasure in the eighteenth century and on Anglo-Scottish writers. She is President of the Eighteenth-Century Scottish Studies Society.

Roy Porter is professor in the social history of medicine at the Wellcome Institute for the History of Medicine. He is currently working on the history of hysteria. Recent books include *Mind Forg'd Manacles: Madness in England from the Restoration to the Regency; A Social History of Madness; In Sickness and in Health: The British Experience, 1650–1850; Patient's Progress* (these last two co-authored with Dorothy Porter); *Health for Sale: Quackery in England, 1660–1850; Doctor of Society: Thomas Beddoes and the Sick Trade in Late Enlightenment England* and *London: A Social History.*

Marie Mulvey Roberts is a senior lecturer in literary studies at the University of the West of England and is the author of *British Poets and Secret Societies* and *Gothic Immortals.* She has edited *Out of the Night: Writings from Death Row,* and co-edited *Explorations in Medicine; Literature and Medicine During the Eighteenth Century; Secret Texts: The Literature of Secret Societies* and *Sources, Perspectives and Controversies in the History of British Feminism.* She is the general editor of three series: *Subversive Women, For Her Own Good* and *Her Write His Name.*

Simon Varey has published numerous books and articles on eighteenth-century literature, history, politics, cooking, and food. His *Space and the Eighteenth-century English Novel* (Cambridge: Cambridge University Press, 1990) has little to say about food but quite a lot about pleasure. He formerly owned a catering business in Los Angeles, masterminding extravagant banquets or preparing frozen TV dinners for those too busy to cook. He still gives cooking demonstrations, which include dishes from Renaissance Italy as well as eighteenth-century England. His current work focuses on medicine in colonial Mexico and its diffusion across Europe in the seventeenth and eighteenth centuries. Simon Varey creates projects that satisfy the life of the mind at the Center for Medieval and Renaissance Studies, UCLA.

Carolyn D. Williams is a lecturer in the department of English at the University of Reading. She is the author of *Pope, Homer, and Manliness: Some Aspects of Eighteenth-century Classical Learning* as well as of numerous articles on various aspects of life and literature from the Renaissance to the end of the eighteenth century.

Index